Reading with Anthropology

Reading with Anthropology

Exhibiting Aspects of New Testament Religion

LOUISE J. LAWRENCE

PATERNOSTER

First published in 2005 by Paternoster Press

11 10 09 08 07 06 05   7 6 5 4 3 2 1

Paternoster Press is an imprint of Authentic Media,
9 Holdom Avenue, Bletchley, Milton Keynes MK1 1QR, UK
and
129 Mobilization Drive, Waynesboro, GA 30830-4575, USA

www.authenticmedia.co.uk/paternoster

Authentic Media is a division of Send The Light Ltd, a company limited
by guarantee (registered charity no. 270162).

British Library Cataloguing in Publication Data
A catalogue record for this book is available from the British Library

ISBN 1-84227-375-2

Cover Design by fourninezero design
Typeset by Waverley Typesetters, Little Walsingham, Norfolk
Print Management by Adare Carwin
Printed and Bound by J.H. Haynes & Co., Sparkford

Contents

Foreword   vii

Acknowledgements   ix

Introduction: Launching an Exhibition   xi

Part I: Reading with Anthropology

1. Anthropology and Biblical Studies: Some Associations and Collaborations   3

2. Reading with Anthropology: A Reductive Pursuit?   17

Part II: Exhibiting Aspects of Scriptural Religion

3. Exhibit 1. Reading with Religious Practitioners: Shamans and Shaman Healers   35

4. Exhibit 2. Reading with Tricksters: Irony, Mystery and John's Jesus   55

5. Exhibit 3. Reading with 'Rituals of Resistance': Willing Deaths and Masculinity   76

6. Exhibit 4. Reading with Women's Religions: Procreation, Suffering and the Domestication of Religion   102

7. Exhibit 5. Reading with Poetry: Modesty, Love and Desire   131

8. Exhibit 6. Reading with Communities of Goods: Morals, Money and Virtuoso Religion   152

9. Exhibit 7. Reading with Food and Memory: Consuming at Corinth   172

10. Exiting an Exhibition   187

Bibliography   193

Foreword

Since the explorations by Mary Douglas on the social rules and interpretative notions of purity in Leviticus, a good number of biblical scholars have been interested in using anthropological tools in order to explore, interpret and understand the biblical text. Fewer scholars have been interested in the larger academic and textual relations between anthropologists and biblical scholars, and only a few have become firmly grounded in both disciplines. The author of this challenging, elegant and creative book is one of those chosen few biblical scholars who have successfully explored the history of anthropological ideas instead of using anthropology solely as a useful tool for interpretation.

Reading with Anthropology is a well-organised textual exhibition of important themes within anthropology and of aspects of the social life of actors in the biblical world. It is a museum piece and an aesthetic creation that expresses Louise Lawrence's convincing knowledge of the biblical text as well as of contemporary social anthropology. Her intellectual expectations are of a high standard when arguing that anthropology and scripture are compatible 'exhibition objects', and as a result 'anthropology is not used as a mere handmaid to biblical interpretation or vice versa. Rather, each discipline has its own particular slant to offer on the selected material' (Introduction).

The themes chosen, namely, religious practitioners, tricksters, rituals of resistance, women's religions, poetry, communities of goods, and food and memory, bring back the consciousness, agency and social powers of those written about within the biblical text. The style is self-reflexive and highly literary, providing an opening to many other themes, texts and social realities still to be explored, cogitated and inscribed.

I am delighted to introduce this book that follows Lawrence's previous steps into biblical studies and literary anthropology, namely, *An Ethnography of the Gospel of Matthew* (2003). This 'exhibition' is of the highest academic standard and has the finesse of an aesthetic creation.

Her ideas and paradigms will certainly mark the field of biblical studies and anthropology because it is one of the few attempts to deal with wide-ranging fields of enquiry rather than with the elucidation of one passage, one social model, or one type of anthropology. Her work brings out the complexities and the intellectual lacunae of biblical studies and anthropology being conceived in isolation.

Dr Mario I. Aguilar
Dean of Divinity
St Mary's College
University of St Andrews
January 2005

Acknowledgements

Exhibitions are not merely the handiwork of their curators. Behind the precisely placed glass cabinets of treasures are a host of others who have contributed in abundant ways to the show. The exhibits of this book are no exception and whilst debts are so inadequately paid by mere mention, it is nonetheless 'seemly so to do'.

Dr Robin Parry, on a cold wintry day in St Andrews, showed interest in *Reading with Anthropology* and subsequently issued a contract with Paternoster Press. For his, Lucy Atherton's and Paternoster Press's munificent patience with me I am very appreciative. I am also hugely indebted to Dr Lawrence Osborn for his professional and rigorous copy-editing of my typescript. Thanks also to the Department of Theology and Religious Studies at the University of Glasgow for granting me research leave to finish this project. Glasgow is a vibrant place to be, and the view of mass renovations of Kelvingrove Museum was firm assurance of the lesser challenge I faced in assembling the showcase of novelties in this book. Thanks also to The Hunterian Museum for allowing me to use their Captain Cook exhibit on the cover of my book and Iona Shepherd's efficiency in sorting out permissions. Due acknowledgement should also be given to Alison Kelly, curator of St Mungo's Museum of Religious Life, who sowed the 'metaphor' of museum exhibitions for me in the first place with her paper at an 'Anthropology and Old Testament Studies Symposium' held in Glasgow last summer.

Dr Mario Aguilar's friendship, interest and input in directing me in all things anthropological and writing a foreword for this book was greatly appreciated. I am also indebted to Dr David Horrell. He read and commented on my manuscript and good-naturedly listened, as always, to my qualms. He has taught me more about an anthropological 'respect for the other' in his friendship and guidance over the years, than anyone has.

On a personal level, thanks to Daniel Morgan for his computer savvy, sense of fun and not letting me take life too seriously. Last but certainly not least, gratitude must be given to my Mum and Dad for all number of remarkable acts and selfless miracles connected with this book. They provide constant proof that I never 'Read with Anthropology', or indeed face anything, alone. For all this and more, 'little bird' and I dedicate this book to them with our fondest love.

Dr Louise Lawrence
University of Glasgow
Lent 2005

Introduction

Launching an Exhibition

Exhibitions, whether of objects or people, are displays of the artefacts of our disciplines. They are for this reason also exhibits of those who make them.

Kirshenblatt-Gimblett

Entering
you will find yourself in a climate of nut castanets,
a musical whip
from the Torres Straits, from Mirzapur a sistrum
called Jumka, 'used by Aboriginal
tribes to attract small game
on dark nights,' coolie cigarettes
and mask of Saaga, the Devil Doctor,
the eyelids worked by strings.

Fenton, 'The Pitt Rivers Museum'

Most people, like me, who have not had the privilege of conducting long-term anthropological fieldwork in 'foreign' lands, learn about such cultures from books and museums. The Pitt Rivers Museum in Oxford is one of Britain's most celebrated collections of anthropological artefacts. Walking around it one enters another world. With its myriad anthropological treasures, one can see, touch and empathise with lives lived quite differently from our own. It is not only the dazzling and beautiful but also the bland and commonplace that reveal in assorted ways how different people across the world live, love, value and believe.

In any museum the viewer is to a certain extent at the mercy of the choices made by the curator. In designing exhibitions curators choose links between artefacts and in so doing guide the narrative context and perceptions of the viewer. In Mark Liddiard's words, in museums 'history as an open-ended experience is invariably organised and constructed for consumption in certain ways' (2004: 15). In the Pitt Rivers Museum objects are exhibited typologically (by themes and purposes) as opposed to cultural and geographical boundaries. In this way different cultures are exhibited alongside one another and meaningful links forged between objects that at first sight could seem totally unrelated. Musical instruments, pottery, masks, jewellery and weapons from a variety of traditions sit side by side, the exhibition plaques and guidebooks providing the connective context between them.

This book is also an exhibition, a carefully designed selection of objects for consumption by viewers. It presents a series of 'exhibits' of selected scriptural texts and material drawn from anthropological sources. I, as curator, forge links between the two artefacts and hope that the novelties displayed in this book's cabinets may cast light on each other in an informative way.

I do not claim organic links between items displayed on account of context, history or culture, nor do I claim to reveal specific knowledge about the particular social contexts of either. My aim is far more modest. Merely, I hope that by viewing selected anthropological data and biblical texts (creatively and, at times, playfully) together, standpoints that otherwise may never have occurred to the viewer may be introduced and probed. Like the Pitt Rivers Museum, my exhibits are all conceived on the basis of thematic (as opposed to historical or cultural) links. This is legitimised to a certain extent by the fact that there is no single consensus among anthropologists about investigative strategies, eclecticism is the hallmark of comparison and analysis (Overholt 1996: 4).

First a few words on the title of this exhibition, *Reading with Anthropology: Exhibiting Aspects of New Testament Religion*. To 'read with' something or someone, is to place oneself alongside another and creatively engage with them. 'Reading with Anthropology' therefore is a positive, empathetic and interdisciplinary pursuit. As anthropology is primarily interested in 'observing' the cultural patterns of human life, monitoring how people live religiously must be seen as a key pursuit in understanding any religious phenomena, not least that presented in the Bible. I specifically chose the word 'religion' for its association with embodied practices. The term 'religion' has also been most commonly used in those schools that work comparatively, placing one form beside another for purposes of research, and thus lends itself to the cross-cultural probing used here.

The exhibition itself is divided into two main parts. Part I, 'Reading with Anthropology', comprises two chapters. The first chapter, 'Anthropology and Biblical Studies: Some Associations and Collaborations' seeks to document briefly some of the major works in this area. The catalogue of research is by no means comprehensive (and on account of my interest is more weighted to New Testament projects) though I provide a further reading list to aid the reader. The second chapter, 'Reading with Anthropology: A Reductive Pursuit?' plots debates regarding the status of social scientific enquiry vis-à-vis faith. Can a discipline such as anthropology have anything useful to say in interpretation of a text hailed as scripture? Is such a pursuit inevitably reductive (seeing faith and religious experiences as nothing more than the result of certain social equations and forces)? In rebutting such a claim I review the work of two individuals, Charles Kraft (1979; 1996) and Douglas Davies (2002), who both imaginatively connect anthropology and theology. I also draw on notions of 'embodiment' and humanity as 'ceremonial animals' (a phrase adopted from Wittgenstein via James 2003) as helpful research perspectives in any anthropological understanding of how people live 'religiously' or 'ritually'. By this I mean a religion that goes beyond particular ways of acting and actually becomes part of the consciousness and sensitivities of an individual. Such connections are easier to decipher with the help of a discipline that can link actions and belief, context and kerygma in an illuminating way for the biblical interpreter. Anthropology is such a pursuit, interested in observing physical and social effects of experiences and beliefs. It is an aid for the interpreter to bring soul and body connected, into view.

Part II, 'Exhibiting Aspects of Scriptural Religion' consists of seven 'exhibits'. When I first conceived of the idea for 'Reading with Anthropology', I chose chapter themes that covered issues of interest in contemporary anthropology and biblical studies. These were as follows: religious practitioners; religion and cosmology; power and violence; sex and gender; body and emotion; ritual/rites; social memory (see Table 1). These various interests respectively provided the implicit perspectives for each exhibit in this book.

Table 1.   Interests and Exhibits

Interest	Exhibit
Religious practitioners	Reading with Religious Practitioners: Shamans and Shaman Healers
Religion and cosmology	Reading with Tricksters: Irony and Social Critique
Power and violence	Reading with Rituals of Resistance: Willing Deaths and Masculinity
Sex and gender	Reading with Women's Religions: Procreation, Suffering and the Domestication of Religion
Body and emotion	Reading with Poetry and Song: Modesty, Love and Desire
Ritual/rites	Reading with Communities of Goods: Money, Morals and Virtuoso Religion
Social memory	Reading with Food and Memory: Consuming at Corinth

Religious Practitioners

Religious practitioners ranging from spirit-possessed visionaries and prophetic founders to establishment-based priestly figures have featured in the ethnography of various religious groups. A fair amount of energy has been put into placing Jesus (along with John the Baptist) in a prophetic framework. It is only recently, however, that the religious identity of the historical Jesus, and indeed the respective pictures of Jesus presented in the gospels, has been shown to share affinities with shaman and shaman healer figures. These types of practitioners tend to exist on the boundaries of society drawing their authority from charismatic as opposed to traditional means. While priests tend to conduct and oversee religious rites and ceremonies on a permanent, 'full-time' basis, in contrast the shaman figure mediates between the earthly and transcendental realms, in an ad hoc and spontaneous manner. This exhibit explores the spirit experience of Mark and Luke's respective portrayals of Jesus. I suggest Mark aligns Jesus with the primitive shaman type of practitioner and Luke presents him as a more collectively orientated shaman healer.

Religion and Cosmology

'Religion and cosmology' represents an anthropological interest in those myths and stories that cultures compose to explain origins and relationships between the natural and supernatural, life and death. These often inform the practice, behaviour and self-identity of the groups addressed by them. So-called trickster narratives (from North American Indian to African societies) variously present a figure that lives on 'boundaries' and has some involvement with origins and creation. The features and purposes of such stories are exhibited with John's picture of Jesus that comprises mystery, irony and, I suggest, 'trickery' dynamics.

Power and Violence

'Power and violence' provides the backdrop of my next exhibit. Notably, Bourdieu saw violence as endemic to social practice, not just confrontation or physical abuse, but also in architecture, exchange of gifts and systems of classification (see Scheper-Hughes 2002: 31). Foucault's thought on how domination is naturalised by certain regimes has also informed anthropology in a number of ways. My exhibit dwells on the complex of themes surrounding domination, violence and masculinity in reference to instances of willing death (both in war and under imperial rule) in the scriptural tradition. I propose that the rhetoric in which certain accounts of willing death are dressed, have certain affinities with 'rituals of resistance' whereby oppressed groups and individuals subvert the efficacy of the violence imposed on them by interpreting them as positive initiations into manhood or another mode of being.

Sex and Gender

Interest in 'sex and gender' has, in light of the development of feminism and women's studies left its mark on many disciplines and research pursuits. In anthropology, projects that give voice to 'muted females' have produced surprisingly rich findings that question the picture of women as a silent 'homogeneous other' so often sustained in ethnography of the past. In my exhibit I present Susan Sered's study of twelve women-centred religions and compare characteristics shared between these with several features of early Christianity. I then go on to introduce a phenomenon that Sered has termed 'the domestication of religion', in reference to the status of women in the early church. This is a process by which 'those who have a great deal invested in interpersonal relationships, and who are excluded from formal power within an institutionalized religious framework, tend to be associated with a personally orientated religious mode' (Sered 1999: 96). This can be equated in part with the gradual assimilation of a religious movement's ideals to the status quo. Women, in such processes are often urged to submit to the broader society's gender expectations.

Body and Emotion

While there has been an increasing interest in the 'body' as a symbolic resource in anthropology, emotion had, until recently, hardly featured at all. Yet this is a necessary and important part of trying to understand attitudes of individuals and groups to external events or dominant cultural ideologies. An interest in the emotional can, in Lutz and White's opinion, 'reanimate the sometimes robotic image of humans which social science has purveyed' (1986: 431). My exhibit takes up this theme in reading the Song of Songs as 'alternative discourse' to the dominant cultural ideology. As Fiona Bowie explains, 'the mindful body is not a static concept, this involves taking account of historical changes, individual agency, and the positioning of the body in terms of hegemonic and alternative discourses' (Bowie 2000: 88). Drawing on comparative material from studies of oral/lyric forms in India and Bedouin society, I seek to show how 'emotion can be studied as embodied discourse only after its social and cultural – its discursive – character has been fully accepted' (Abu-Lughod & Lutz 1990: 13).

Ritual/Rites

Ritual has been one of those concepts whose meaning in anthropology is polyvalent. I take ritual in its broadest sense to be 'performed commitment' and 'sanctified activities'. This is not to confine 'ritual' to the enactment of 'religious' rites (circumcision, baptism) alone, but rather also to include ordinary, human practice to which certain meanings can be ascribed and how through such actions religious awareness can be absorbed into the base identity of an individual. Ronald Grimes touches on this relationship in his provocatively titled book *Deeply Into the Bone: Re-Inventing Rites of Passage* (2000). He submits that bodily and collective means of meaning making (in rites, ritual and everyday life) allow actions to become part of the very essence of people's identities. Like archaeologists who can discover elements of a person's social life (diet, occupation, etc.) from their bones, so individual and religious 'bodies' can also be seen to be socially formed. Actions and beliefs in such cases are not 'skin deep' but inscribe themselves within the dense marrow of people's lives. In this sense I compare the 'ritual' of sharing possessions in the early church with similar actions in the Qumran and Hutterite movements, and document how this action is inscribed into the very 'bones' of each individual.

Social Memory

The ways in which practices and traditions are embodied, sustained and transmitted have come under anthropological scrutiny in recent years. Material aspects of cultures have been seen as particularly important sites of construction of 'incorporated memories', as opposed to a text-based tradition of memory (inscribed). I provide a comparative reading of a recent ethnography that takes food and memory as its subject matter with Paul's advice to the Corinthians regarding their celebration of the Lord's Supper. This ritual meal should not solely be seen as representative of something else; rather, due acknowledgment must be given that the social and sensory aspects of eating, embodies and educates believers in their identity in, and remembrance of, Christ's sacrifice for them.

I, as curator, provide the connective context between the constituent parts of each exhibit. My method is hybrid and eclectic, but no apologies are made for that here. Also, I am candid that some of the anthropological studies comprise Christian influenced groups (Hutterites, Shakers, etc.). Akin to the utilisation of a sect model (itself derived from the study of Christianity) there is an inevitable circularity of interpretation involved here. This is not, however, to render comparisons totally valueless. Looking at behaviours and religious embodiment is an interesting and promising pursuit. Common ground shared by traditions need not dictate results nor be screened out of comparative exercises.

Some of the exhibits may make strange, even uncomfortable viewing at times. However, interdisciplinary pursuits like museums are 'places for confrontation, *experimentation* and debate' (my italicisation, Karp & Lavine 1991: 3). They are forums for the present not just temples dedicated to the past. As such, viewers must be open to change and challenge. In the words of Duncan, museum visitors 'bring with them the willingness to shift into a certain state of receptivity ... a particular kind of contemplation and learning experience and demanding a special quality of attention' (Duncan in Karp & Lavine 1991: 91). A uniting theme of all the exhibits here is an interest in the consciousness, agency and social powers of those catalogued in the scriptural texts studied. One hopes that you, as exhibit viewers, will also be able to imagine something of the flesh and blood lives, inscribed in the respective texts by viewing them through this anthropological prism. I also hope that you will be spurred on to pursue some of the questions posited here and explore some of the avenues merely pointed at throughout the journey.

In many ways the metaphor of exhibitions also informs our understanding of social and collective memory and identity, a field museums share with scripture. Both museums and books of scripture seek to impart a particular view on the past for a community and in so doing contribute to the shaping of the future. The British Museum in 2003 launched an exhibition entitled 'The Museum of the Mind: Art and Memory in World Cultures' illustrating just this. Roman coins, marble portraits, carvings from the Congo and many other objects in different ways contributed to memory within groups. MacGregor in his preface to the exhibition catalogue, correspondingly wrote:

> For individuals, as for communities, it may be said that memory is identity. At the very least it is an essential part of it. To lose your memory is, quite literally, no longer to know who you are, and we have all witnessed the consequences both in individuals and in communities. For both, a life without memories is so diminished as hardly to count as life. All societies have therefore devised systems and structures, objects and rituals to help them remember those things that are needful if the community is to be strong – the individuals and the moments that have shaped the past, the beliefs and the habits which should determine the future. These monuments and *aide-mémoire* point not only to what we were, but also to what we want to be.
>
> MacGregor 2003: 8

It is no coincidence that biblical studies and anthropology have asked new questions in response to contemporary issues (post-colonialism, feminism, etc.) and through such endeavours have actually reconstructed our memories and images of the past. By viewing history and sacred texts, from slightly different angles, one is also open to re-evaluating our present assumptions and worldview.

It is hoped that the artefacts witnessed in this book will prove that anthropology and scripture provide compatible 'exhibition objects' and prompt at least some new perspectives and questions when these are viewed together. Anthropology is not used as a mere handmaid to biblical interpretation or vice versa. Rather, each discipline has its own particular insights to bring on the selected material. Anthropology and biblical texts tell us about the behaviours, cultural assumptions and experiences of particular communities different from our own. Both make the interpreter realise that their own context is not the measure of all things. Both teach us about 'foreigners' but at the same time also add to our understanding and remembering of who we are: people of particular social situations but also citizens of a rich and plural human race and world.

Enough said by way of introductions – let the 'reader' understand ...

Part I
Reading with Anthropology

1

Anthropology and Biblical Studies

Some Associations and Collaborations

> No man is an island, entire of itself; every man is a piece of the continent, a part of the main.
>
> J. Donne

> The objects of anthropological knowledge – society, culture, belief, gender, law and so on – have never been exclusively anthropology's own.
>
> N. Thomas

The scholar today has more freedom and opportunity to peep over disciplinary parapets than ever before. The academic world is no longer a mosaic of autonomous subject areas, but a tapestry where the threads of different research areas can be woven alongside one another. This 'blurring of genres', to use Geertz's famed phrase, has not been uncritically welcomed by all. Trudging through what some have seen as an indigestible 'subjects soup', fears have been raised that practitioners can neither be certain nor even know their particular discipline's contribution any more. Such scepticism has led to lengthy self-examination and, in some cases, identity crises for a number of subjects.

Anthropology and biblical studies have been no exception. At base, both these have an interest in the shaping of meaning in human existence, and as such have touched, shared and disputed grounds with law, politics, economics, literary criticism and others. However, provided research is not 'undisciplined', surely the great inheritance of 'interdisciplinarity' has been the innovative, rich and original readings and questions that have been produced over the last few years? Just like Alice discovering the marvels of Wonderland, would the treasures of advocacy, liberation, feminist, literary and social-scientific analyses (to name but a few), ever have been discovered if biblical exegetes had not boldly peered beyond the historical-critical box?

This chapter constitutes a brief introduction to those social-scientific interpreters of the Bible that have creatively used, adopted and 'read with' perspectives from anthropology. The works cited are by no means comprehensive, and given my own interest in New Testament studies, belie a bias to what my Old Testament colleagues devilishly refer to as 'the appendix' to the Bible.

What is Anthropology?

anthropology n.—study of mankind, esp. as manifested in societies and customs

Oxford English Dictionary

Anthropology is etymologically derived from the Greek *'anthropos'* (human) and *'logos'* (word/message) and is essentially the study of humankind. The anthropological discipline has traditionally been subdivided into four pursuits. First is physical anthropology, which is interested in the heritage and evolution of humanity; second, archaeological anthropology, which has as its focus prehistoric societies and cultural development; third, linguistic anthropology, which endeavours to show language as a foundation stone of societies; and fourth, socio-cultural anthropology, which involves the comparative study of different cultural facets, values and traditions.

Malinowski designated the pursuit of 'understanding the other' as central to the anthropological endeavour. This 'other' was often seen, as Evans-Pritchard famously stated, as 'primitive'. However, casting the 'other' (the anthropological subject) as 'foreign' or 'exotic' was questioned in Said's project on 'Orientalism' (see Lawrence 2004). As a result of this, in Rapport and Overing's terms, 'anthropology is now in an "age of self-reflection", a process through which it often joins other post-colonial voices in a critique of the grand narratives of modernism' (2000: 10). This statement implicitly attests to the fact that a research strategy that focuses on 'otherness' is necessarily a narrative that operates with some form of exclusion. To overcome this division one has to be braced not only to encounter, but also be changed by our interface with different social and cultural situations. To study the 'other' as 'merely other' with no openness to change our own perspectives in the process of interaction is no triumph, especially in this 'post-9/11 world'. Understanding the other and their motivations is not only 'nice' but also 'necessary'.

Today anthropologists can be found working not only in isolated tribal groups but also throughout the industrialised world. Many work close to home, even conducting research in their own contexts, so-called autoethnography. Reed-Danahay defines this as 'a form of self-narrative that places the self within a social context. It is both a method and a text, as in the case of ethnography. Autoethnography can be done by either an anthropologist who is doing "home" or "native" ethnography or by a non-anthropologist/ethnograper' (1997: 9). Increasing globalisation has contributed to this 'blurring of subjects', because it has dissolved many conceptions of regional isolation and led to 'transnational and multinational identities become increasingly common' (Klass & Weisgrau 1999: 5).

Anthropology's traditional interest in the 'native's' viewpoint is shown in its basic methodology, which distinguishes between *emic* perspectives (documenting the insider's point of view) related to fieldwork description and *etic* perspectives (represented by the external observer/researcher), involving analysis, comparison and systematisation (McCutcheon 1999: 17; Harris 1976: 329–50). In the past, anthropology popularised participant observation and cross-cultural comparison. Anthropologists observe the totality of relationships between people within a social unit, often by living among them during fieldwork, and document their research in 'ethnography', literally written reports about people (see Atkinson 1990). Anthropology, while involved in close fieldwork analysis, is also, with its interest in the comparative tradition, dealing with a broader picture than, for example, the micro-specific research preoccupying an archaeologist. Such comparisons allow the anthropologist to see poignant convergences as well as divergences between cultures. They believe that the key to understanding a cultural feature involves viewing it alongside similar features in other situations. By such comparative exercises one is stimulated to view the tradition one is investigating in alternative ways.

While numerous attempts have been made to situate Christianity in relation to Jewish and Graeco-Roman traditions and culture, in such projects cultural neighbours in physical contact with the movement, or traditions which have directly impacted the movement, rather than remote cross-cultural comparisons, have been the norm. One wonders whether a certain bias against comparing scripture with other cultures and religious traditions has been behind this interpretative trend? Eilberg-Schwartz in his celebrated book, *The Savage in Judaism* (1990) rejects such imbalance, and is a robust defender of cross-cultural comparison in exegesis. He provides two main reasons for his standpoint. First, such analysis provides creative perspectives to 'read with', second, cross-cultural analysis is an invaluable aid in reconstructing and imagining historical worlds which are not accessible or for which we have incomplete evidence. In his words,

> Comparative inquiry features second-order reflection that transforms the way in which interpreters think about and therefore analyse cultural traditions … I discovered a plethora of new models for thinking about Israelite practice and beliefs that had not been employed by interpreters of Israelite religion … ethnographies have convinced me that comparative inquiry was indispensable for interpreting cultures of the past … historians by necessity engage in the task of reconstruction … the archaeology of culture involves the interpreter in the attempt to imagine how incomplete literary remains may reflect or distort a cultural reality of which they once formed a part. The cultural historian is by necessity engaged in archaeology of culture.
>
> Eilberg-Schwartz 1990: 91–92

One may still feel, however, that those subjects and traditions selected for comparison must have some significant connections (either being produced in similar circumstances, from a similar time frame or region) to hold weight. However, at such a point one must concede anthropology has been a lot freer in its comparative work, even if biblical studies has, in comparison, been much more constrained. (Perceived) links in the end are always dependent on the interests of the interpreter; it is he/she alone who must provide reasons for the utility of looking at a selected ethnography alongside another, whether that be on geographical, traditional, thematic or other bases.

Social-Scientific Criticism

social science—scientific study of human society and human relationships

Oxford English Dictionary

John Elliott has provided the following generally accepted definition of social-scientific exegesis:

> Social-scientific criticism of the Bible is that phase of the exegetical task, which analyses the social and cultural dimensions of the text and of its environmental context through the utilization of the perspectives, theory, models and research of the social sciences.
>
> Elliott 1995 [1993]: 7

Social-scientific criticism can be linked with historical-critical paradigms, in that it variously tries to find out about the dynamics of social situations and contexts in which biblical texts were produced and received. There is a diversity of approaches that fall under the rubric of social-scientific criticism. Elliott (1995 [1993]: 18–20) has for example distinguished the following five categories.

- *Social Realities* – Largely a descriptive pursuit, illustrating some feature or features of ancient society with no concern for analysing social data.

- *Construction of Social History* – Again largely a historical / descriptive enterprise, picturing details of a particular period, group or movement.

- *Social Organisation* – Analysing social forces that lead to particular social forms by using the insights of social theories.

- *Social-Scientific Modelling* – Projects explicitly using social-scientific 'models' to interpret biblical texts.

- *Social and Cultural Scripts* – Studies of the construction of social values operative in a particular cultural environment.

The first two pursuits seem more in line with a social history approach. The others, however, with their explicit use of insights from sociology and anthropology, seem more neatly to represent a distinctively social-scientific approach. The latter, in Philip Esler's opinion, realise that the social-scientific perspectives adopted are 'heuristic tools, not ontological statements' and as such 'are either useful or not, and it is meaningless to ask if they are true or false' (Esler 1995a: 4). What is more important, it seems, is how these social-scientific theories and insights allow the interpreter to see material in a different light and account for different dynamics displayed in the texts studied.

But what is the particular contribution of anthropology to social-scientific study? It is often said that sociology studies industrialised societies while anthropology focuses on the study of tribal peoples. In reality these boundaries are far more fluid. More important to note is the difference between the respective methodologies of each. Sociology tends to produce frames based on quantitative methods and surveys while anthropology, as shown above, prizes fieldwork, description and comparison (on the differences between the two see Lang 1985; Rogerson 1984 [1979]; Tidball 1983).

Until recently the most creative work on the interface between biblical studies and anthropology was in reference to the Old Testament. One can speculate on myriad reasons for this, but perhaps the most obvious is that ancient Israel provided more ready reminiscence with tribal societies in which anthropologists traditionally worked, unlike the plural and heterogeneous environment of the New Testament. As I have explained elsewhere (2004), research on Israel's tribal structure, folklore, values, symbolics and institutions have variously been informed by anthropological comparison (Robertson Smith 1969 [1889]; Dalman 1928–39; Noth 1960; Gottwald 1979; Lang 1985; Eilberg-Schwartz 1990). Israelite kinship, slavery, purity laws, sacrifice and prophecy, to name but a few interests, were all brought into sharper focus under the anthropological lens (see contributions in Lang 1985; on prophecy, see Culley 1981; Buss 1981: 9–30).

Broader comparative projects in Old Testament Studies have included Proffitt's (1984) anthropological analysis of Moses and the book of Exodus as a revitalisation movement similar to other such groups in North American Indian contexts. Lasine's (1986) review of literary and anthropological theories in relation to biblical texts, particularly the mythological, has also been important. Anthropologists themselves also found the Old Testament to be fruitful 'field' for anthropological harvests (Eliade 1964; Evans-Pritchard 1965; Davies 1977). For example, Fiensy (1987) documents Evans-Pritchard's project of comparing Nuer culture of Africa with the Old Testament. Douglas's study of Levitical purity laws hardly needs mention as a celebrated 'great' among anthropological studies of the Bible (Douglas 1966).

The long tradition of anthropological research in Old Testament Studies has, inevitably, stimulated a fair amount of critical reflection. Those projects working from structural-symbolic perspectives were accused of painting the worlds of the Old Testament as static 'photo-shot' pictures, with little eye on their dynamism, development and change (See Lemche 1985; Perkins 1992). Others (most significantly

Rogerson 1979) took anthropological studies of the Old Testament to task for drawing conclusions about ancient Israel that were based on unsustainable or refuted anthropological theories.

In contrast, sociology has been most widely used in New Testament studies. Witnessing to this, the *Anchor Bible Dictionary* provides an entry on the 'sociology of early Christianity' but does not include an entry on anthropology. Similarly, Blasi, Duhaime and Turcotte's recent collection, *Handbook of Early Christianity: Social Science Approaches* (2002) is bereft of any substantial use of anthropology in the twenty-seven contributions; sociology and psychosocial pursuits dominate discussion. In marked contrast, Stegemann, Malina and Theissen's recent edited work, *The Social Setting of Jesus and Gospels* (2002) does provide a wealth of cross-cultural and anthropological readings. Also, a book I co-edited with Mario Aguilar, *Anthropology and Biblical Studies: Avenues of Approach* (2004) documents the findings of an international conference held in St Andrews, Scotland on the interface between these two specific disciplines. Within New Testament studies it is true to say that anthropological comparisons have had their most notable press in the project of understanding and bridging the cultural gaps that exist between interpreter (exegete) and interpreted (the New Testament). This perspective has stimulated countless projects that have sought to understand the 'foreign' nature of the texts and peoples encountered within them.

Navigating Foreign Worlds

HSBC Bank has an amusing television commercial. It features a young man leaving a bunch of carnations on the bike of a girl he adores. The advert goes on to indicate that, in Italy, carnations are associated with death. We see old women looking in horror at the carnation adorned bike, and they in turn bring tributes to the scene, weeping and wailing. The object of the man's affections then opens her door and is met by the curious scene, the old women, at the sight of the girl, faint. The advert ends – 'At HSBC we never underestimate the importance of local knowledge.'

In a related vein, the last chapter of Acts tells how Paul and his travelling companion arrived at the Island of Malta and were warmly greeted by the people there (28:1–6). The word used to describe these people is *barbaroi*, variously translated in dictionaries as barbarian, foreign, strange and non-Greek. The NRSV renders it as 'native': a word that was popular in anthropology in times past, to denote indigenous peoples who were historically the subjects of anthropological fieldwork. Both the advert and the Acts encounter beautifully illustrate the anthropological assumption that different cultures hold different expectations and understandings of customs, morality and values. The man thinks carnations are a symbol of love not death, but this perspective is not shared by the culture he is in. The Maltese 'natives' interpret Paul's curious encounter with a viper in the first instance as evidence that he is a murderer (*phoneus*, v. 4). However, when Paul killed the poisonous creature in the fire, the people hail him as a god (*theon*, v. 6). To understand both viewpoints one has to understand the cultural perspectives from which they interpret the incident. The anthropological dictum that one needs to try and 'contextualise' the response before one can try and understand it seems particularly appropriate in each case.

The champions of the move to use cultural anthropology in New Testament studies, are a group of scholars collectively known as the Context Group, a largely North American movement (on the development of this group see Esler 2004). Spearheaded by Bruce Malina, and stimulated by his 1981 work *The New Testament World*, these scholars defend the use of cross-cultural models in exegesis and seek to avoid the 'twin monsters' of anachronism and ethnocentrism. Anachronism is the representation of something as existing other than at its proper time. An anachronistic statement would be, for example, 'Alexander the Great set his digital watch alarm for lunch time'. Ethnocentrism is interpreting other cultures from one's own perspective and assuming a superiority of one's own culture over others. An example of this would be a Scotsman who claimed that all cultures not promoting men to wear skirts are somehow morally deficient (for further discussion on anachronism and ethnocentrism see Rohrbaugh 2002; Craffert 1995; 1996). The Context Group assume that cultural anthropology, based on studies of the Mediterranean region, enables the interpreter to correlate at least in part, values of that area, with ancient Mediterranean contexts and situations. Abstraction in turn provides the raw material for the construction of a model. The models posited within the script include the following (for comprehensive analysis of cultural scripts, see Lawrence 2003).

- *Honour and Shame:* Honour denoted the socially approved and expected attitudes and behaviour in areas where power, sexual status and religion intersect. Accordingly, honour (either ascribed or acquired) comprised two basic and balancing elements: the assertion of worth and the acknowledgement of that worth by others. Since shame was dependent on views of the group, it was claimed to function as a measure of social sanction in the kin-based collective social structure of the Mediterranean.

- *Anti-Introspective Self:* People within an honour culture are outwardly (publicly) orientated rather than internally orientated (shame-based rather than guilt-based). As a result, people afforded little significance to individual consciousness and thought.

- *Agonistic Interaction and Challenge-Riposte:* Cultures that hold honour as their core value are inherently competitive (agonistic). Accordingly, males defending their honour in public engage in a social confrontation known as challenge-riposte, in which an evaluating audience accords honour to one or other of the participants.

- *Limited Good:* This refers to the cognitive conviction in small, closely knit groups that all goods (including immaterial elements such as health and precedence) exist in limited supply. This in turn results in the perception that one party's gain can only occur by another's loss.

- *Dyadic Personality:* Dyadic personality, as opposed to individualist personality, is a discernment of self, established by and dependent upon the assessments of others.

- *Sexual Division of Labour:* Honour is associated primarily with male kin representatives and is symbolised by blood, lineage, name and physical attributes. Such qualities are subject to constant social challenge in the public sphere. In contrast, females have to be sexually exclusive (shame in a positive sense), compliant, submissive and humble and are confined to the home and private sphere.

- *Evil Eye:* A cultural reflex that wards off envy, particularly of honour. Such a response is necessary in a limited good environment.

Many projects have produced schematic readings of biblical texts (even entire books) in light of the cultural map plotted above (Malina & Rohrbaugh 1998; Malina & Pilch 2000; Neyrey 1998). For example the scandal of the cross has been interpreted in light of the cultural values of honour and shame (Neyrey 1996) and as a ritual of status transformation (McVann 1993). The relationship between the individual and group as a determinant of personality in the Mediterranean has also been scrutinised (Malina 1981: 51–70; 94–121; 1996; Malina & Neyrey 1991: 67–96; 1996). The evil eye has been linguistically and culturally investigated in relation to selected biblical passages (Elliott 1988; 1990; 1992; Derrett 1995). Similarly, the limited good ethos has been discussed and linked to the social institution of patronage in the ancient world (Malina 2001 [1981]: 81–82; Moxnes 1991). Such work has forcibly injected a 'cultural shock' to exegetes and warned them of the folly of interpreting 'alien' texts as mere reflections of their own cultural contexts and assumptions.

Selected Anthropological Analyses of the New Testament

In a different situation altogether, Claude Lévi-Strauss discussed totem objects as 'good to think with', allowing groups to ponder and contemplate their own condition. In a similar vein, anthropology has provided biblical scholars with myriad 'resources to think with'. Texts have been mined for relevant data before bringing comparative material regarding the theme under question to bear on it. Subjects addressed have (to name but a few) included the structure and purposes of ritual in the early church; kinship; purity and pollution; disease and healing; comparison of religious practitioners; witchcraft accusations and magic.

Van Gennep's work on rites of passage and Victor Tuner's perspectives on liminality and *communitas* of rites have variously informed biblical readings. Neyrey (1995), for example, has drawn a distinction between rituals (single actions) and ceremonies (repeated actions). The purposes of rituals, for example, baptism and the Lord's Supper in the Pauline churches, have been investigated (Horrell 1996; MacDonald 1988; Meeks 1983); even ritual transformations on mountains (Hanson 1994).

Kinship (a subject that has been seen by some to be as central for anthropology as the nude is for art) has also featured in analysis of religious groups. The importance of the family and household as the identity label of the early Christian church has been particularly illuminated by categories of fictive kin and household respectively (Osiek & Balch 1997; Esler 2000b). Destro and Pesce have built upon this interest and constructed the ethos of kinship in relation to discipleship and movement in John's Gospel (1995).

Purity and pollution have also been firmly set on the exegete's agenda since Douglas's celebrated work on Jewish law (1975; 1992

[1966]; 1996 [1970]). In New Testament studies the cultural importance of boundary maintenance, policing 'matter and people out of place' and Jesus' transcendence of traditional grounds for enforcing purity rules has been outlined (Neyrey 1986a). Others have utilised Douglas's work on cosmologies and grid/group analyses to investigate community contradictions and innovations (Lucien 1984; see also Carter's recent reading of Paul through Douglas's theories, 2003).

There has also been a considerable rise in interest in illness and healing through the adoption of resources from medical anthropology seeking to understand the world of peasant societies and their social conceptions of disease and wholeness. John Pilch has been at the forefront of these moves (1985; 1986; 2000a; see also Elliott 1988: 60–66; 1992; 2000). The powerful realisation that disease is not only physical (the primary assumption of the Western scientific mindset) but also profoundly social is imperative in understanding the transformations effected by Jesus, on behalf of the sick and unclean. In Pilch's words 'Jesus reduces and removes the experiential oppressiveness associated with such afflictions. In all instances of healing, meaning is restored to life and the sufferer is returned to purposeful living' (2000a: 14).

Religious figures have also provided comparative material for investigation of the religious identities and dimensions of New Testament figures. Davies has seen Jesus as a healer (1995), and Malina and Neyrey have seen him as a magician (1988). Pilch has compared Jesus with a shaman (1993; 1998; 1995; 2002; see also Craffert 1999; DeMaris 2002) and Ashton has conducted a shamanic analysis of Paul's experiences and identity (2000).

Anthropological concerns have also made a mark in historical Jesus studies, particularly within the constructions of members of the Jesus Seminar. Crossan's methodology, for example, involves a 'macrocosmic' method, which draws on social anthropology concerning a wide variety of themes (honour and shame, ecstatic religion, healing, power, magic, protest movements) as well as microcosmic analysis of literary sources (Crossan 1991: xxviii–xxix). Similarly, Borg has constructed his picture of a spirit-led Jesus along similar lines to anthropological studies of those controlling spirits and undergoing vision quests: 'a "spirit person", a "mediator of the sacred", one of those persons in human history to whom the Spirit was an experiential reality' (Borg 1993 [1987]: 32).

The respective pictures presented of Jesus by Borg and Crossan are of course comparative constructions. We will not bump into any historical

'Mediterranean Cynic, Jewish Peasants' or identical 'Spirit-driven Sages'. But this is not to say that particular elements of Jesus' character and mission are not brought into greater relief by the anthropological analyses of these respective scholars.

Anthropological studies of witchcraft and magic have also been brought to bear on particular situations within the early church tradition (Esler 1994; Neyrey 1986b; 1988). Witchcraft and sorcery accusations for example have informed understandings of disputes, both among early Christians and with Jews (Malina 1991), also in interpretation of the book of Revelation (Duff 1997; Elliott 1993: 261–76). Related to an interest in linguistic conflict and exchange has been the development of work that looks into secrecy and lying as powerful actions in an honour culture that puts premium importance on the public sphere (Pilch 1992a; Pilch 1994; Botha 1998).

Having introduced some of the associations and collaborations between biblical studies and anthropology, I want to briefly suggest some methodological pointers for future interaction between the two. It should have become clear to you that I wholeheartedly affirm the use of anthropology to overcome cultural difference in biblical interpretation. However, there are pitfalls; therefore, we must tread cautiously.

The most obvious limitation in the adoption and application of predefined models (whether they are highly abstracted cultural values such as honour and shame or more general conclusions regarding shamans, speaking in tongues and the like) is that of determinism. Once evidence is viewed within the framework of a particular model, it is difficult, if not impossible, to consider viewpoints that do not fit that framework (Horrell 2000; Esler 2000a; Lawrence 2003: 37–39). This is not to say, however, that some sort of interpretation of context is unimportant or fruitless. Rather a balance between micro and macro scale dynamics is needed. This is particularly true given the recent critique of the culture concept in anthropology (Aguilar 2004), which argues for recognition in anthropological studies of individual diversity, as opposed to proposing grand and unified cultural schemes accepted in the same way by everyone. While Geertz may have been right at one time to stress, in symbolic terms, that culture constitutes human beings 'caught in webs of significance', now ideological concerns make contemporary anthropologists retort, 'who is weaving the web and who is just suspended in it?' In this respect, interest in individual resistance to dominant cultural frameworks is central. In his study of ethnographic practices for the twenty-first century, Denzin constructs the following vision for contemporary ethnography:

Ethnographies will not attempt to capture the totality of a group's way of life. The focus will be ... slices, glimpses, and specimens of interaction that display how cultural practices, connected to structural formations and narrative texts, are experiences at a particular time and place by interacting individuals.

Denzin 1997: 247

Of course, anthropological readings of the Bible also share the problems that plague social-scientific analysis of the Bible as a whole. Derek Tidball, in particular reference to sociology, identifies these as follows (1983: 20–21): First, there is a lack of relevant evidence in the biblical text for social conclusions to be drawn. Second, there are no avenues for gaining more information or conducting further field research open to the biblical exegete. Third, is the danger of parallelomania (two different cultures being assumed to resemble each other on the basis of certain similarities). The last of these is perhaps the most serious for anthropological research that works from comparison. However, as long as one reads comparatively, with humility, in order to cast fresh light on, rather than dictate or presume to wholly understand patterns, hazards can be ameliorated to some degree.

Overholt, in his study, *Cultural Anthropology and the Old Testament* (1996) described three attractions of anthropological research that seem crucial in such amelioration of criticisms, even before analysis has a chance to get started. First, he notes that it is important to take account of agency (namely individual actions) as well as social structure. This is especially important in light of the destabilising of the culture concept as a unified, static entity (see Aguilar 2004). Second, Overholt commends those perspectives that recognise that social life contains within it contradictions and inconsistencies. Not every person in a culture submits to a cultural script, there are different viewpoints. Third, he applauds those working with what he terms a 'non-positive epistemology which holds that anthropological description does not mirror social reality, but rather provides one of several possible maps that can guide us in our attempts to understand society' (Overholt 1996: 5). This is especially instructive for the present project. In the past I have been particularly critical of those who claim to uncover the 'truth' about Mediterranean society and values by abstracting from modern ethnography of the area (Lawrence 2002; 2003). The world(s) of the Bible are not simply the world(s) of the Mediterranean (or any other part of the world) today. However, if one is willing to provide comparisons without the straitjacket of positivism, one is open (not enslaved) to the possibilities hinted at in the comparative process. The exhibits of this book, which are not predicated on any claim whatsoever to reveal '*the* culture', '*the* values' or '*the* situation' of the texts in view (if ever such an endeavour is possible in the first place), are a case in point.

Conclusion

Ben Witherington closed *Women in the Ministry of Jesus* (1984) with the declaration that his book stood as an 'open ended beginning, rather than a self-contained end' (1984: 131). In many ways the projects alluded to here provide similar invitations. Thanks to their insights, it is now duly acknowledged that our assumptions as Western readers should not be uncritically transferred to our interpretation of scriptures. Recourse to anthropology, a discipline that works from the simple but effective assumption that one cannot understand particular actions or beliefs without encountering other instances of such behaviour across the world, seems particularly relevant in such cases. It helps us straddle the divide between reading people of ancient texts as pale reflections of ourselves and seeing them (and other peoples of the world today) as radically 'other' from us. Its potential contributions in our world, so often plagued by social and cultural unawareness and prejudice, should be obvious.

Suggestions for Further Reading

For general introductions to the aims and agendas of social-scientific criticism, see Elliott (1993); Horrell (1999); Martin (1999); Wortham (1999). With specific reference to the Old Testament, see Chalcraft (1997); and with reference to the New Testament, see Esler (1994); Pilch (2000b); Rohrbaugh (1996); Stegemann, Malina and Theissen (2002); Blasi, Duhaime and Turcotte (2002).

Specifically on the use of anthropology and biblical studies, see Leach (1982) and Lawrence and Aguilar (2004). On the use of cultural anthropology in Old Testament studies, see Overholt (1996). For a collection of essays on anthropological approaches to the Old Testament (mainly written by anthropologists), see Lang (1985). For critical reflection on the use of anthropology in reference to ancient Israel, see Rogerson (1979). On the cultural script of Mediterranean worlds in reference to the New Testament, see Malina (2001 [1981]) and Pilch (1999).

2

Reading with Anthropology

A Reductive Pursuit?

For many Christians, the term anthropology is either an unknown term or one that they associate with those who attack Christianity ... I often have people ask me, 'How can you be both an anthropologist and a Christian?'

C. Kraft

The most basic contribution that anthropological understanding of culture – post-modern or not – makes to theology is to suggest that theology be viewed as part of culture, as a form of cultural activity ... Like all human activities, it is historically and socially conditioned; it cannot be understood in isolation from the rest of human socio-cultural practices.

K. Tanner

These quotations from Charles Kraft and Katherine Tanner provide a departure point for our journey. They propose that anthropology and theology both have at their heart an interest in human life, culture and experience. However, the two have not always been seen as compatible pursuits, indeed some claim that assumptions underlying their respective enquiries are diametrically opposed.

Social science is, according to the *Oxford English Dictionary*, 'the scientific study of human society and social relationships'. Note the focus on human and terrestrial elements as opposed to transcendent. In contrast, the dictionary definition of scripture is as follows: 'the sacred writings of Christianity contained in the Bible – from Latin *scriptura* meaning writings'. While the term 'sacred' introduces a holy, 'set apart' element (perhaps denoted in subject matter or its status as revelation, words of God) it is also true that scripture itself results from human cultural activities. It documents the lives and social experiences of particular religious groups in diverse environments. The sacred and social should not and cannot be conceived in isolation.

In this chapter I will briefly introduce the 'reductionism critique' and provide a review of two scholars who, in different ways, have actively countered such criticisms and viewed anthropology and theology together in creative, illuminating ways. First, Charles Kraft, a Christian missionary who uses anthropology in cross-cultural encounters; second, Douglas Davies, an anthropologist and theologian who has engaged both disciplines in a rich and fruitful way to shed light on traditional Christian doctrines. I will then seek to outline two main elements that will ground subsequent readings in this book, namely, 'embodiment' and humanity as 'ceremonial animals', respectively derived from Fiona Bowie and Wendy James. These concepts in turn provide the central axis on which subsequent chapters are hinged. It is my contention that anthropological approaches offer biblical exegetes some ways to unite practice and belief, body and soul, experience and institution, culture and gospel.

'Reading with Anthropology': A Reductive Pursuit?

Davies voiced a virtual truism when he claimed 'Christian theology could not function without God, while anthropology operates per-fectly naturally without it' (2002: 1). It is unsurprising that a disci-pline that was perceived not to *need* God was also seen by some as a discipline working *against* God. Thus was born the reductionist critique, social science was 'reductive' vis-à-vis the transcendent. The *Concise Oxford Dictionary* provides the following definition of reductionism,

> reductionism *n*.—often derogatory, the practice of analysing and describing a complex phenomenon in terms of its simple or fundamental constituents, especially when this is said to provide a sufficient explanation.

John Milbank (1990), a key figure in the 'Radical Orthodoxy' movement, claims that religion, spirit and theology in the hands of the social scientist becomes little more than a product of particular social circumstances. More importantly in his opinion, it sets up a counter-narrative to a theological metanarrative, and as such should be rejected. Milbank fears that nothing but a 'residual place is left for Christianity and theology within the reality that is supposed to be authoritatively described by such a [social-scientific] theory' (Milbank 1990: 2).

The historical uneasiness between social science and theology of course goes back to the opinion held by social-scientific forefathers. Feuerbach, Durkheim and Freud all played a part in popularising the dictum that theology, while claiming to be about God, is at base about humanity (Davies 2002: 2). More recently in the great sociologist Berger's terms, social scientists primarily observed religious actions but were not interested in questions of a correlate transcendental reality. Their academic outlook in this sense was a form of 'methodological atheism' (Berger 1967: 179–85). On account of this some may say it is unsurprising that some have boycotted social science as 'taboo' in any discussion that wishes to value or affirm the reality of God, religious experience or belief.

On the surface at least, corroborating this position, James cites Evans-Pritchard's 1959 lecture 'Religion and the Anthropologists' in which he claimed disapprovingly that most anthropologists were either atheists or agnostics bereft of 'an ear' (a musical metaphor) for the religious experiences of those studied (James 2003: 126). James goes on to tell us that 'in his analysis of the Nuer, Evans-Pritchard appropriated language of the Bible as part of his project of presenting Nuer religion as one way of understanding the nature of God; and thus claiming the attention and respect of Christian believers' (James 2003: 126). While this implicitly provides evidence that some anthropologists (i.e. Evans-Pritchard) were actively trying to shake off a bias against belief within the discipline, his comments also attest that he saw himself as an 'enlightened' exception to the rule.

However, while some anthropologists may, in times gone by, have been staunch atheists (Frazer's *Golden Bough* set out to disprove claims of the Bible) most anthropologists would probably now be classified as neutral as opposed to anti-transcendental and faith claims. In Fiona Bowie's words:

It is an etic rather than an emic perspective on a religious culture. As anthropologists we are interested in what people say is the truth, the way people think the world works, their understanding of the mysteries of God or gods and their actual behaviour.

2003: 49

Social-scientific criticism actually arose in order to redress an imbalance from another direction, namely an inordinate importance being put on thought and belief to the neglect of physicality and society. To use Robin Scroggs's powerful phrase, New Testament studies was dogged by a 'methodological docetism' (cited in Horrell 1999: 6), it interpreted the fledgling Christian movement as 'disembodied' from its social situation and context.

Esler (1995a) has been a particularly prominent voice in bridging bodies, souls, social processes and faith. He submits that the theological appropriation of social-scientific research requires 'an understanding of contemporary Christian theology with which historical results might be brought into conjunction' (1995a: 15). He cites George Lindbeck's work *The Nature of Doctrine, Religion and Theology in a Post-Liberal Age* (1984), which builds on perspectives from anthropology to construct a theory of religious belief and action as a language of cultural suppositions. In such a framework the religious believer is seen to learn to embody a tradition's story, life and message in culture and practice. The social sciences can therefore offer important vistas to the social life of belief. Tanner, as a pupil of Lindbeck, also provides recent work on the pertinence of the culture concept to contemporary theology. In a post-modern way, she traces the potentially fruitful interaction that can be enjoyed between the two. For Tanner, 'theology is something humans produce' (thus anthropologists are interested in it) and 'like all human activities, it is historically and socially conditioned; it cannot be understood in isolation from the rest of human socio-cultural practices' (Tanner 1997: 63).

Paul Tillich's work on a *Theology of Culture* (1959) should also, of course, be mentioned at this point. His important work linked sacred and secular realms by interest in 'ultimate concern' that in his opinion pointed to the divine. His existential starting point valued human experiences and saw God as the ground of all being. In his words 'every joy is joy in God. In all preliminary concerns, ultimate concern is present . . . the religious and the secular are not separated' (Tillich 1959: 42).

While theology and social sciences have been seen by many to be explosive and damaging to each other when used collaboratively, I hope that some of the avenues above have shown that this certainly need not be the case. Yes, it is true that one is primarily interested in the social, the other open to the transcendent. But two different starting points and research agendas on one particular issue need not mean a battle for primacy by each discipline. Rather, each can contribute something original and provide a more holistic reasoning and understanding of the subject matter to hand.

Dialogues Between Anthropology and Theology

Salamone and Adams have posited the methods of what they term 'The Anthropology of Theology' (1997; 2000). In their opinion this pursuit is differentiated from the anthropology of religion (which they perceive as focusing on institutions) by placing more emphasis on semiotics (the analysis of comprehension through signs), values and morality. In Adams's words, an anthropology of theology 'is the study of meaning behind central tenets of faith, the systems of values, and of moral and ethical codes' (Adams 1997: 2). Critically they argue that 'theology' should not be restricted to Christian perspectives alone, but rather should address 'questions posed by any modern religion' (Adams & Salamone 2000: 4; on a theology of culture, see Van Rheenen 1997). I am not convinced that a neat division between 'religion' (as institutional practice) and theology (as morals, values and beliefs) can be sustained. However, their point that thought, just as much as action, is important within enquiry of this sort is helpful. The comparison of diverse religious traditions within the 'anthropology of theology' is also illuminating. Two other scholars, who have devoted much of their professional lives to fostering links between anthropology and (Christian) theology, are Kraft and Davies. Both aptly illustrate the possibilities for cross-fertilisation of ideas between the two disciplines and both unite action, morals and belief in their work.

Charles Kraft: Missionary and Anthropologist

Kraft, as a missionary and anthropologist, sees anthropology as the most important discipline for dealing with non-Western cultures. He provides ten reasons why anthropology is crucial to the cross-cultural witness he is involved in (Kraft 1996: 4–13) and cites vivid examples of the hazards involved in cross-cultural misunderstandings.

> What should a cross-cultural witness do when he discovers that presenting Satan as a dragon (Rev 12) to Chinese results in their regarding him positively? Or presenting Jesus as the Good Shepherd in parts of Africa results in their understanding him to be mentally incompetent? Or telling the story of Jesus' betrayal results in Judas being regarded as a hero?
>
> Kraft 1979: 14

While Kraft's main interest was 'translating' scriptural assumptions and ideas for the benefit of receptor cultures, if one transposes his points to a project trying to understand the 'different' and 'foreign' worlds of the Bible, important insights are also gained.

First, Kraft points out that 'anthropology deals with concrete behaviour' (1996: 4). Anthropology as a behavioural science observes what people do and say without necessarily judging them. This is important given the different worldviews of the Bible. We could, for example, feel uneasy with talk of demons and devils, etc. but this is no reason to try and explain such beliefs away or attribute them to the 'primitive' assumptions of the scriptural authors.

Second, Kraft shows that 'anthropology has for the most part focused on non-Western cultures' (1996: 5). This has obvious importance for his project of making the Bible make sense in non-Western environments. However, it is also important for biblical studies, which has for the most part been dominated by Western scholarship. Anthropology bestows the biblical interpreter with what I have elsewhere termed 'a taste for the other' (Lawrence 2004: 9), and in so doing widens our gaze, from our own narrow cultural context, immeasurably.

Third, Kraft notes that 'culture is the anthropologist's main category' (1996: 6). Definitions of culture are notoriously difficult to pin down, but in general terms it seems culture consists of social customs and expectations into which individuals are socialised. Not that everyone is a social robot, but nonetheless there are general norms to which people are socialised to accept and live out. We have to try and discover the cultural assumptions and values of those we seek to understand. It is also important, in light of Edward Said's warnings against the perils of Orientalism, that we do not prize our own culture as more refined or developed than others.

Fourth, Kraft submits that 'anthropology takes a holistic view of communities' (1996: 7). Anthropology forges links between cultural life, experience, family, religion, politics, etc. In Kraft's words 'people are like fish swimming in cultural water … the culture in which people exist must be taken into account, people must, furthermore, be treated holistically' (1996: 8). This is particularly important in cultures such as those represented in the Bible where one cannot, and should not, separate realms of family, religion and politics. However, while acknowledging the existence of general patterns of socio-cultural life one must not assume that every individual embodies 'culture' in the same ways (see the critique of the culture concept in anthropology in Aguilar 2004c).

Fifth, Kraft praises the empathetic nature of anthropology, which 'provides a perspective by which to view communities' and see them 'not simply a[s] subject' (1996: 8). Anthropology can bring a cross-cultural perspective to our reading of biblical texts. Since scripture itself consists of texts from other times, places and cultures, its 'otherness' should not be overlooked. We need to cultivate a cross-cultural perspective if we are to involve ourselves with what is going on in the text.

Sixth, Kraft claims 'anthropology focuses on communication' (1996: 10). Here he emphasises the fact that anthropology focuses on people in relationships with others across cultural parapets and boundaries. Only by trying to ponder on the nature of our encounters with the Bible, can we hope to avoid falsely characterising those populating biblical worlds.

Seventh, Kraft sees anthropology distinguishing between forms and meanings (1996: 10). This, Kraft believes, means that we do not just see a practice as sacred (for example, the community of goods – the purposeful pooling of money and material possessions by members of a group), but rather that the meanings flowing through the practice are brought into sharper focus in comparison.

Eighth, he praises anthropology for emphasis on the worldview of those studied (1996: 11). Anthropology sees interconnections between all facets of a person's experience and does not seek to question or disprove the reality of each worldview; actions and thoughts are intimately related and should not be divorced from one another.

Ninth, Kraft sees anthropology's research method of participant observation (1996: 12) as reclaiming an experiential dimension to study. This is of course slightly more difficult in relation to texts. We cannot live among a community; however, it does give salutary warning that the interpreters must try, in all possible ways, to immerse themselves within the text and the assumptions that are presented in it.

Finally, Kraft believes that anthropology can deal with cultural change and development (1996: 12–13). It does not just see societies as static, photo images, despite its interest in participant observation. It wants to construct a diachronic, as well as synchronic, perspective. Plotting changes and developments (for example, leadership patterns, attitudes to women) would be significant here. For both the one transmitting the Bible into different cultural contexts and the one interested in discovering the different cultural contexts assumed in the Bible, anthropology makes, on the basis of Kraft's work, a trusty travelling companion.

Traditionally, of course, anthropologists were very sceptical of missionaries, not least because they were seen to disregard native worldviews and pursue colonialist strategies and initiate cultural change. Stipe in his essay 'Anthropologists Versus Missionaries: The Influence of Presuppositions' (1999) cites Keesing's stereotypical pictures of missionaries and anthropologists to make this point vividly:

> The caricatured missionary is strait-laced, repressed, and a narrow-minded Bible thumper trying to get native women to cover their bosoms decently; the anthropologist is a bearded degenerate given to taking his clothes off and sampling wild rites.

Keesing cited in Stipe 1999: 12

However, while the missionary may have traditionally been viewed negatively in anthropology, some of their presuppositions have been extremely informative vis-à-vis social-scientific analysis of the Bible. Their realisation that one had to understand the culture of those among whom you worked is central. Moreover, the form of missionary that Kraft embodies (trained in anthropology as well as Bible transmission) shows the reflective and reciprocal relationship between the disciplines and their mutually informing agendas. His work seems vital not only for transposing text to diverse cultures today, but also for looking through the window of the text to the diverse cultures that lie behind it.

Douglas Davies: Anthropologist and Theologian

Davies in his recent book, *Anthropology and Theology* (2002) also brings the two disciplines into fruitful dialogue. He shows how anthropological reflections on self, society, symbols and rituals have something to say to Christian ideas regarding the human condition, worship and practical theology. He also looks at how anthropological theorising on the body, death and sacrifice can cast new light on traditional Christian doctrines of incarnation, atonement and salvation. His major focus is on Anglicanism but reference is also made to Roman Catholic and Greek Orthodox traditions within his book.

Davies draws on anthropological work from the nineteenth century (including evolutionists such as Tylor), more recent symbolic approaches (Geertz, Douglas, Sahlins) and contemporary anthropological debate. At all times his project does not seek to reconcile or conflate anthropology and theology. In his various discussions they stand as autonomous perspectives, which nevertheless have respectively pertinent things to say on the subject matters at hand. For example, he links embodiment with the doctrine of the incarnation and merit-making with soteriology in underlining the important anthropological mirroring of key Christian doctrines. He submits that 'it is because the "real meaning" is grounded in the "inalienable gift" of Jesus as God's son' that we can conceive of Christ as 'given but never given away' (Davies 2002: 53).

He also investigated the efficacy of sacrifice in reference to embodiment and nominated participation and substitution as two central concepts in understanding this. In reference to the former, he cites Lévy-Bruhl's work on how primitive people were participators in their natural environments. In reference to the latter he discusses Evans-Pritchard's ideas of the 'substitutionary' nature of sacrifice in Sudanese sacrificial ideals: 'Substitution of cattle for people is possible because of the prior degree of Nuer participation in cattle, both practical and conceptual' (Davies 2002: 96).

Davies goes on to discuss ritual, symbolism, sacrament and spiritual gifts in illuminating ways from the dual perspective of anthropology and Christian theology. His stimulating book ends with the galvanising call that both anthropology and theology can, and should, be speaking to (though not merging into) each other in research. He concludes,

> In the present state of knowledge the venture of furnishing meaning and of being attentive to our very existence, with simplicity but without naiveté, demands that anthropologists and theologians acknowledge that they have much to ponder as the conversation continues.
>
> Davies 2002: 209

If it is true that the combining of interests of anthropology and theology yields rich harvests of understanding, what particular 'categories' of thought bridging both disciplines can be helpful as we begin our journey? While Kraft saw the intersection between text and living community, and Davies saw the intersection between anthropological theory and Christian doctrine, I take my stepping stones to be embodiment and the profound ritualistic nature of human living evidenced in the Bible and other communities across the world.

Embodiment and Humans as 'Ceremonial Animals'

Morris Beaman, a historian, once remarked that 'history gets written with the mind holding the pen'. He then wondered 'what would it look like, what would it read like, if it got written with the *body* holding the pen?' (cited in Csordas 1999: 184). This analogy seems to be expressing similar sentiments to those propagating social-scientific analysis as one way to counter an inordinate focus on mind and theology in biblical studies. I have adopted two concepts, 'Embodiment' and 'Humans as Ceremonial Animals' as frameworks to 'read with' in subsequent exhibits in this book.

I initially derived the concepts of 'embodiment' and humans as 'ceremonial animals' from two female anthropologists: Bowie and James. In Bowie's view, religion is intimately related to embodied social experience (2003). She explores ways in which spirituality is transmitted through inscription on the body as well as the mind, bringing external, observable aspects of religion and the interior realm of personal experience together. She sees the body as a medium of interpretation for spiritual experiences. In this perspective, anthropology is not denying reality of belief in God but actually studying how 'being religious' or 'having faith' is *embodied* in society and practice.

Wendy James's recent book, *The Ceremonial Animal* (2003) (a title adopted from Wittgenstein's writing) attempts to show how people are socially and ritually formed throughout their lives. Ceremony is perhaps a word that evokes sociality and practice more than 'culture' does in present anthropology. In James's opinion we 'may share a sense of wonder and curiosity about the nature and history of our imaginative, sometimes fierce but always vulnerable species' (2003: viii).

Both theorists have contributed to my own thinking in different ways on how practice, performances and social memory are intimately related to religious belief and experience.

Embodiment

Bowie in her recent article 'An Anthropology of Religious Experience: Spirituality, Gender and Cultural Transmission in the Focolare Movement' (2003) draws on her experiences as both anthropologist and a member of Focolare. She is particularly interested in 'understanding the body as a medium of interpretation for spiritual experience' (2003: 50). She sees that spirituality embodied within the movement 'transmitted through inscription on body as well as mind' bridges 'external observable acts of religion and the interior realm of personal experience' (2003: 50).

An anthropological interest in the body is of course nothing new. It can be traced back to the now classic works of Robert Hertz (1960 [1909]) who famously showed the social pre-eminence of the right hand and Marcel Mauss (1973 [1935]) who documented various bodily techniques. Bowie herself draws on Mauss's ideas of bodily performances and *habitus*, 'learned ways of acting that become internalised so as to appear natural' (2003: 54). Grimes's metaphor, referred to in the introduction, of ritual embedding itself 'Deeply into the Bone' is also relevant here.

Following on from these innovations, Scheper-Hughes and Lock in their article 'The Mindful Body: A Prolegomenon to Future Work in Medical Anthropology' (1987) present three perspectives from which the body is viewed in anthropology (1987: 6). First is 'a phenomenally experienced individual body-self'; second, 'a social body, a natural symbol for thinking about relationships among nature, society and culture'; third is 'a body politic, an artifact of social and political control'.

The individual body involves the worlds of individual experiences. Scheper-Hughes and Lock cite Mauss's important work on the embodied self in both health and sickness, distinct from other individual bodies (1987: 7). The social body concept owes much to the celebrated work of Douglas and her analysis of the symbolic use of the body for social purposes (1975; 1992 [1966]). In her opinion 'the body in health offers a model of organic wholeness; the body in sickness offers a model of disharmony, conflict and disintegration' (Douglas discussed in Scheper-Hughes & Lock 1987: 7). The body politic is interested in the control of both individual and collective bodies. Scheper-Hughes and Lock refer to Foucault's important work in this area in showing that in polities 'the stability of the body politic rests on its ability to regulate populations (the social body) and to discipline individual bodies' (1987: 8).

The importance of a heuristic interest in the body can hardly be overestimated in light of the above. The body literally 'embodies' belief, cultures and values.

It is a form of communication – the language of the organs – through which nature, society, and culture speak simultaneously. The individual body would be seen as the most immediate, the proximate terrain where social truths and social contradictions are played out, as well as a locus of personal and social resistance, creativity and struggle.

Scheper-Hughes & Lock 1987: 31

One of the foremost contemporary theorists on the body in anthropology is Thomas Csordas. He sees a crucial difference between understandings of the body alone and what he terms 'embodiment'. In his opinion the body 'is a biological material entity and embodiment is an indeterminate methodological field defined by perceptual experience and by mode of presence and engagement in the world' (Csordas 1999: 182). Embodiment in Csordas's opinion can 'be elaborated for the study of culture and the self' (1990: 5). Csordas explains,

> Embodiment begins from the methodological postulate that the body is not an object to be studied in relation to culture, but is to be considered as the subject of culture, or in other words as the existential ground of culture.
>
> Csordas 1990: 5

It is in this sense that 'a theory of practice can best be grounded in the socially informed body' (Csordas 1990: 7). That 'the locus of the sacred is the body' (Csordas 1990: 39) should be evidence enough that one reading the Bible would do well to 'read with the body' and focus on the body as a canvas and channel of significant religious boundaries and beliefs.

Body images and concepts are also important 'food for thought'. It has been noted, for example, that different cultures 'think with' different parts of the human body. Scheper-Hughes and Lock cite the example of the liver, which 'absorbs a great deal of blame for many different ailments among the French, Spanish, Portuguese and Brazilians' (1997: 17). They also cite Muller who amusingly writes 'when an Englishman complains about constipation, you never know whether he is talking about his regularity, his lassitude, or his depression' (Muller cited in Scheper-Hughes & Lock 1997: 17). Bodily fluids are also important symbolic resources. Blood, for example, is important in constructions of health and social well-being (Scheper-Hughes & Lock 1997: 18).

The body even represents cosmological or other natural phenomena in some cultures. For example, the Dogon of Western Sudan see the village 'from north to south like the body of a man lying on his back. The head is the council house, built in the Centre Square. To the east and west are the menstrual huts which are "round like wombs and represent the hands of the village"' (Scheper-Hughes & Lock 1997: 21). Csordas concludes,

> To work in a paradigm of embodiment is not to study anything new or different, but to address familiar topics – healing, emotion, gender or power – from a different standpoint. Embodiment is about neither behaviour nor essence *per se* but about experience and subjectivity, and understanding

these is a function of interpreting action in different modes and expression in different idioms.

Csordas 1999: 184

Humans as 'Ceremonial Animals'

James (2003) takes as her starting point the fact that humans embody beliefs and practices in their day-to-day lives. She is interested in what could be termed the cultural choreography of life. She discusses Godfrey Lienhardt's work, *Divinity and Experience: The Religion of the Dinka*, published in 1961, in which he investigated experiential impacts of different religious events (James 2003: 126). In brief, these Southern Sudanese people constructed images of divinities from their social experiences, particularly those related to life and death. Moreover, Lienhardt saw rituals as something that could shape experience and form moralities, a point that would later be taken up in Rappaport's celebrated work on *Ritual and the Making of Humanity* (1999). In Rappaport's opinion performance of particular practices brings into being the values and commitments of the order of life of which ritual is a part. In his words,

> In attending to ritual's form we must not lose sight of the fundamental nature of what it is that ritual does as a logically necessary outcome of its form. In enunciating, accepting and making conventions moral, ritual contains within itself not simply a symbolic representation of social contract, but tacit social contract itself. As such, rituals ... guards and bridges boundaries between public systems and private processes, [and] are the basic social act.
>
> Rappaport cited in Lambek 2002: 465

James also approvingly cites Davis's 1982 edited work, *Religious Organisation and Religious Experience*, which takes as its subject, experience, rather than institutions or systems. One particularly interesting essay in Davis's edited book is by Ruel, entitled 'Christians as Believers' (1982: 9–31). He investigates the meaning of 'belief' in Christianity, which transformed Hebrew 'trust' in God to a particular propositional 'belief that' ... Jesus was raised. He traces the meaning of belief in Christianity from the New Testament to present day and hails it as a pre-eminent concept central to Christianity. Furthermore, Ruel proffers that the interpreter may need to reject Western ideas of belief with its background in metaphysical concepts and rather concentrate on practice. He even outlines 'shadow fallacies' that haunt fieldwork with Christian assumptions. Ruel submits that those questions about belief as we understand it may make little sense to other religious traditions and, as he shows, may mean different things in different periods of Christian history. He sees a marked contrast, for example, between Christian belief (as credal statements) and Judaism, which hinged its relationship on covenant obligations. He also views Islam as closer to Christianity on this point in 'submission' to one God as a believer – *mu'min* (Ruel 2002: 109).

Therefore reductionism vis-à-vis faith and belief may also be a very Christian criticism. Anthropology has excelled at discovering information about largely non-Christian communities and this perhaps gives it important credentials in providing a control on enquiries into social aspects of Christianity. It can ask different questions from those preoccupying Christian theologians and investigators, and also not just confine religion or God to the 'religious' spheres (a division that could only properly be understood in secular modernity). For people of the Bible, religion infiltrated all areas of life. James's emphasis on the human experiential part of religion is important in realigning this focus. Humanity as 'ceremonial animals' links both actions and thoughts.

Eilberg-Schwartz, in a similar vein, noted that anthropology's historical interest in primitive traditions often meant it concentrated on the symbolic affiliations of day-to-day activities. Thus eating, sex and excretion could themselves be valued 'religiously' (1990: 236). In his view, to dismiss aspects of so-called 'low' culture is to dismiss aspects of embodied religion and, in James's terms, misunderstand humanity's ceremonial nature. Moreover, it is by looking at other people's experiences that new questions can be asked. In Eilberg-Schwartz's words, 'like detectives, interpreters of historical cultures are better equipped to decipher cultural traces the more exposure they have to different kinds of cases' (1990: 238).

While comparison of any kind does not uncover social laws (if there are indeed such laws at all) it does allow one to recognise that different people in different times and places can in certain respects resemble each other. In view of this fact, it seems hard to disagree with Eilberg-Schwartz's conclusion that 'since such similarities do exist and since they are interesting, they should find a place in the larger picture we construct of humanity' (1990: 102).

Conclusion

Bowie and James make no assertions regarding the truth or otherwise of the spiritual beliefs of the communities they studied, rather they see that rituals and bodily performances can serve as powerful mediums of the sacred. Such observations are *not* reductionist vis-à-vis faith, but rather constructivist vis-à-vis embodiment and rituals associated with belief. This is corroborated by Kraft's point that anthropology can remind the theologian and biblical scholar of behavioural aspects of life as opposed to philosophical (Kraft discussed in Grunlan & Mayers 1988: 273). This in turn can inform one's relationships with others.

Both Bowie and James give an invitation to investigate what could be termed 'The Practice of Religion', namely, the observance of different ways in which humans live their tradition's way of life, remember their tradition's sacred stories and values, and live out their tradition in their day-to-day lives, individually, socially and politically. The following 'exhibits' with their corresponding interest in embodiment and the ceremonial nature of human beings within the Bible constitute attempts to respond to this open invitation and vision.

Part II

Exhibiting Aspects
of Scriptural Religion

3

Exhibit 1. Reading with
Religious Practitioners

Shamans and Shaman Healers

Curator's Notes

This exhibit displays anthropological work on religious practitioners – shamans and shaman healers – alongside Mark's and Luke's respective depictions of Jesus. It is inspired by John Pilch's innovative work in this area.

It is difficult for us, modern … as we are, to imagine the repercussions of such a spectacle in a 'primitive' community. The shamanic miracles not only confirm and reinforce the patterns of the traditional religion, they also stimulate and feed the imagination, demolish the barriers between dream and present reality, open windows upon worlds inhabited by Gods, the dead and the spirits.

M. Eliade

I'm more spiritual now than when you met me in 1985. I've changed a lot. It is partly because I now see the ancient power of shamanism, and believe in the shaman's ability to cure, but it is also because I myself saw a spirit last year at a sacred lake.

M. Balzer

Marcus Borg's quotation of a colleague's complaint that much work on the New Testament is like a flat tyre from which 'all the *pneuma* had gone' (1993 [1987]: 26) bemoans the lack of interest in early Christianity as an 'experiential religion' (see Johnson 1998). Yet the New Testament world is populated by supernatural beings, documents the 'seizure of man by divinity' (Lewis 1989: 15) and assumes the manifestation of transcendence at various junctures in its narratives. Furthermore, it presents charismatic, visionary and revelatory phenomena as central parts of both Jesus' and the early church's lives, not to mention assigning both with powers of healing, exorcisms and miracles.

This exhibit initiates what Jonathan Smith terms 'a disciplined exaggeration in the service of knowledge' (Smith cited in Ashton 2000: 214). Such an interpretation involves an overt focus on those characteristics of Jesus that parallel a shamanic typology to the neglect of other aspects of his identity not featured within this model. I compare the respective pictures of Jesus in Mark and Luke with selected anthropological studies of magico-religious practitioners, namely, the shaman and shaman healer. Studies of cross-cultural figures in their contexts operating from similar cosmological assumptions as the New Testament are enlightening. For, as I. M. Lewis in his *Ecstatic Religion: A Study of Shamanism and Spirit Possession* asked 'How else can we understand "other cultures" except comparatively in terms of our own concepts, constructs and language?' (1989: 14). We cannot hope to empathise or participate in the gospel portrayals of Christ unless we also cultivate an ability to 'think with religious and spirit experiences'. The shaman and shaman healer models seem to be viable avenues to develop such sensitivities.

Some tentative steps have been made in this area with regard to presenting Jesus as a shaman. However, little has been done on the applicability of the more communally orientated shaman healer typology, nor on the specific aid of such models in understanding particular gospel portrayals of Jesus and their relation to the 'religious' experience of the groups to whom each text was addressed. But this is undoubtedly an important aspect, for as Larry Hurtado submits, 'earliest Christianity was characterised by a rich and varied assortment of religious experiences … [which were] perceived by recipients as revelations' (2000: 183, 192). More importantly, he sees these experiences as central elements behind religious innovations (in particular the cultic veneration of Jesus). In short, for Hurtado, religious experiences stimulated Christological development in the tradition. It is not unreasonable then to propose that these experiences could also have prompted analogies to be drawn between the spirit experience of Jesus in his earthly life and the post-Easter church's experience of spirit in their communities.

The Transformation of Jesus' Experiences in Tradition and Text

The gospels do not constitute self-written memoirs of Christ's own psychological life, but rather the purposeful presentation of this experience by others. Jesus is an agent in the evangelists' texts and how they respectively present his religious and visionary experiences offers important clues to their understanding of his identity and the sort of spirituality that these authors wanted to impress on their readership. We know that those involved in the formation of early Christian traditions were enlivened by charisma, bolstered by visions and privy to experiences of the resurrected Christ. Paul has revelatory experiences of Christ, reflecting divine glory (2 Cor. 12:1; Acts 16:9; Acts 18:9). In Acts, Stephen is given a vision of 'the glory of God and Jesus standing at the right hand of God' (Acts 7:55–56). Also having visions in Acts are Ananias (Acts 9:10); Cornelius (Acts 10:3) and Peter (Acts 10:11) (see Hurtado, 2000: 199). Presumably these experiences also 'retrospectively' left a hallmark on the early Christian biographies of Jesus; experiences and social situations formed and reformed traditions; community experiences could be retraced back onto accounts of Jesus' life. (For narration of one event in a manner designed to recall another, see Charity 1966 and Jasper 1993: 51).

In social science, links have been made between ecstatic, mystical experience and the emergence of creativity. Distinctions have accordingly been drawn between an experience in itself and the conceptual interpretation put onto it. Hurtado argues that 'certain powerful religious experiences themselves produce significant innovations in religious traditions and such experiences, though shaped by social and cultural forces, are not merely confirmations of religious ideas otherwise generated and are also not necessarily manifestations of psychopathology' (2000: 192; see also Holm 1982: 50). 'Retrospective interpretation', that is interpretation influenced by tradition arising after the experience, seems particularly illuminating in relation to the gospels. Here in the portrayals of the evangelists, the 'pre-Easter Jesus' is shown to initiate powerful spiritual experiences and provide access on behalf of the community to God. In C. Keller's words such texts 'discuss the path towards a realisation of the ultimate knowledge which each particular religion has to offer and which contain statements about the nature of such knowledge' (Keller 1978: 77).

Whatever the historical experience of Jesus, by the time traditions have been dedicated to 'gospel' his visions and experiences are portrayed and documented with community concerns in mind. These played a part in the spiritual and ethical formation of believers and spoke of their own visions and experiences establishing continuity between this 'spiritual guru' and the tradition formed in his wake. This is not, however, to discount the historicity of the experiences per se. John Ashton in his recent study of Paul in light of a shaman model implicitly attests to the importance of the antecedent shamanic elements of the earthly Jesus' ministry. In his words: 'if I am right about Jesus I am more likely to be right about Paul, because of the real possibility of an inherited debt' (2000: 62). The early church's charismatic and visionary experiences were presumably seen to compare, at least in part, with Jesus' own strong sense of the Spirit.

Ashton goes on to argue that Paul's experience on the Damascus road 'was an instance of merkabah mysticism' (2000: 85). Of course it cannot be uncritically assumed that merkabah mysticism (a Jewish tradition variously rooted in, and focused on, ascent to God's chariot and throne) is flatly replicated in the New Testament. Often the enormity of the task of communion with God stressed in merkabah traditions (for example, navigating the tiered heavens) does not easily parallel the more immediate access to the divine enjoyed by Jesus and Paul, but the similarities should nonetheless not be overlooked. Ashton also compares shamanic features with aspects of Paul's theology, including possession by sin and indwelling in Christ. However, Ashton is careful to admit that spirit experience and shamanic qualities are not the only notable facets of Paul or Christ's portrayal, indeed from the point of view of their impact upon the tradition, such experiences, he believes, are secondary (Ashton 2000: 62). 'Higher' Christological motifs left a deeper mark on Christian theology. It is rather to say that these areas were ones in particular that could provide important links between the spiritual life of Jesus and his followers. The crucial difference between these, of course, was that while Jesus experienced the immanence of God, the substance of the church's religious and visionary experiences was Jesus as resurrected Lord.

Introducing the Shaman and Shaman Healer

If anthropology's central interest is to confront and somehow understand the 'other', then study of 'supernatural' experiences has de facto affirmed the credibility of their task. Religious types are all 'etic' terms and concepts – abstracted from a body of comparative materials, which facilitate cross-cultural comparisons between similar traits and features across a number of contexts.

The term 'shaman' is derived from the Tungus people's word, *saman*, meaning 'one who is excited, moved or raised' (Lewis 1989: 51). Shamans and shaman healers enjoy, as Winkelman suggests, an almost 'quasi-etic status' in anthropology. Hutton cites four definitions regularly used in contemporary work on shamanism:

> In one, shamanism is the practice of anybody who contacts a spirit world while in an altered state of consciousness. A second limits it to specialist practitioners who use such contacts at the behest of others. A third attempts to distinguish shamans from other such specialists, such as 'mediums', 'witch doctors', 'spiritual healers' or 'prophets', by some particular technique.... To some the definitive characteristic is that shamans exert control over the spirits with whom they work, while to others it is the ability to undertake a personal journey into an alternative reality and to accomplish tasks there.... The fourth definition stands on its own, being the use of the expression shamanism, to characterise the native religions of Siberia and neighbouring parts of Asia. This is the only one to lack logic in itself, because shamanism (by any of the first three usages) represents only one component of these religions, and rarely the dominant one.
>
> Hutton 2001: vii–viii

Several anthropologists have objected to the conception of shamanism due to its generality. Geertz famously characterised it as a dry and insipid notion, which drained the spark and life from ethnographic accounts. Michael Taussig has also tried to deconstruct the idea from a post-modern perspective (see D'Anglure 1996).

However, while conceding that all definitions of shamans, or any religious practitioner, are nothing more than theoretical types, based on abstractions from a variety of cross-cultural data, it does not mean such categories are useless. Shamanism, in all its diversity, at base denotes 'a cross-cultural construct, used to group together [similar] beliefs and activities across the world' (Hutton 2001: vii). Mircea Eliade's lengthy cross-cultural catalogue of shamanic data was perhaps the most impressive collection of comparative traits to illustrate this point (see also Winkelman 1990: 309).

It is also important to note, that while ethnographic study of particular environments is central to anthropology, fieldwork is often predicated on a theoretical basis or the testing of an abstracted generalisation. If this were not the case there would be no hope of drawing constructive conclusions as regards cultural difference. Ashton makes an important distinction in this regard between 'genealogical comparisons', namely, ones in which the things compared share some organic link, and 'convergent resemblance'. Here, certain characteristics are shared in common across a number of cultures and environments, but no direct link in history or development can be established. He uses the illustration of 'the use of metaphor' to unpack the meaning of convergent readings. These, like metaphors, 'draw attention to particular features of whatever it is that they are focused on without involving any claim, either explicit or implicit, that this is the only way of looking at them' (Ashton 2000: 58). It is in this sense that exhibiting Jesus and figures of the early Christian movement, alongside 'shaman/shaman healer figures' in Siberia, Japan, the Arctic, Polynesia, Mexico and Africa becomes a legitimate exegetical enterprise.

The shaman is a master or mistress of the spirits. Lewis cites the colourful Polynesian designation of the shaman as 'a godbox' (Lewis 1989: 49). Hultkrantz sees the shaman as 'a social functionary who, with the help of guardian spirits, attains ecstasy in order to create a rapport with the supernatural world on behalf of his group members' (cited in Davila 2001: 44). The shaman is a commanding, captivating individual who often acquires power through manipulation and high regard from others. Crisis or illness often accompanies the appointment of the shamanic individual. Symbolic associations with death, rebirth or journeys into another realm and unions with spirits through trance states are also frequently described (Lewis 1989: 51).

The areas where both shaman and shaman healers share characteristics are in the spheres of power and magico-religious activity. Both control the spirits, an act that Davila has identified as 'the *sine qua non* of shamanic competence' (Davila 2001: 197). Shamans and shaman healers act as healers, diviners (seeking knowledge by supernatural means) (Lewis 1989: 49) and psychopomps (spiritual guides to individual's soul) and crucially respond to needs and concerns in their community (Winkelman 1990: 318). Differences between the two are pre-eminently in appointment and education (shamans are trance-led; shaman healers are ritual-led), and their respective power and authority channels. The shaman operates individually while the shaman healer operates via a community or group. Features of the respective types as identified by Winkelman (1990: 318) are figuratively portrayed in Table 3.1. Significant differences are italicised to bring distinctions into sharper relief:

Table 3.1. Comparing Shamans and Shaman Healers

Characteristics	Shaman	Shaman Healer
Appointment and education	Vision quests, visions	Vision quests, visions
	Training involving trance	*Trance and ritual training*
	Status recognised by clients (spirits)	*Ceremony recognises status*
Ability	Spirit power controlled	Spirit power controlled
	Healing and divination	Healing and divination
'Spirit' associated activities	*Hunting magic*	*Agricultural magic*
Forms of Power/ Authority	*Charismatic leader*	*No political power*
	Individual practice	*Collective/group practice, specialised role*

As can be seen in Table 3.1, the main differences between shamans and shaman healers are quite subtle, based on the specialized roles of each and their respective contexts. Shamans are individualistic, their performances impulsive and their context – hunting/gathering environments. Shaman healers in contrast are involved in organised group activities, often concerning professional training. Their context is developed agricultural or pastoral realms, and their outlook institutionalised and collective, with hierarchical patterns present. Winkelman proposes developmental links between the two types of individual, and building on this division Davila suggests that they could be called 'hunting' and 'agricultural' shamans respectively (2001: 299).

Davila (2001) used this typology in his study of the Jewish Hekhalot literature. He designates the producers and recipients of these texts as comparable with shaman healers who develop techniques of ritual power as opposed to the charismatic seizure of the individual by divinity, characteristic of shamans. But what light would this typology cast on the gospel portrayals of Jesus? Of course the agrarian setting more neatly parallels the environment of the gospels, than does the hunting-gathering society. Contexts aside, however, if one thinks of the shaman/shaman healer as points on a continuum rather than two mutually exclusive types, certain features of each can be aligned with gospel presentations, though only the 'shaman' type has hitherto been adapted within interpretations of Jesus' identity.

Many have noted how the shaman provides important parallels with Jesus for whom the theatre of history is not closed to supernatural influence. Fiona Bowie, in her *Anthropology of Religion*, opens her chapter on shamanism with the bold statement that 'Jesus is a shaman' (Bowie 2000: 190). P. Craffert in his 1999 article 'Jesus and the Shamanic Complex' also sets out tentative links between the two: Jesus' baptism was seen as an initiation into shamanism; his ascents to heaven were compared with shamanic journeys and prayer and meditation shown as shamanic trance techniques. Craffert also points out other traits that could be reminiscent of the typology. First, Jesus was accused of insanity (Mk. 3:21), second, some saw him as being possessed by an evil spirit (Mk. 3:21) and third, he frequently withdrew into isolation (Mk. 1:12–13; Mt. 4:11; Lk. 4:1–13).

It is John Pilch, however, who has done most work in this area. His recent essay 'Altered States of Consciousness in the Synoptics' (2002) takes as its subject religious experience as a foundation for religious behaviour in the gospels. He cites the Human Relations Area Files (HRAF) at Yale University, which estimate that 80 per cent of inhabitants of the Mediterranean region experience altered states of consciousness, which can in turn promote religious behaviour (2002: 104).

Pilch follows Townsend's (1999) picture of shamanism as constituting the following: direct contact/communication with spirits; control/power over spirits; control of altered states of consciousness; sky journeys; abilities channelled to help communities (Pilch 2002: 107). Accordingly he identifies five sequences in the gospels that reflect altered states of consciousness. These are the baptism, temptation/testing, walking on the sea, transfiguration and resurrection appearances (Pilch 2002: 109–11).

Of course, one of the methodological pitfalls involved in such an exercise involves the age-old problem of 'parallelomania'. While comparisons can be strong in respect of some traits, weaknesses must also be catalogued. In order for the legitimacy of any comparative religion exercise to be confirmed, one must acknowledge both similarity and difference. This is not to say that the biographies of Jesus might not be brought into sharper focus by a shamanic typology, but it must also be recognised that many elements identified in this type are not replicated by gospel portrayals. The extensive teaching and parable discourses, not directly related to the cultivation of altered states of consciousness, do not easily fit with the paradigm. Also, while apocalyptic elements, particularly visionary experiences, may have close parallels with shamanic traits, an eschatological perspective is not well documented in shamanic study. Shamans realise the communion between natural and supernatural in the present. While Jesus of course does this as well, his talk of kingdom as a future reality perhaps fits less tightly with the shaman/shaman healer framework.

These caveats notwithstanding, here broad comparisons will be drawn between the portrayal of Jesus and just two areas of the shaman/shaman healer model that do seem to provide positive comparisons. First is selection and training, which I will compare with the synoptic accounts of Jesus' baptism and experiences in the wilderness. Second is the trance, which I will compare with the transfiguration narrative. At all times it will be kept in mind that our texts do not present accounts of the religious experiences of Jesus per se, but rather retrospective portrayals of these experiences for the benefit of the post-Easter reader. I will tentatively suggest that the Marcan Jesus, having more individualised experiences, reflects the most primitive religious type of shaman, whereas the practical techniques and community orientation of Luke's Jesus provides more ready resonance with the shaman healer type.

Selection and Training

Initiation as a shaman and shaman healer share key common features, which confirm that the practitioner has 'transcended the profane condition of humanity' (Eliade 1964: 85–86). Both figures during this initiatory stage are threatened by visions of destruction that often involve a testing by spirits. The motif of death and dismemberment is common in such circumstances (Eliade 1964: 56). In Lewis's terms 'the shaman's initial crisis represents the healer's passion, or as the Akawaio Indians themselves put it "a man must die before he becomes a shaman"' (Lewis 1989: 63).

In Mark, the baptism acts as a foreword for the whole gospel (Matera 1995: 231). It presents Jesus' spiritual initiation as opposed to any details of physical descent. God declares Jesus as his son (Mk. 1:11) and the singular verbal form *eiden* indicates that the vision was experienced by Jesus alone. 'Seeing' in the context of the heavens as R. Guelich points out, often connotes a visionary experience in other New Testament texts (Acts 10:11; Rev. 19:1) (Guelich 1989: 35). Its central importance lies in affinities with the Hebrew Bible's hope for an era of salvation where God would come down and liberate the world (Is. 42:1) (Hooker 1991: 48). Equally the term *schizō*, as is often stressed, powerfully conveys the violent rending apart of the heavens and the transcendental intervention in the scene. This was a common motif to signify the descent of God to earth in deliverance (Is. 64:1). The mention of clouds also finds echoes in Jewish theophanies (Ex. 16:10; Num. 11:25), though Jewish comparisons are not the only ones to be affirmed here. Mark's account also finds 'convergent comparisons' with the initiation of the Lakota shaman who reports:

> The kingbird said, 'Look, the clouds all over are one-sided, a voice is calling you'. I looked up and the two men were coming down singing:
>
> 'Behold him; a sacred voice is calling you. All over the sky a sacred voice is calling you.' I stood gazing at them and they were coming from the north; then they started toward the west and were geese.

Demallie cited in Davila 2001: 58

In Mark, Jesus is presented as an entirely passive recipient of communication initiated by the divine. Yet, as E. Malbon suggests, for this evangelist 'the heavenly and earthly are through him [Jesus] now as close as parent and child' (Malbon 1991: 82). It is not insignificant that this 'passion narrative with an extended introduction', to cite Kahler's celebrated phrase, also encourages the believer to take up their cross, die and transcend earthly concerns. Dying to the self and being reborn through baptism became a central symbol of early Christian discourse. Just as Christ had experienced tragic dismemberment and death at crucifixion, only to experience the ultimate rebirth in resurrection, so, like the shaman's initiation, the Christian was called to death of self as a pre-cursor to spiritual transformation.

Turning to Luke's account, we see Jesus born as a result of the intervention of the Spirit, owing his very identity to this force (Lk. 1:35). Davila notes that while a shaman's call is often imposed from spirits, for some, powers may be hereditary, or determined from childhood by the presence of a shaman's mark, 'a special characteristic on the initiate's body' (2001: 55). This seems to throw some light on Luke's infancy narrative. As such, as Dunn correctly argues, Luke's depiction of Jesus does not flatly affirm incarnational Christology. His intention is rather to 'describe the creative process of begetting, not that which is begotten. It is this failure or refusal to do that further step which marks Spirit Christology off from Wisdom Christology and Logos Christology' (Dunn 1998: 76). Dunn concludes 'Spirit Christology was only a Christology of a man inspired' it was 'not however, the only Christology' (1998: 77).

In Luke, Jesus' spiritual awakening and initiation is shown in contrast to Mark's passive reception, as a direct result of prayer. Redactionally, Luke 3:21 speaks of the heavens opening as opposed to Mark's violent ripping asunder of the heavens associated with eschatological expectations (Ezek. 1:1; Is. 64:1) (see Schweizer 1984: 78). Luke adds that the Holy Spirit descended on him in bodily form in 3:22. It has been speculated that Luke emphasised that it was the Holy Spirit in Luke 11:14–23 to rebut any claim that Jesus acted by the power of an unclean spirit (see Evans and Sanders 1993: 28ff). The adverb *sōmatikō* served to underline the Spirit's descent as a dove upon Jesus, affirming the experience as 'real and enabling' (Evans & Sanders 1993: 29). Interestingly, Johnson suggests that Luke schematised features of the baptism experience with the annunciation. Both include a message delivered from the heavenly realm and the similar invocation of the power of God overshadowing both Mary and Jesus. As a result of these elements, Johnson writes 'in the baptism perhaps the dove is the hovering symbol that enables the reader's imagination to pull these elements into a single focus' (1991: 71).

It has long been recognised that from a Graeco-Roman perspective the narrative would exhibit Jesus as a distinguished person of superior excellence, with the dove being especially emblematic of beneficence. The presence of the Spirit as an embodied dove would appeal to Graeco-Roman interest in 'demonstrations of power' (Danker 1988: 96). Additionally many commentators highlight the possible link of the dove symbol with Genesis accounts, where the spirit is shown 'hovering' over the waters (Gen. 1:2), or see the account as a prefiguring of Pentecost. Schweizer suggested that the reality of the coming of the Spirit is depicted geographically in the image of the dove descending from the Father to the Son, similar to the descent of flames of fire on the disciples in Acts 2:3 (1984: 79). Green also makes this link and views the baptism as an anticipation of the subsequent empowering of Jesus' followers in Acts (Green 1995: 44–49). So while the words from God clearly distinguish the relationship of the Son to God from that of the community, nevertheless their experiences are reflected in this paradigmatic scene.

R. E. DeMaris's recent essay, 'The Baptism of Jesus: A Ritual-Critical Approach' (2002) also provides interesting reading in this respect. He conjectures that 'the followers of Jesus may have introduced the baptismal rite into the story of his possession because of the stigma attached to spontaneous possession' (2002: 138). He cites Erica Bourguignon's global study of dissociational states. She defined two main ways that cultures view altered states of consciousness (1973: 13–133). First, trance (absence of soul from the body and travel to an alternative realm) and second, possession trances (permanent entry of spirit into persons). In short, 'the trancer sees, hears, feels, perceives and interacts with another; the possession trance *becomes* another' (my italicisation, DeMaris 2002: 147). Bourguignon links trance states to less structured hunter/gatherer contexts and possession with more hierarchical and agricultural contexts (Bourguignon 1973: 147). DeMaris argues that associated states of consciousness are triggered by ritual activity and as such the baptism rite could have triggered a visionary experience: 'In this circumstance, therefore, the orientation of the social sciences towards patterns and scenarios instead of specificity and detail proves to be the historian's boon rather than bane' (DeMaris 2002: 152).

The temptation narratives can also be paralleled with the shaman's and shaman healer's initiatory integration, disintegration and testing by the spirits. In Mark 1:12–13, Jesus is sent into the wilderness by the Spirit that descended on him at the baptism. The force of the language is instantaneous and arresting giving the notion of Jesus being totally driven by the Spirit, 'throwing' him into the wilderness (Mk. 1:12). It is also not insignificant in shamanic terms that Mark's Jesus is shown to be with wild beasts. This calls to mind a number of elements. Revelation 11:7 pictures beasts representing satanic powers and the opponents of God in a similar way to Daniel's famous dream (Dan. 7:12). The divine power of Pythagoras to soothe wild beasts and traditions of wild beasts not attacking Apollonius of Tyana may also be called to mind (Gundry 1993: 55). More interesting for present purposes is the fact that in many shamanic initiations, animals are shown to play a key role. This could be as part of the testing period, for example, a bear devouring parts of the body (Rasmussen 1908: 306), or simply the incarnation of a spirit in bodily form (Eliade 1964: 93). In a number of myths and legends the hero is accompanied or carried away by an animal. Eliade suggests that animal references are another way of showing that the shaman can 'forsake his human condition … in a word to die' (1964: 93). Eliade also suspects that the presence of animals 'in a manner re-establishes the situation that existed *in illo tempore*, in mythical times, when the divorce between man and the animal world had not yet occurred' (1964: 94). This is even more persuasive if Mark's account can be found to echo Adam's testing by the snake (who in later Jewish interpretation became Satan, see e.g. *Apoc. Mos* 17:4) or Adam's peace and unity with the beasts in Eden (Gen. 2:19–20) (Marcus 2000: 169). Richard Bauckham's 1994 essay 'Jesus and the Wild Animals (Mk 1:13): A Christological Image for an Ecological Age' also concurs with this sort of picture. He sees hierarchy and division between humanity and creatures being overcome in Jesus' messianic peace. He writes:

> There is no reason of doubt that first-century people who were well aware that they shared the world with wild animals, would be interested in this aspect of salvation for its own sake … in contrast to restoration portrayed in Jewish literature, the animals are not said to fear him, submit to him, or serve him…. The concept of human domination over the animals as domination for human benefit is entirely absent.
>
> Bauckham 1994: 20

Following the baptism experience, in contrast to Mark's spirit-driven Jesus, Luke's Jesus is led to the wilderness 'full of the Holy Spirit' (Lk. 4:1). Luke's choice of language thus brings out more clearly that the Spirit is not something external which drives him, but rather something endemic to his own character and identity. Luke's account also accentuates the wilderness wandering as a testing period in contrast to Mark's pithy desert experience. Borg has drawn parallels between the Lucan account and other 'testing' periods in Jewish tradition, for example Moses and Elijah who also journeyed into the solitude of the wilderness. Such wanderers Borg suggests underwent extended periods of fasting and meditation, all of which produce 'psychological experiences of the sort, which many traditions call vision quests' (Borg 1993 [1987]: 43).

The dialogue in Luke is also more developed than in Mark with a powerful presentation of the struggle between two kingdoms, God and evil (Lk. 4:5–6). Furthermore, an extraordinary vision seems to be implied in viewing all the kingdoms of earth 'in an instant'. Garrett in her study of the devil in Luke extensively discussed this struggle. She stressed the statement highlighting Luke's understanding of Satan as the 'ruler of this world' using *oikoumenē*, meaning inhabited world, as opposed to the more universal *kosmos* (Garrett 1989: 38) thus defining the confines of his rule. As Johnson similarly observed, the devil has real *exousia* over those he rules and his shadow kingdom 'parodies that of God, enabling him in his challenge to this Messiah to counterfeit the courage of God's realm' (Johnson 1998: 76). Luke's Gentile readers would also not escape noticing the three vices portrayed within the temptation: love of pleasure, love of possessions and love of glory. These were typical vices often used in association with temptations of an inspired individual. Thus the fact that Jesus refused them would 'mark him out as a *teacher* capable of teaching virtue' (my italicisation, Boring, Berger & Colpe 1995: 195). Luke's conclusion to the section – 'the devil departed from him until an opportune time' (Lk. 4:13) – is also significant. Satan's power was wretchedly fragile when face to face with the Son of God, yet Satan's rule would not be vanquished completely in the foreseeable future at least (Garrett 1989: 108). In overcoming the temptation to self-glorification, the Lucan Jesus, like the shaman healer, teaches important lessons to the reader. First that his overcoming of temptation was on their behalf, moreover his was an exemplary path to be followed by them. The subsequent irony of conquering through death, showed the subversive nature of this glory.

While Bultmann labelled the temptation narrative a legend (1921: 271–75; see also Schiavo 2002), contra Bultmann it does not seem unreasonable, in view of the traditions concerning wilderness experiences and the link between ascetic practice and altered states of consciousness, that the evangelists believed Jesus did experience this. Convergent comparisons can be drawn between this event and shamanic experiences attested in ethnography. Mark's Jesus seems to show more characteristics of possession by the Holy Spirit, his experience is more violent, more spontaneous. Furthermore the implication is that the clients (spirits) recognise who he is immediately (not least because the first thing Jesus does is exorcise). Luke's Jesus seems to undergo more 'practical training'. Prayer is shown as central to the provocation of the experience; furthermore by making the baptism vision a public announcement of who Jesus is, it almost makes us believe that Luke is constructing a 'ceremonial' recognition of Jesus' status to his readers. The collective dimension is also emphasised in Luke's account of the 'sending of the seventy' in which Luke describes Jesus having a vision of 'Satan fall from heaven like a flash of lightning' (Lk. 10:18) when he saw his followers exorcising demons. This saying is unique in the gospels and as W. Kümmel suggested seems to recount an actual visionary experience rather than just a metaphor or vivid turn of speech (Kümmel cited in Fitzmyer 1989: 167). Significantly it has been suggested that while the Greek verb *theōreō* was used in an earthly sense to mean 'to see', it also conveyed in Greek literature a religious sense of revelatory or visionary sight. The assurance that the disciples' names are written in heaven stresses the importance of Jesus to work through the life of the community so that they, through him, attain the certainty of salvation. In short, in Mark, Jesus' selection corresponds more to the selection and training of a shaman, in Luke, it looks more like the initiation of a community-orientated shaman healer.

Trance States

Shamanic cosmology often conceives of the universe as multi-tiered. Eliade notes that in such contexts:

> the universe in general is conceived as having three levels – sky, earth, and underworld, connected by a central axis.... It is through this hole that the gods descend to earth and the dead to the subterranean regions; it is through the same hole that the soul of the shaman in ecstasy can fly up or down in the course of his celestial or infernal journeys.
>
> Eliade 1964: 259

Shamanic trance is a particular characteristic of the shaman and shaman healer. Other religious specialists may experience altered states of consciousness, but the shaman alone does so for the benefit of the community or group. Shamanic ecstasy is identified as a class of altered state of consciousness involving (a) voluntary control of entrance to trance; (b) post-trance memory; and (c) trance communicative interplay with spectators (Peters & Williams cited in Jakobsen 1999: 10). Accordingly, Horwitz defines a shamanic individual as:

> Someone who changes his or her state of consciousness at will, in order to journey to another reality, a non-ordinary reality, the world of the spirits ... to ask for help, power, or knowledge ... mission accomplished, the shaman journeys back to ordinary reality where she uses or dispenses the newly gained knowledge and/or power.
>
> Horwitz cited in Jakobsen, 1999: 9

While spirit possession involves loss of consciousness and memory and is therefore a disassociated state, trance journeys do not involve such loss. Shirokogoroff, in his description of the Tungus, especially highlights the importance of the company of believers who witness and participate in shamanic trance experiences. He writes 'in almost all forms of shamanistic performance, when the ecstasy of the shaman and the excitation of the audience are needed ... several technical methods are used' (Shirogoroff cited in Jakobsen 1999: 13).

Both evangelists show the transfiguration event as part of the visionary experience of the disciples (Mk. 9:2–8; Lk. 9:28–36) and as such can be associated not only with the trance state of Jesus, but also the community. In order to cultivate the necessary preconditions for trance states, both shamans and shaman healers practice particular trance-invoking behaviours: fasting, isolation, citation of particular words, etc. Such practices serve to remove the shaman from the worldly sphere. In Blackler's terms,

> In so far as they are painful, in so far as they remove both body and mind from their accustomed habits, in so far as they require very great strength of will to accomplish, they may be properly described as ascetic ... these disciplines can be broadly classified into three: fasting, cold water and the recitation of words of power.
>
> Blackler 1965: 85

Mark and Luke document similar practices. Mark's Jesus frequently withdraws from public places (Mk. 3:7) and Luke presents him developing a mystical relationship with God through his reliance on prayer and meditation (Lk. 6:12; 9:18). Both show Jesus spending time fasting in isolation in the wilderness.

As noted above, many scholars have argued that the transfiguration can be compared with other ecstatic experiences. It is significant that this event takes place on a mountain, as this was traditionally regarded as a place for divine communication to occur, and was also often symbolic of power (Dan. 2:35). Also important, as Eliade notes, is the shamanic conception of the universe being conceived as having three levels – earth, sky and underworld, connected by an axis often figured as a tree or mountain (Eliade 1964: 259). Through the mountain motif, the brightness of Jesus' garments and the cloud and voice, significant parallels are also drawn, with, among others, Moses' encounters with God (Ex. 19:16ff). This is particularly shown in the reference to a cloud that traditionally represented the *shekinah*, the presence of God (Hooker 1991: 216). The reference to the cloud (Lk. 9:34) also seems to imply that this covers the apostles bringing them into the radiance of glory and providing revelation to them, crucially providing the community link so central to the shaman typology.

Luke makes a number of redactional alterations from Mark (Marshall 1978: 381). In verse 28 it is characteristically stressed that Jesus went up a mountain to pray, thus implying once again that the transfiguration occurred 'as a divine response to Jesus' communion with God in meditation' (Barton 1992: 88). It is during this intimate moment with the divine that Luke presents Jesus being transfigured. J. Behm suggests that Luke dropped Mark's verb *metemorphōthē* because it most likely would have been understood in a Hellenistic way. He sees the 'ecology' of this verse being in the encounter of Moses whose features were alight, because he had been speaking to Yahweh on Mount Sinai (Ex. 34:30) (Behm discussed in Marshall 1978: 383).

In contrast to Mark, Luke also offers a fuller discussion with Moses and Elijah concerning Jesus' identity, glory and suffering. Luke presents these figures as appearing, like Jesus himself, in glory (Lk. 9:31). Linked with this, Luke also presents the actual conversation between the three concerning Jesus' *exodus* (Lk. 9:31), a term that itself rekindles for the reader liberating images of the exodus from Egypt. Marshall notes it can alternatively be used as a euphemism of death; 'in the eyes of the foolish they have died, and their *departure* was thought to be a disaster' (Wis. 3:2) (Marshall 1978: 384).

It is often noted that Luke uses a narrative exclusionary scheme for the disciples showing that they, unlike the reader, were not able to listen to this conversation because they were asleep. However, equally important to note is the fact that sleep is a common trait associated (both physically and metaphorically) in the ecstasy of seers in Jewish tradition (Dan. 1:7; 1 En. 13:8; 2 Bar. 52:8 – 53:1). Yet, as Fletcher-Louis perceptively notes, here we have the reverse in that the encounter awakens the disciples. He suggests that this is because Luke wants to show the transfiguration not merely as visionary but rather as a reflection of post-resurrection appearances and the physicality of the ascension experienced by the community of faith (Fletcher-Louis 1997: 28). Nonetheless in the narrative, the disciples did, after waking up, see the glory of Jesus and interpret this as a divine revelation.

It is also commonly suggested that the transfiguration is a post-Easter vision that is put into a pre-Easter context (Hurtado 2000: 201). This may well be true and is particularly important given the perspective of mystical writings and the link between religious experience and creativity. It is also important to note, however, that even if this account presents a post-Easter event, it was nevertheless seen as viable to insert such an experience into a narrative of the pre-Easter Jesus' experience. Rowland (2002) conjectures that there is a theological development at play but that this could still be rooted in a real, authentic experience in the life of Jesus. In his opinion, the ascended, glorified, resurrected Christ need not be completely cut off from the reality of a transfiguration vision in Jesus' own experience.

In a similar vein, Ashton, in his 2002 William James Lecture, available online, stressed that experience of the post-Easter Christ found some antecedents in experience and remembrance of the earthly charismatic Jesus. Moreover, he sees that the pre-resurrection experience of Jesus somehow informed and laid the groundwork for the post-Easter experiences of the resurrected Christ. Gundry lends weight to this perspective in his plea that 'we should not speak of transferring luminosity, and with it authority, from the exalted risen Jesus to the earthly Jesus before the latter's death and resurrection.... [The] two [pictures of] Jesus do not compete' (Gundry 1993: 472). More importantly for the communities that read these texts, it was the spirit-filled shamanic Jesus who more closely paralleled their own charismatic experiences and visions. It was, however, the glorified, resurrected and ascended Lord that these same communities felt compelled to worship and adore. Paul, for example, talks about a certain person in Christ being taken up to Paradise and hearing things that cannot be heard (2 Cor. 12:4). Philippians 1:19 also portrays ascent to describe the desire to 'depart and be with Christ'. In short, Jesus was the focus of early Christian trance and heavenly journeys.

In the Name of the Father, Shaman and Holy Spirit?

Comparisons with shamans, shaman healers and their communities do not tell us about Jesus' own experiences, but they can suggest some occurrences that may be reflected in the texts we have. Cross-cultural comparisons of traits can illuminate our perspective in fresh and creative ways. The spirituality of both Mark and Luke ultimately has to do with a sense of divine presence. The evangelists' constructions in response to religious experience both encouraged readers to interpret and affirm their spiritual visions and consciousness and turn to God. In Mark's Gospel the religious experience of Jesus marks him out as a chosen eschatological agent of God in whom the divine is active. His individual experiences seemed to correlate with the typology of the most primitive framework of the shaman. In contrast, Luke's Jesus is primarily represented as a prototype of active spirituality with the central importance of prayer being emphasised repeatedly through the gospel as the necessary precondition for an experience of the divine. Most notably, Luke's Lord's Prayer is presented as Jesus' practical paradigm of how to pray (Lk. 11:1ff.). Through the use of the term 'Father', Jesus encourages his disciples to understand God not as far removed from their existence, but as one who could be known intimately as their own father. This again stresses that the Lucan Christology has a strong exemplary quality: Jesus' life of regular communion with God in prayer prompts his disciples, and at the discourse levels also his reader, to follow his example. Because of the collective witness and orientation of many of the religious experiences of Luke, and the dissemination of the powers of exorcism and healing to many followers, the Jesus of Luke seems more fully to parallel the shaman healer type (Spencer 1963: 329). Jesus, like shaman healer figures, is empowered through his experience of the Spirit and consequently crosses earthly/heavenly boundaries. He heals, exorcises demons and witnesses intense mystical and ecstatic manifestations of God's presence, but crucially these visions are also witnessed by the reader and at times witnessed by other figures in the story. Through these, the community 'share' these experiences and are additionally taught strategies (for example, disciplined prayer) by which they also may be subject to spirit direction.

The shaman/shaman healer frameworks can also provide interesting convergence with the witness of other early Christian authors and communities. Interestingly, the metaphor of spiritual marriage between Christ and church found in the New Testament (2 Cor. 11:2; Rev. 19:7; 21:2; 22:17) can also find parallels in shamanic ethnography. From Carib-speaking Indians, Buddhist Bramans to Songhay in West Africa this image of marital intimacy between community and spirit is used (Lewis 1989: 53). Also common is the use of blood terminology to reflect the community/divine relationship. In Lewis's words 'here the shaman or devotee is described as a child (a son or daughter, according to sex) or occasionally as a younger sibling of the spirit' (1989: 56). How appropriate therefore that the early church used fictive kin terminology to describe their self-identity as 'children of God' (Mk. 10:2 Mt. 5:45) who lived as brothers and sisters in Christ (Mt. 12:50; Mk. 3:35).

No less important, as mentioned above, is the fact that the ceremonial initiation rite into the Christian community, baptism, draws on symbols of dismemberment and death common in shaman/shaman healer types. The individual dies to the old self in baptism and is born again into resurrection glory to 'walk in newness of life' (Rom. 6:4). It is this life wherein experience of the spirit becomes potent and central. Furthermore, individuals are no longer seen as individual beings, but participators in a new communal body of church and Christ, in the spirit.

Additionally, the cultivation of an ability to 'think with spirits' by way of the shaman/shaman healer model also affirms the experiences of some contemporary global reading of the Bible. African interpreters, living in an environment whose cosmology provides resonance with the New Testament, can offer interesting avenues of research in this regard.

For example Bobby Loubser's study on 'Possession and Sacrifice in the New Testament and African Traditional Religions' (2004) investigates conventions of oral culture in African traditional religion, with a view to understanding the literary formation and genres of New Testament texts. He explores the functioning of texts in a 'world of spirits' and designates the Holy Spirit as an agency of 'memory and discernment' who is 'instrumental to textual formation'. The link between 'thinking with spirits' and the reality of the 'Holy Spirit' is also mentioned by Dunn, who notes that in abandoning, or demythologising, such references we may overlook 'the *mysterium tremendum* open to us in these texts' (Dunn 1998: 68).

All in all, the comparative anthropological data on magico-religious practitioners can provide fresh perspectives for the exegete. They help us to re-imagine a cosmology entirely different from our own. They also help to reclaim the category of experience in the lives of ancestors of faith and, to cite Borg's colleague's analogy once again, to inflate the tyre of New Testament studies with the '*pneuma*' it has at times seemed to lack.

It is important to note, however, that 'shamanic' or 'Spirit' Christology will never produce an incarnational Christology. One cannot begin to talk 'in the name of the Father, the Shaman and the Holy Spirit'. Nevertheless, a shamanic model does allow particular elements of Christ's experience as portrayed in the gospels, and more particularly its relationship to early Christian religious experience, to be explored. Theologians' focus is often restricted by traditional formulas of the divine/human Christ, and consequently overlooks the vivid and magnetic picture of the spirit-possessed Jesus of the synoptic gospels. Dunn, in a different context, lends support for this viewpoint when he stated 'whatever its value in past centuries, the static Christology of Chalcedon does not do justice to the dynamic Christology of the New Testament' (1998: 51).

Mark and Luke both present Jesus with a shamanic vocation, experience and features, precisely because it was this feature of Jesus that could find parallels with early Christian experience of healing, exorcism, revelation and visions. This Jesus was the one who initiated their intense experience of the divine. But it is also true to say that this Jesus, being the subject of early Christian visions, came to be the subject of their own visions and spirit experiences. To find the grounding of this development one must look beyond a shamanic typology.

4

Exhibit 2. Reading with Tricksters

Irony, Mystery and John's Jesus

Curator's Notes
This exhibit displays elements of trickster narratives from West Africa to Winnebago Indians, alongside John's presentation of Jesus, which is characterised by irony, joking and illusion.

To be fooled and tricked, to treat the illusory as reality, is to be subordinated and subjected to the control of the prankster or trickster, be this a deity, a demon or a human being. However to see the reality behind the illusion, to be the unmasker as well as the masker is to exercise dominance and superiority.

B. Kapferer

Imagination is the capacity to give reality to culture, and to keep inventing social worlds anew.

J. Preston

According to the *Oxford English Dictionary*, a trickster is a 'deceiver or rogue'. This definition makes 'Reading with Tricksters' an unlikely enterprise for the biblical interpreter. *The Encyclopedia of Social and Cultural Anthropology* may hold more clues for the utility of such an exercise. It defines a trickster as follows:

Trickster n.—in folklore and mythology, a character that plays clever tricks on other characters. Often taking the form of an animal such as a fox or coyote, the trickster can represent downtrodden elements of a community or the triumph of good over evil.

Barnard & Spencer 1996: 626

Anthropological interests in cosmologies and worldviews first stimulated this exhibit. Imagination of worldviews is a key anthropological concern. I take worldview to constitute the basic outlook or conception of life, 'a particular system of values, beliefs and attitudes' (Rapport & Overing 2000: 395). This 'system', however, need not be systematic; at times elements can be contradictory (indeed most trickster narratives inhabit boundaries and highlight contradictions). In such cases, worldviews can serve to mediate between diverse viewpoints, alleviate cultural dissonance and prompt changes in perspectives.

It is my contention that John's Jesus, his words and miraculous actions share notable features with the 'trickster' figure in anthropology. Such persons inhabit liminal realms, are often conceived as messengers of the divine, upstage and wield power over enemies and frequently subvert social boundaries. I submit Jesus' trickster nature in turn fosters the cultivation of a 'trickster imagination' within John's readers, initiating a process of transformation in their reading strategies, perspectives and worldview. I propose that the Gospel of John constructs a world that is 'liminal' and 'anti-structural' (concepts I derive from Victor Turner's work). His readers, in accepting the call to be 'born from above', must also occupy a 'liminal' space.

Introducing the Trickster

Ethnography documenting trickster figures relates to areas as diverse as North America, Greece and West Africa. The trickster is an 'etic' category used by anthropologists to speak about a certain type of being who appears in many myths, narratives and folktales across the globe. As with the previous exhibit, it should be candidly stated at the outset that a trickster, like a shaman, is an anthropological construct. It is a term whose broad appeal to scholarship is its usefulness in allowing features of certain individuals in diverse socio-cultural contexts to be compared. The term itself derives from study of a figure in North American Indian mythology who was 'a selfish buffoon', who, while often preoccupied with his own physical needs, nevertheless also played important roles in the development of civilisation, for example, bringing fire. Others see the trickster as a cultural hero, who outwits stronger opponents and is celebrated by the people (Carroll 1984: 106). Ricketts even proposed a developmental relationship between the buffoon and the hero. He saw the former being more likely to appear in simple societies and the latter in contexts where religious systems are more developed. The latter 'lack the physical appetites that make trickster-fixers so "human" and which lead them to behave so foolishly' (Ricketts discussed in Carroll 1984: 112).

Explicitly connecting anthropological thinking on cosmologies and worldview with tricksters, Paul Radin (1972 [1956]) saw the trickster myth of the Winnebago Indians as a comment on the 'role of chaos and ambiguity in creation myth'. In short, it allowed people to think through some inconsistencies in their view of the world and provided 'a frank recognition and acceptance of human ambivalence' (Radin cited in Lambek 2002: 244). The almost satirical streak of some trickster tales presented, for Radin, evidence of sceptical critique by some individuals in societies. Similarly, Lewis Hyde in his study *Trickster Makes This World: Mischief, Myth, and Art* (1998) reflects on the trickster as 'the mythic embodiment of ambiguity and ambivalence, doubleness and duplicity, contradiction and paradox' (1998: 7). In this respect he is a figure that not only crosses over boundaries but can also play a role in constructing boundaries. He notes, 'in several mythologies, for example, the gods lived on earth until something the trickster did, caused them to rise to heaven' (1998: 7).

In African mythology Eshu and Legba are tricksters who are the sole mediators between human beings and the gods. These figures also have shrines built in their honour. Interestingly, these shrines are often built outside the village or physical boundaries of the group associated with them (Carroll 1984: 123). Some have suggested this is to reflect their guardian roles in relation to humans. However, Carroll proposes a different view:

> The invariable placement of Eshu/Legba shrines outside the boundaries of the household or the village is simply a way of disassociating Eshu/ Legba from human society, that is, from culture. In other words, the invariable placement of Eshu/Legba shrines outside the boundaries of important social groups (like household or the village) establishes the same disassociation with 'culture' that is established in the case of other tricksters with solitary animals.
>
> Carroll 1984: 124

In view of the above diversity, one wonders whether it is possible to provide a comparative framework for such figures. Hansen has done a great service in this respect in his recent work, *The Trickster and the Paranormal* (2001). Therein he helpfully lists common characteristics of trickster figures that are presented in Table 4.1. Diversity should breed caution in relation to neat typologies, for as Camp states, 'there does not seem to be any one ideal trickster type. Rather, any given trickster may comprise a shifting combination of several but not necessarily all, characteristics of the general type' (Camp 1988: 15). Despite these reservations the following characteristics do provide a neat point of reference for subsequent comparison.

Table 4.1.   Trickster Characteristics

Characteristics	
Boundary crosser	Disrupts norms / crosses boundaries / does not conform to the establishment
Disorderly	Courts disorder / loss of status / seen as buffoon or cultural hero
Deceptive	Deceives larger and more powerful beings / inverts situations to own benefit
Tells stories cloaked in mystery	Tells stories that are irrational and need decoding / brings divine messages
Miracles and signs	Performs supernatural manifestations

'Tricksters' in Biblical Studies

Anthropologists have identified circumstances when trickster characters arise as those in which persons are deficient in authority or influence in political, economic, religious or domestic spheres. Afro-American slave tales, for example, share many characteristics in common with trickster frameworks: 'in the context of slavery, the figure of the trickster reveals a mechanism of praise for those who are able to turn a system of oppression on its head through ridicule of those in control' (Steinberg 1988: 6). It is unsurprising therefore that substantial use has been made of the literary trickster trope in biblical studies, or 'archetype' to use Jung's term, by feminist interpreters in a 1988 *Semeia* volume entitled, *Reasoning with the Foxes: Female Wit in a World of Male Power*. These feminist readings concur that, due to their marginal position, women as a group can seek to accomplish aims through alternative ways; deception and trickery are examples of such avenues (Exum & Bos 1988).

Power and authority are of course key issues in such circumstances. Those that have to resort to the 'subversive' practice of trickster narratives to re-imagine their world and see their own bad situations in another light are the underdogs of social situations. Steinberg seems correct to assert 'stories of tricksters in the Bible appear to be explorations of the instability of the power brokers in society' (Steinberg 1988: 1). By commenting on social problems of order and disorder, marginals can re-imagine their adverse social circumstances. In Ashley's words, 'carnivalesque behaviours, like role reversals, seem to act out protest against the politically powerful, while at the same time consolidating the established order' (Ashley 1988: 114).

Boyarin and Boyarin in their 2002 book, *Powers of Diaspora*, provide very interesting insights regarding 'trickster' characteristics in the self-construction of Diaspora Jews. They root this identity in the narratives of Esther and Judith respectively. These women 'save themselves and the Jewish people by seducing and deceiving a powerful male gentile' (Boyarin & Boyarin 2002: 37). They voice similar sentiments to the feminist contributors to the *Semeia* volume, in seeing trickster themes as part of a 'politics of resistance' and suggest that: 'Jews identify themselves as a people with these heroines, and thus as female, with the appropriation of tactics of survival that belonged "by nature" to women' (Boyarin & Boyarin 2002: 37). They cite Levine's construction of feminine self-understanding in Diaspora Judaism, which, like tricksters, inhabits a 'middle' space, between boundaries. They write:

> On the one hand, it [the female body] is the vulnerable body, the body that is invaded, penetrated and hurt. On the other hand, it is the fecund body, the body that interacts with the world and creates new life – in short, a perfect representation of the dangers and powers of diaspora ... no wonder then, that the disaporic people imagine themselves as female.
>
> Boyarin & Boyarin 2002: 38–39

Boyarin and Boyarin's study continues by tracing a shift between Judaism presented in Tobit and later rabbinic formulations. The former conceives of Israel as a male figure, however the rabbis can conceive of themselves and Israel in female terms (Boyarin & Boyarin 2002: 39). Boyarin and Boyarin see this as a shift from a context in which the primary concern was policing purity boundaries in the face of impinging chaos to one in complete contrast, which presents the breaching of borders producing life. This shift, in their opinion, constitutes a move from 'one in which diaspora and feminisation of the social body are seen only as a threat to one in which they are celebrated (however warily) for their ethical and creative possibilities … Tobit is dreaming of an immediate end to diaspora; for the Rabbis it has become the condition of their lives as Jews' (2002: 39). The border itself becomes a source of creativity rather than taboo.

If trickster themes are more often associated with 'creative' transcending of boundaries and borders, rather than protection of them; furthermore, if those 'displaced' turn creatively to trickster themes as commentaries on their positions, is there first, any mileage in seeing John's presentation of Jesus reflecting trickster ideas? Second, are there any insights into the messages and worldview that John seems keen to impress on his readers that can be illuminated by reference to this theme?

John's Trickster Jesus

Returning to the typology of trickster characteristics noted above, John's Jesus certainly does seem to provide comparative possibilities. First, disruption and boundary crossing is part and parcel of John's narrative and Jesus' mission. Jesus straddles and mediates between heaven and earth, above and below, the Father and the world. He embodies nonconformity to the establishment. He disregards social and religious conventions (speaking with the Samaritan woman; healing on the Sabbath; cleansing the temple) in order to reveal an alternative world order. Jesus declares that his revelation and word alone makes clean (Jn. 15:3). His identity and spirit ameliorates distinctions and boundaries. Likewise, he tosses Pilate's question aside regarding kingship: 'My kingdom is not of this world. If my kingdom were from this world, my followers would be fighting to keep me from being handed over to the Jews' (Jn. 18:36). He thus transcends cosmological, religious, social, political and racial boundaries.

Second, Jesus courts loss of status and allegations of disorder from his enemies. They accuse him of having a demon (Jn. 7:20; 8:48, 52; 10:20), however, while dismissed by them as 'a selfish buffoon' others hail him as a 'cultural hero': 'these are not the words of one who has a demon. Can a demon open the eyes of the blind?' (Jn. 10:21). More prominent is Thomas's legendary salute, 'My Lord and My God' (Jn. 20:28).

Third, cosmic trickery is rooted at the heart of John and involves deception of the 'prince of this world'. God in the form of man, lifted up on a cross, will cast out the prince of this world (Jn. 12:31). Though Jesus succumbs to his enemies, it is all due to the divine ordinance of events; the prince of this world has no effectual power over him (Jn. 14:30). As a direct result of his glorious passion and resurrection, the Spirit 'will prove the world wrong about judgement, because the prince of this world is condemned' (Jn. 16:8, 11). In his exchanges with worldly foes, particularly the Jewish authorities, Jesus also inverts conflict situations to his benefit. He gets the logical and theological better of them in arguments (Jn. 5:17; 7:14–28; 9:35–40); he performs wonders that cannot be assigned to demonic powers (Jn. 10:21); he is a skilful negotiator who seems always to have the last word.

Fourth, mystery riddles his ministry, indeed 'he was in the world, and the world came into being through him; yet the world did not know him. He came to what was his own, and his own people did not accept him' (Jn. 1:10–11). Jesus speaks in coded and symbolic language, water, life, truth, spirit are just some of the double-voiced words within the narrative, which leave unbelievers blind, but bestow on those open to the message the faculty of spiritual sight (Jn. 9:39). Misunderstandings on the story level, such as the exchanges with Nicodemus and the Samaritan woman, also serve as catalysts for the reader's deeper enlightenment. Jesus embodies the divine message, indeed he *is* the divine: 'the words that I say to you I do not speak on my own; but the Father who dwells in me does his works. Believe me that I am in the Father and the Father is in me' (Jn. 14:10–11).

Finally, Jesus manifests the supernatural; indeed it is through him that creation is brought into being. This has some parallels with Babcock's study that reveals how in many cultures trickster narratives form part of the sacred heritage concerning the creation of the world. Pelton in his study of the trickster in West Africa likewise sees such figures as, 'beings of the beginning, working in some complex relationship with the High God; transformers, helping to bring the present human world into being; performers of heroic acts on behalf of men' (Pelton 1980: 15).

If the fact that the logos is an agent of creation and embodies God on earth was not enough, John's Jesus also performs his miraculous signs (Jn. 2:1–11; 4:46–54; 5:2–9; 6:1–14; 6:16–21; 9:1–12; 11:1–44). Collectively these explain and defend the belief that through Jesus believers have access to life. In the words of Rensberger:

> Jesus performs only seven miracles in the fourth gospel, but they are distinctive in being life-giving acts.... These works of life-giving love and power demonstrate that Jesus is a window to God, and they give a glimpse through that window to the character of God.
>
> Rensberger 2001: 22

Those who are recipients and witnesses of signs and miracles are shown to believe (Jn. 2:11; 4:53). After his resurrection Jesus' words are confirmed (Jn. 2:22); those who believe do not perish but have eternal life (Jn. 3:15, 18; 5:24; 11:24; 12:46). The signs explain that belief is John's desired response for his readers (Jn. 1:7). Belief in Jesus denotes belief in the Father (Jn. 14:10–11) for Jesus reveals the Father. Indeed the gospel as a whole is written 'that you may come to believe that Jesus is the Messiah, the Son of God and that through believing you may have life in his name' (Jn. 20:31).

One interesting application of the trickster theme, to which I am particularly indebted, is J. Berenson Maclean's 1999 Society of Biblical Literature seminar paper entitled 'A Tale of Two Weddings: The Divine Trickster in John' (available online). Although she did not elaborate extensively on the anthropology of the trickster figure, Maclean nonetheless recognised in John's Jesus particular attributes of such a character. Concentrating on Jesus' first sign in John (and a comparative reading of tricks in Jacob's wedding narrative) she argues:

> Because the miracle is not fully revealed in the story – only the servants and the disciples are apparently privy to Jesus' deeds – Jesus' actions remain on the level of undetected trickery for the steward, the groom, and the wedding guests. The steward believes that the groom has deceived him by withholding the good wine until the end of the party; the groom we should imagine is equally surprised at the steward's comments, for he has no knowledge of a reserve of excellent wine.
>
> Maclean 1999

Maclean continues that 'the trick introduces the Johannine theme that Jesus' ministry divides humans into two groups – those who are in the know and respond favourably and those who simply cannot understand'. For Maclean 'tricksterism is revealed to be at the heart of Jesus' glory' (1999). Jesus is a transformation of God into man, just as other tricksters transform into forms of animals, change sex and the like. If John's Jesus can indeed be fruitfully exhibited with trickster, how does this sort of Christology impact our understanding of John's Gospel?

John's Celebration of Liminal Space

Tricksters occupy space between social boundaries. I have suggested above that the creativity of John's presentations of Jesus also exploits this placing. Here I suggest that John's readers are likewise 'in the world, but not of it'. They occupy a place of otherness – a liminal space.

Barbara Babcock popularised the notion of liminality in anthropological studies of tricksters. It is not insignificant that she worked under Victor Turner and that his conception of liminal space is one in which her trickster-figure seems quite at home. She sees the trickster standing in 'immediate relation to the center in all its ambiguity ... and for this we not only tolerate this margin of mess, this enemy of boundaries, we create and recreate him' (Babcock-Abrahams 1975). George Hansen likewise submits that liminality and ambiguity is the trickster's particular province (2001). But how, if at all, does 'ambiguity' relate to John's Gospel?

John's prologue tells us much about the gospel's overall perspective. The events it narrates go far beyond the limits of normal human experience. The backdrop is eternity; the players include the divine; the realm is above. It tells of the mystery of the incarnate one, coming to earth and pitching his tent among us (Jn. 1:14). Jesus himself reflects and embodies God's presence within the world. Those who want to follow him and become children of God are born 'not of blood, or the will of the flesh or the will of man, but of God' (Jn. 1:13).

Early on in the gospel we are presented with the famous exchange between Jesus and Nicodemus in which Jesus teaches that 'no one can see the kingdom of God without being born from above' (Jn. 3:3). This causes no small confusion for poor Nicodemus who mistakenly interprets birth as the physical re-entry into his mother's womb (Jn. 3:4). Jesus continues his enigmatic explanation and speaks of being born of water and spirit (Jn. 3:5–9). One is not sure that Nicodemus grasps the situation any better by the end of the exchange (Jn. 3:9), but as many commentators suggest, misunderstanding on the story level invites deeper understanding on the part of the reader regarding being 'born from above'. Talbert describes the situation thus:

> The answer is not by individual mystical ascent into heaven (v.13a) but by
> virtue of the descending-ascending Son of Man (vv.13b–21). How does the
> descent-ascent of the Son of Man enable it? This text does not explicitly say
> how, but later in the Gospel the reader is told. It is by the Spirit that is given
> after Jesus' glorification (7:37–39; 20:22) and made possible by it (16:7). 'It
> is to your advantage that I go away; for if I do not go away, the Counselor
> will not come to you; but if I go, I will send him to you'.
>
> Talbert 1992: 102

The invitation to be 're-conceived' in another dimension calls to mind Victor Turner's explorations of anti-structure and liminal space. Turner enjoys classic status in anthropology. His celebrated works on rites of passage, building on the thought of Van Gennep, have been particularly influential. He saw the middle transitory stage of these rites, in which the subject was called out of the world but not yet reintegrated back into it, as liminal (derived from the Latin term for threshold – _limen_). Turner's conception of liminal space was derived from fieldwork on Ndembu ritual, particularly the initiation of a chief. By virtue of similar clothing and actions within this rite, distinctions between sexes and persons (particularly the chief and the rest of the community) were transcended. The collective body of people in Turner's opinion formed 'a repository of the whole gamut of the culture's values, norms, attitudes, sentiments and relationships' (Turner 1991 [1969]: 103). In such liminal occasions, Turner witnessed an intensely holistic and collective vision shared by the group's participants.

Structures, statuses and social norms are all suspended in the liminal realm. While this in effect could strip an individual of their identity and make them marginal to the world, ironically often individuals occupying this realm enjoy profound social relationships or _communitas_ with each other. Turner did not reserve this analysis for rites of passage alone, but saw persons and even communities (such as ascetics, monastic orders and even revolutionaries) as permanently embodying liminal space (being liminoidal). Such people 'took on the stigma of the lowly and unkempt, the vagrant and ostracised, the mad and simple.... Life was conducted so that they may replace social-structural obligation and differentiation with a sense of true human bonds, based on personal relations of love, equality, spontaneity and freedom' (Turner discussed in Rapport & Overing 2000: 234).

If we take the invitation issued to Nicodemus to be 'born from above' 'in water and spirit' as an invitation for the reader to embark on a journey of gradual embodiment of a liminal identity (similar to the boundary identity of the Jewish Diaspora elucidated above by Boyarin and Boyarin) what other features of John's worldview could be part and parcel of the scheme?

First, most directly, features surrounding the symbols of water and spirit provide an air of 'otherness' for readers of the gospel. Previous to the Nicodemus exchange, Jesus has provided symbolic 'new wine from water' in the sign of the wedding feast at Cana. The reader learns that Jesus gives living water (Jn. 4:10; 7:38) 'springing to eternal life' (Jn. 4:14) that stands in contrast to physical liquid. Similarly, spirit denotes things divine (Jn. 4:24) that stand in contrast to fleshly and material substances (Jn. 6:63). The Spirit is the agent of truth. However, the Spirit is not recognised or admitted into the social space of the world. It can only hope to reside in the world in the receptacle bodies of believers: 'This is the Spirit of truth, whom the world cannot receive, because it neither sees him nor knows him. You know him, because he abides with you, and he will be in you' (Jn. 14:17).

All the language of separation or otherness from the world within the gospel would also link in to Turner's conception of separation from social structures. Examples of such language and ideas are not hard to find in John (Jn. 15:19; 16:33; 17:14). The most obvious theological motif connected to this is the ascent/descent motif. Wayne Meeks's masterly study connected this motif to the marginal self-identity of Johannine Christians who felt themselves to be 'in the world not of it'. Adele Reinhartz in her book, *The Word in the World* (1992) has elaborated on this theme and tells what she calls 'The Cosmological Tale of the Fourth Gospel'. This is a threefold tale involving the 'word's relation with the world ... before the creation of time'; 'the word's entry into the world'; finally the word's departure from the world' (1992: 17). She elaborates on this tripartite scheme as follows:

> First, the Word is the Son of the Father. Second, his entry into the world served a specific purpose, described as making the Father known and enlightening the world (1: 9). Third, his coming engendered the desired response among many, which as a result enjoyed benefits such as becoming children of God and receiving grace upon grace.
>
> Reinhartz 1992: 18

In many ways this tale provides a prototype of Turner's ritual analysis. Jesus himself is separated from his own realm (above) and descends to earth to reveal the Father. This stage is liminal. He invites others to join him in this liminal space and *communitas* is enjoyed by those receptive to his message. He awaits his return to the Father, as glorified son, and will send the Spirit to his own while they wait for his return. Reinhartz sees the cosmological tale imprinted on the whole drama of the gospel and reads John 10:1–5, the image of the sheepfold, as a microcosm of the macro-cosmological story.

> The gate has two functions. First, it is the way through which the legitimate shepherd gains entry to the sheepfold and thereby also access

to the sheep. It is also the means through which the shepherd, as well as
the sheep, leaves the sheepfold.... If we see the paroimia as a symbolic
reference to the cosmological tale, in which the sheepfold is the world,
then it would appear that it is the incarnation by which Jesus enters the
world, and it is the passion, including the crucifixion, resurrection and
ascension by which he leaves it. The events therefore are the means by
which Jesus crosses the threshold between this world and the realm of
the Father.

Reinhartz 1992: 81

However, if Jesus mediates between God and the world, his ministry
nevertheless also involves reintegration in heaven. This is not the case
for believers at least in the immediate future. They are called to occupy
liminal space in the world until Jesus comes again: 'Though not of
the world, they remain in the world, protected from the evil one until
their shepherd will return to lead them out of the fold to their Father's
house' (Reinhartz 1992: 104). The reader also participates in liminal
reading space, for the return of the shepherd has not occurred. They also
are called to exist in the world, but stand apart from its assumptions,
structures, hierarchies and worldviews. They must have heaven, not
earth, on their minds. The *communitas*, the bond uniting the liminoid
readers of John, is of course love. Those called out of the world must
love one another as Jesus has loved them (Jn. 13:34) for this is his greatest
commandment (Jn. 15:12).

   If then the reader is invited to change perspective and enter liminal
space, how does the text itself inscribe otherness in its readers? How
does it seek to defamiliarise them with perspectives of their own world?
If commentators are right that John's Jesus provides a prototype or
exemplar for his readers, for example, as the ascending and descending
redeemer who embodies their marginality, then surely the narrative
presentation of his 'trickster' doings will also comment on or change
the reader's perspective.

   Maclean (1999) is also insightful here. She connects the trickster nature
of John's Jesus to the status of John's community. Citing Edwards, she
sees trickster tales promoting 'welfare of the community by reflecting
the values of the oppressed' and unmasking the 'vulnerability of power
as defined by the current social hierarchy'. In this vein, trickster tales
are powerful weapons of the weak, the marginal and those who feel
they have been sidelined by society. She links this with the so-called
Johannine community's break from the synagogue.

J. L. Martyn (1979) initiated reading John's worldview on two levels. First, the surface-story concerning Jesus and second, a deeper level, which reflected the situation of John's intended readership, the so-called Johannine community who had just experienced expulsion from the synagogue on account of the *Birkath-ha-Minim* clause inserted into the synagogue prayers following the Jamnia council. Whether or not a break had actually taken place, relationships between the Christian and Jewish communities were, it is claimed, tense. Such a context explains the polemic against the Jews in the gospel and the dualistic language of light/darkness, life/death and flesh/spirit. Many interpretations have read the gospel in light of their preconceived picture of the social situation of John's community.

Wayne Meeks's now classic essay 'The Man from Heaven in Johannine Sectarianism' (1986 [1972]) is one example of such a reading. Meeks, like other interpreters using the sociology of knowledge (Gager 1975: 9–12; Kee 1980: 22–26; Esler 1994: 6–12; MacDonald 1988), sees the community situation in which the text was written as central. Meeks's work has been invaluable for those imagining the sectarian identity of John's community, whose worldview (centred on their descent/ascent mythology) had dictated that salvation and life come from 'above'. Due to their marginal status, the Johannine Christians felt out of place in the world. Meeks is keen to stress that the gospel is not a projection of the group's situation. 'On the contrary, the Johannine dialogues suggest quite clearly that the order of development must have been dialectical: the christological claims of the Johannine Christians resulted in their becoming alienated … that alienation in turn is "explained" by a further development of motifs' (Meeks 1986 [1972]: 164).

Whatever the specific circumstances however, it is certain that an air of separateness and the 'trickster' questioning of authority power structures is breathed within the fourth gospel. Furthermore, the use of the trickster figure as a survival strategy is an elegant response to symbolic and actual subjugation that demeans an individual or community's basic convictions and values. Jesus the divine trickster unmasks the vulnerability of the powerful (of this world) while providing the powerless (of this world) with a new creative perspective on their liminality. Just as certain Jewish authors had commented on the fecundity of being 'dispersed' – 'betwixt and between' spheres – from one land, but displaced to another, so John comments on his community's symbolic space.

Trickster Imagination

The faculty necessary for creative transformation is of course human imagination. So-called 'trickster imagination' has been a key theme in anthropological theorising, not least in Preston's essay, 'The Trickster Unmasked: Anthropology and the Imagination' (1991). He, like Goodman (1978: 7–16), contended that no worldview was entirely novel, but always built upon existing ideas, objects and relations, for 'comprehension and creation go on together' (Goodman cited in Rapport & Overing 2000: 392). Beidelman likewise sees imagination as crucial for developing stories amongst those who perceive themselves to be located on margins or between boundaries. Beidelman defines imagination as 'the picturing of characters and events in the mind's eye in a manner or form resembling but significantly different and removed from reality' (1980: 33). Furthermore he notes qualities of such narratives as follows:

> These stories are odd, not in the sense that they do not represent recognised characteristics, feelings, motives and roles, but in the sense that whereas in real life these cannot all be properly judged and met by the same person in one situation, here they are clearly defined and resolved. Indisputable, unambiguous moral judgements and permanent resolutions must remain imaginary so long as a person lives.
>
> Beidelman 1980: 33

Preston illustrated the reconception of the world along four dimensions in trickster 'imagination-provoking' narratives. These dimensions were spatial; temporal; morphological; comprehensive (Preston 1991; see also Rapport & Overing 2000: 394). How does John's narrative appear through these lenses?

Spatial

Preston saw that elements of the world could be re-imagined spatially by magnification or reduction. Space is an incredibly important social-scientific concept. We inhabit space from cradle to grave. Landscapes and places can accordingly be examined 'as symbolic fields', 'maps of meaning', 'ways of seeing', and 'read as texts' (Watts 1992: 122).

Within the gospel, spatially and theologically heaven is the homeland of the word (Jn. 6:38), the place from which the Son of Man descends (Jn.

1:51; 3:13) and the Spirit comes (Jn. 1:32). For those 'born from above' it is the place from which life and nourishment comes (Jn. 6:32–33, 50–51, 58). It is literally and ideologically contrasted with the world below (Jn. 3:31) and its structures and norms. In many ways the vista from the beginning of the gospel is 'above' and 'before' earth. The reader in effect comes to see their origin in the story with the word, before creation. In this sense what is spatially 'above' becomes their homeland (Jn. 17:14), and heaven becomes the remembered place referred to throughout the narrative. Such places, in Gupta and Ferguson's words, serve 'as symbolic anchors of community for dispersed people' (1992: 11). They submit: 'This has long been true of immigrants, who use memory of place to construct imaginatively their new lived world. Homeland in this way remains one of the most powerful unifying symbols for mobile and displaced peoples' (Gupta & Ferguson 1992: 11). If for John, heaven is imagined as the homeland of the reader, the status of the world is far more ambiguous, even 'defamiliarised'. On one level, *kosmos* variously refers to the entire world, the arena into which the Word enters and departs (Jn. 1:9; 8:26; 10:36; 11:27; 16:28; 17:11–12; 18:37), or a created entity brought into being through the Word (1:10; 17:5, 24). On another level, the world is seen as a public domain – to which one must show oneself, and also the domain of revelation of God through Jesus (Jn. 7:4; 12:19; 14:19, 22, 31; 17:6, 13, 21, 23; 18:20).

There is also a very negative stance towards the world. Ashton proposes a twofold negative spatiality. First, what he has termed a vertical dualism: the world is shown as opposed to heaven (1991: 207). Second, the horizontal dimension whereby those belonging to the world are unreceptive and in darkness (Jn. 1:5, 10). The evilness of the world is shown through the metaphor of darkness (Jn. 3:19), which is explicitly contrasted with the light Jesus brings (Jn. 8:12; 9:5; 12:46). Furthermore, the world is cast as rejecting Jesus and his message (Jn. 7:7; 14:7; 15:18; 17:14) or being alien to things from above (Jn. 8:23; 14:27; 15:19; 16:20; 17:9), for Jesus' kingdom is not of this world (Jn. 18:36). The world is a domain that Jesus must overcome (Jn. 16:33) but wherein those he calls his own (Jn. 13:1) must still live for the time being (Jn. 17:15–16, 18). Despite this bleak, 'dark' picture, Jesus is shown as saviour of the world (Jn. 1:29; 3:16–17; 4:2; 12:47) who gives his flesh for the life of the world (Jn. 6:33; 6:51). All these diverse perspectives must be synthesised and co-ordinated by the reader. It makes incumbent on them the responsibility to respond and believe.

The spatial metaphor also operates in so-called Johannine indwelling, whereby the spirit of truth indwells in believers (Jn. 14:15), and the

Father and Son 'will come to them and make our home in them' (Jn. 14:23). The realisation that the divine is potentially 'here' at their reading experience is underscored by the importance put on the encounter with Jesus in the text. Culpepper is instructive here. He notes that places, Cana (Jn. 2:1), Capernaum (Jn. 2:12), Judea (Jn. 3:22), Aenon near Salim (Jn. 3:23), Sychar (Jn. 4:6), etc. are all presented in the narrative. In contrast the immediate 'here' (ōde) occurs in dialogue with Jesus alone (1983: 27), serving to emphasise the importance of response by the reader. Resseguie is insightful on this theme. In his opinion:

> The narrator shapes familiar settings to express an unfamiliar, new or otherwise strange point of view. Inside space is secure space and this is hammered home with unmistakable regularity in the images of the sheep-fold and garden … Space is used to effectively communicate the dilemma of trying to bring dissonant, unappeasable voices in harmonious unity with the voice of the good shepherd.
>
> Resseguie 2001: 106

He continues, 'other familiar settings – seas and mountains – are used to express an ideological point of view. Distance communicates estrangement. And so the disciples' separation from Jesus is a struggle for survival' (Resseguie 2001: 107).

Temporal

Imagination along temporal lines in Preston's view progresses through montage (situations being presented as kaleidoscopic), simultaneity (events being juxtaposed) and the presentation of different events in the past and future. In this sphere the Spirit (*pneuma*) has an enormously important role to play. John the Baptist sees the Spirit descend on Jesus (Jn. 1:32–33). Jesus calls everyone to be born of water and Spirit to enter the kingdom (Jn. 3:5); this is contrasted with those born of flesh (Jn. 3:6). At 'the hour', an eschatological term, true worshippers are shown to worship the Father in Spirit (Jn. 4:23–24). Additionally, the Spirit is explicitly connected with life (Jn. 6:63). The Spirit is a spirit of truth (Jn. 14:17; 15: 26; 16:13) who will lead believers in truthfulness.

Morphological

Transmutation, animation and materialisation of certain elements are recorded here. Themes of this sort seem particularly well suited to understanding Johannine irony. As Kieffer reveals, the reader is called to 'elucidate the misunderstandings ... riddles and the Johannine irony' (Kieffer 1999: 57). The irony of the blindness of the Pharisees is shown in John chapter 9. The sinner who is blind believes Jesus is the Son of Man (Jn. 9:35–38) ironically the Pharisees cannot see (Kieffer 1999: 60). Continuing the optic metaphor, light and darkness can in part be seen to coalesce with day and night. Light 'virtually replaces the proclamation of the kingdom as the object of the gospel promise' (Ashton 1991: 214). 'Bread and water, the staple necessities of life, are natural symbols of supernatural life' (Ashton 1991: 219). Dokka likewise submits: 'One cannot toil ... long ... before seeing the double effect of creating heavenly metaphors of normal human life – and of recreating a normal human life out of the heavenly metaphors' (1999: 106). He admits that there are elements in the gospel that would seem to indicate strong and hostile pressures from outside the group. However, he also recognises:

> The language in which these themes are clothed is, however, heavily 'mythological'. It draws on ideas about transcendent powers and hidden origins, and it transforms what we take to be worldly matters into grand hypostatic powers engaged in cosmic drama. The pressure likely to have been felt by the Johannine community was, in a literary reading, basically of a mythological nature. Most exegetes concerned with the actual state and ideology of the Johannine group work on the assumption that this mythically worded pressure can be translated fairly easily into sociology. It is far from obvious, however, how this pressure was related to social realities.
>
> Dokka 1999: 99–100

The worldview can provide 'psychological reinforcement' and certainty in times of uncertainty and comfort in times that could appear as crisis points. Often rituals are used for such purposes (funerals would be a case in point). Other means of reinforcing the worldview are also brought into play. The 'I Am' sayings, for example, play an important role in affirming certainty in Jesus' role and identity; and accordingly the legitimacy of the reader's belief in him.

Comprehensive

Comprehensive imagination involves changing the world in terms of focal depth, distortions and overall decisions regarding the world. This category therefore involves all of the above. As Martyn recognised in John,

There are dramas taking place both on the heavenly stage and on the earthly stage. Yet these dramas are not really two, but one drama ... one might say that events on the heavenly stage not only correspond to events on the earthly stage, but also slightly precede them in time, leading them into existence so to speak. What transpired on the heavenly stage is often called 'things to come'. For that reason events seen on the earthly stage are entirely enigmatic to the man who sees only the earthly stage. Stereotopic vision is necessary, and it is precisely stereotopic vision, which causes a man to write an apocalypse.

Martyn 1968: 127

As a result of this, Ashton has likewise asserted that 'Jesus' task is not just to talk about God, but to establish his glory. The concept of God's glory comes from the Old Testament theophanies, which were manifestations of God's power and authority to individual human beings and followed in every case by an event of exceptional significance' (Ashton 1991: 405). Jesus, for John, 'is the plan of God, his grand project for humanity (the word) made flesh and his glory made manifest. This is the very essence of apocalyptic' (Ashton 1991: 406). Dokka accordingly sees this gospel asking people to effect 'a distancing from the world verging on the absolute, and a deep unity with the world, also verging on the absolute'; 'securely above the world and defencelessly one with it' (1999: 106–107).

One particular way in which the Johannine Jesus is comprehensively remodelled in contrast to the synoptic figures, is that he performs no exorcisms. Unlike in the synoptics where Jesus is shown to publicly fight evil, cast out demons and overcome 'Satan' in his mission (not least at the temptation), in the Gospel of John the role of the devil is not as developed. Those against Jesus are shown to be in league with the devil, for example, Judas who will betray him (Jn. 6:70; 13:2). Also, Jesus casts his opponents as children of the devil (Jn. 8:44) and they in turn accuse Jesus of having a demon (Jn. 8:48, 52; 10:20). The prince of this world (Jn. 12:31; 14:30; 16:11) is presumably a reference to the devil.

After surveying a number of inadequate theses why the fourth gospel features no exorcisms, Twelftree forwards his own perspective. 'Jesus is never portrayed as relying on a source of power/authority outside himself in performing miracles' (Twelftree 2001: 139). He notes that the balance tips away from the synoptic exorcist to the practitioner of signs, which shows that 'God is himself at work in these acts of Jesus, and through them his character is disclosed' (2001: 140). In contrast to the in-breaking of the kingdom in the synoptic gospels shown in the exorcisms, in the fourth gospel the entire ministry can be seen to be a battle with Satan:

> To put the matter sharply, on the one hand, in the synoptic traditions the battle with Satan is centred during the public ministry of Jesus, in his exorcisms. But then it is severely attenuated in the passion narrative. The reverse is the case for the Fourth Gospel. The battle with Satan permeates the proleptic ministry of Jesus, reaching its climax and realization in the cross event – the grand cosmic exorcism.
>
> Twelftree 2001: 141

Ronald Piper's recent work on this theme links the absence of exorcisms to community rivalry. Demonic language is reserved for 'demonising one's opponents' (Piper 2000: 265); moreover 'believers define themselves over against him (Satan) and his sphere of influence' (Piper 2000: 275). Drawing an interesting anthropological perspective on this issue is Kapferer's study of *Exorcism and the Aesthetics of Healing in Sri Lanka* (1991). Kapferer submits that Buddhist exorcists are masters of illusion and trickery. He writes,

> Through their artifice and skill they can give rise to the illusory and disruptive powers of the demonic. But in their mastery of illusion they can also control the demons and expose the falsity behind appearances.
>
> Kapferer 1991: 158

He notes how demons (conceived as community opponents) can disguise themselves behind other masks (appearing as something else), yet the exorcist can see through this. He writes, 'the ability of demons to control and dominate through illusion is contained in processes which resolve the contradiction between the apparent order of their form in appearance and the disorder which lurks behind it' (Kapferer 1991: 176). Kapferer goes on to describe the characteristics of humans who are subject to demonic illusion. These individuals often manifest disorder within themselves and in their relationships with others. Moreover, they are:

> deluded by the illusion of demonic power when their perception of a wider cosmic unity, its hierarchy and principles of order, is obscured or restricted.

It is through a conscious and reflective awareness of the hierarchy of the cosmic order and the further principles according to which the cosmic hierarchy finds its essential unity, that the demonic illusion and the power of demons can be broken.

Kapferer 1991: 177

Could it be, in alignment with Twelftree and Piper's conclusions, that the entire ministry of Jesus in John constitutes an overcoming of Satan and a rejection of those who opposed Christianity and thus needs no explicit exorcism accounts? This could perhaps be one of the central 'tricks' of this gospel. By overriding any 'illusion of demonic power' for the readers, they in turn are freed to reconsider their position in the cosmic order and break demonic illusion – a trick par excellence. By showing readers the usefulness of their liminal position, the gospel also serves to reduce any conception whatsoever that demonic power is a potent force in the era of the 'word becoming flesh'. By re-imagining worldviews in light of specific changes, conflict is resolved and cultural dissonance is eliminated. As Wallace noted in reference to worldviews:

Where mutually contradictory cognitions (including perceptions, knowledge, motives, values and hopes) are entertained, the individual must act to reduce the dissonance. While theoretically, he can do this by changing the real world in some respect, so as to modify the data coming in, he may also achieve the same effect by modifying his perceptions of self and of the real world in such a way that one horn of the dilemma is no longer recognised.

Wallace cited in Kraft 1979: 57

The prince of this world is defeated, those 'children of light' born of the will of God not flesh, have nothing to challenge their sense of belonging to a new community, standing apart from the world's assumptions and values.

Tricksters and John's Worldview

In diverse cultures across the world, trickery is one way in which individuals and communities that do not have power within the institutionalised structures of society can express their viewpoints, rationalise their situations and accept their position. Like these, John's narrative is also carefully constructed to capitalise on, and show the creativity inherent in the reader's liminal position. They, like the trickster Jesus, are called to live on boundaries, exist in a world that is foreign to them, live remotely from their homeland, which is above. Transformation along spatial, temporal and morphological lines and a presentation of Jesus with features of irony and ambiguity also promotes certain awareness within the readers. Sight only seems to be available through recognising misunderstanding; the world is only understood in contradistinction to heaven; Jesus' identity is only revealed through knotted riddles and unexpected turns of events. Like other marginal status people who use such stories to effect mental or symbolic rather than actual social change, John's Gospel beckons its readers to re-imagine the world, and their place in it.

However, as noted above, the trickster is only an analyst's construction. Beidelman made a similar point when he argued that broad characteristics or functions of 'tricksters' in cross-cultural analysis should not be sought, but rather 'we may ask what texts suggest about a particular society's mode of thought and organisation, rather than raise questions about tricksters in general' (Beidelman 1980: 28). This has certainly been the case here. Various dimensions of imagination and aspects of Jesus' character in John have produced fruitful convergence with broad trickster characteristics. There is a Chaco myth about a trickster rubbing against a tree and being shredded by the tree's thorn. He then takes his heart, intestines and stomach and transforms them into plants for human sustenance (Carroll 1984: 117). One cannot but recall, when hearing this narrative, John's Jesus becoming life-giving water and bread for his people. Such resonance between formulations, myths and perspectives seem to confirm the legitimacy of at least an attempt at viewing tricksters and John's 'Word' in concert.

5

Exhibit 3. Reading with 'Rituals of Resistance'

Willing Deaths and Masculinity

Curator's Notes

Anthropological thinking on masculinity, honour and violence (interpreted by the oppressed as rites into manhood) is brought to bear on instances of willing deaths, both in war and imperial contexts, in scriptural tradition.

Masculine power lay at the core of imperial ideology.

S. Fischler

A representation created with the intent of humiliating has been reversed into one of honour, manhood and moral superiority.

J. Peteet

The themes of violence, masculinity, death, resistance and honour (those situations in which a public conferral of status is granted) seem particularly well suited 'to read with' willing deaths (situations in which an individual openly embraces their own destruction) in scriptural tradition. This exhibit, after briefly introducing the complex issues surrounding the categorisations of 'willing deaths' as 'suicide' or 'martyrdom', will introduce traditional ideas of honour precedence (reputation affirmed before others on account of power, social status or prestige) and its link to situations of conflict and masculine ideals (for the distinction between honour precedence and virtue, see Lawrence 2002; 2003).

It is my contention that the willing death of Samson (Judg. 16) displays traditional concerns for honour precedence, manliness and war as a sacred activity. His conflict with the Philistines is presented in 'ritualised' terms. His actions in the temple of Dagon are 'sacred' acts of resistance, with Yahweh being with him. In contrast, the deaths of Saul (1 Sam. 31), Abimelech (Judg. 9), Ahithophel (2 Sam. 17), Zimri (1 Kgs. 16) and Judas (Mt. 27:4–5) are foils to this construction, documenting 'men behaving badly'. In exegetical sections I draw heavily on Droge and Tabor's celebrated study, *A Noble Death: Suicide and Martyrdom Among Christians and Jews in Antiquity* (1992).

The exhibit will then go on to explore the ways in which ethnography reveals how techniques of positive aggression against others are not the only forms of 'riposte' to perceived assaults on status and domination from alien powers. Some subjugates wage war with symbolic as opposed to physical means. For the oppressed victims, for whom physical retaliation is not an option, symbolic reversals of status (even in situations of death) are often the only avenues of resistance open to them. Julie Peteet's study, 'Male Gender and Rituals of Resistance in the Palestinian Intifada: A Cultural Politics of Violence' (1994) has been instrumental for me in constructing this perspective. Peteet revealed how youths subject to beatings in the occupied West Bank transformed their experiences of humiliating violence into rituals constituting initiations into manhood. This symbolic move formed a 'creative and dynamic act of resistance' (Peteet 1994: 31).

It is my contention that the Maccabean martyrs (2 Macc.; 4 Macc.), Jesus and the martyrs featured in Revelation, exhibit a strategy akin to what Peteet termed symbolic 'rituals of resistance' to domination: namely, a certain acceptance of the violence inflicted upon them but a rejection of the efficacy of that domination by commentary on the failings of the oppressors. These people reinterpret their experiences, like the youths on the West Bank, as rites of initiation into another mode of existence and as such reject the efficacy of the violence and projects of demasculinisation enforced upon them.

Introducing Willing Deaths: Cross-Cultural Problems of Classification

suicide n.—intentional killing of oneself, an instance of this; person who does this; action destructive to one's own interests or reputation etc. (L *sui* of oneself, –CIDE)

martyrdom n.—sufferings and death of martyr; torment

Oxford English Dictionary

Distinguishing between suicides and martyrdoms in the ancient world is no easy task, for the classification of such events often depends solely on the perspective of the labeller. As Droge and Tabor astutely noted 'one person's martyr was another person's suicide and vice versa' (Droge & Tabor cited in Brettler 2002: 5). In modern English usage, reflecting a mainly industrialised and individualist provenance, a suicide is often construed as the act of a depressive individual. Rational, scientific thinking no doubt added to the opinion that suicide was due to psychological instability or despair with life. Durkheim speculated on the reasons for the highest suicide rates of the world occurring in Western developed nations. In his *Le Suicide* (1951 [1897]) he explored 'individualistic' dynamics: first, the egoistic situation in which a person felt detached from a community; and second, the anomic situation in which strong collectively held values and norms were lacking.

The definitions of martyrdom in modern English, in contrast, imply some sort of vicarious sacrifice for others, or sacrifice for a cause. 'Martyr' is derived from the Greek word for 'witness' (*martus*). A judicial setting is the predominant context of the word in the Septuagint. The wider semantic range of martyrdom including persecution, affliction and loss of life seems to have been a later development in second-century Christian thinking (Brettler 2002: 3). As the above attests, definitions are culturally specific and when applied to different cultures could risk ethnocentric and anachronistic conceptions.

Ethnography reveals that the meanings and classifications of 'willing deaths' are open to different interpretations across the globe. Nils Rettersol, working in the Norwegian centre for 'Suicide Research and Prevention', helpfully documents work on the cultural history of suicide (1998), itself diverse and wide-ranging. To name but a few, in Aztec society suicide is prized; there is even a divine being dedicated to the act of self-destruction (Ixtab) who is traditionally depicted with a noose around her neck (see Farberow 1975; Cormack 2002). Eskimo societies accept willing death as socially beneficial in certain situations (Rasmussen 1931). For most nomadic tribes the elderly and sick who conceive of themselves as a burden to the rest of the group, kill themselves or stay unprotected and alone in the wilderness in order to induce death. This reflects altruistic motives in Durkheim's terms, whereby the needs of the group are valued above the needs of the individual. Trobriand Islanders' attitudes to certain willing deaths can also be understood in light of these social dynamics (Malinowski 1926). For example, willing death is an acceptable indictment of an offending spouse in problem marriages and a public example of the contravention of collectively held norms. Also, in parts of India (until relatively recently) the act of sutee, whereby a widow would fling herself on the funeral pyre of her husband, was seen to guarantee blessedness for them both. In feudal Japan, Hara-kiri (a Japanese ceremonial disembowelment) could atone for dishonour (or avoid humiliation through the contravention of values held dear by the group). Similarly Junshi (willing death carried out after the death of a superior) was seen as an ultimate gesture of allegiance to an esteemed deceased person (Robertson 1999).

The ancient world also provides myriad resources for investigating and categorising willing death. Graeco-Roman traditions reveal a plurality of positions on this issue. Recent work by historians has revealed that Latin and Greek did not have equivalent words to our suicide (which is itself a relatively late term derived from the Latin 'suicidum' around the 1500s), nor did their words for such acts necessarily harbour negative connotations (Van Hoof 1990: 136). Indeed some have claimed 'the absence of a completely hostile usage' with regard to self-inflicted death in classical vocabulary (Van Hoof 1990: 141). Van Hoof suggests that Greek had a number of words for self-killer; however, none of the words stood solely for the killer of self, but more often killer of kin.

In ancient Greece self-inflicted death was rejected if seen to contravene the will of the gods. Socrates, while dying at his own hands, argues such deaths could never be justified unless divinely willed (Brickhouse & Smith 2002). Roman drama, in contrast, specifically links such deaths with honour. If one found oneself in an intolerable situation, one could produce one last act of defiance by killing oneself. Likewise, those dying in battle were praised. Carlin Barton's contribution to Margaret Cormack's edited collection Sacrificing the Self (2002), entitled 'Honor and Sacredness in the Roman and Christian Worlds' (2002: 23–38), illustrates how seeming failure, capture and death could be transformed by the Romans into a symbolic pattern of redemption. Through death, persons could recover sacred honour (2002: 24). She writes,

> The Romans rarely identified with or wanted to be seen as victims, even in the direst circumstances. And so their stories of the vindication of honor are designed not to elicit pity, not to reveal a victim, but to reveal an unconquered will.
>
> Barton 2002: 27

What of the attitudes to willing deaths in scripture and Jewish/Christian thought? In the Christian tradition, an explicit rejection of 'suicide' as a crime can be traced to Augustine (354–430 CE) who saw such acts as offences against divine will. Indeed the only instances in which such acts could be accepted, in his opinion, was in response to a divine request (hence his acceptance of Samson's death as legitimate). While an explicit rejection of suicide (even a definition of suicide) came much later than the biblical period, what of martyrdom?

Marc Brettler in his essay 'Is there Martyrdom in the Hebrew Bible?' (2002) is particularly helpful here. Brettler adopts the five characteristics of martyrdom drawn up by Droge and Tabor in their 1992 book on noble death (Brettler 2002: 4). These are as follows:

- Martyrdoms reflect situations of opposition and persecution.

- The choice to die is viewed by the authors as necessary, noble and heroic.

- These individuals are often eager to die; indeed, in several cases they end up directly killing themselves.

- There is often the idea of vicarious benefit resulting from their suffering and death.

- The expectation of vindication and reward beyond death, more often than not is a prime motivation for their choice of death.

Brettler argues that martyrdom as defined above is not found in the Hebrew Bible at all. In coming to this conclusion, he explores situations of resistance to foreign rule (situations of opposition and persecution). First, in the pre-exilic situation reflected in the Book of Kings, he studies Hezekiah as an example of extreme resistance: 'he dared to oppose the mighty Assyrians, the great imperial power of his time that had overrun much of the ancient world' (Brettler 2002: 9). However, Hezekiah does not kill himself. He then looks to the Persian and Greek eras reflected in the books of Esther and Daniel respectively (Brettler 2002: 6). He writes, 'although the book of Esther introduces the element of national persecution, a fundamental element of martyrdom, this book is ultimately anti-martyrdom – the Jews of Esther redefine themselves as political victors rather than victims' (Brettler 2002: 13). It is only in a situation of actual extreme persecution, as presented by the later parts of the Book of Daniel, that Brettler perceives 'the coalescence of all the factors necessary for true martyrdom, and the first descriptions of martyrdom as a religious ideal in Judaism' (Brettler 2002: 16). Full-scale violent oppression allowed this to develop. Brettler writes:

> It is only in the final chapters of the Book of Daniel, representing the very latest of the canonical books of the Hebrew Bible, that all the necessary elements for martyrdom come together, as the notion of resurrection is first clearly seen in the Bible (Dan. 12:2–3).... This shift to full-scale religious persecution is the last missing piece that allowed the idea of martyrdom to develop. The persecution is referred to in the typically difficult and obscure language of the concluding chapters of Daniel, which state concerning Antiochus: 'He will have great strength, but not through his own strength. He will be extraordinarily destructive; he will prosper in what he does, and destroy the mighty and the people of the holy ones' (Dan. 8.24). The entire period is conceived as an era of 'wrath'.
>
> Brettler 2001: 15

Brettler is largely convincing in his arguments. If the Book of Daniel contains the seeds of a conception of martyrdom, it flourished in the Maccabean period and later impacted early Christian thinking on the sacrifice of Jesus and those who died on his account. Barton is once again insightful here in forging bonds between Roman thinking on transformation through suffering and death, and similar thinking by the early Christians.

> For the Roman, as for the early Christian, the victim was conspicuously central and active: the more actively voluntary, the more effective the sacrifice. Sacrifice exalted the victim and rendered him or her divine.... The Roman gladiator could recognize the Christian Perpetua's gesture of baring her throat, because it was his gesture.
>
> Barton 2002: 30–31

Martyrdom then, like suicide, risks anachronistic connotations in some instances in the Hebrew Bible. However, later Jewish writings and early Christian thinking on deaths in persecution can be seen to reflect what we would recognise as 'martyr-like' qualities. In an attempt to avoid some of these semantic pitfalls, for the purposes of subsequent discussion the more 'neutral' term of 'willing death' shall be used. This allows one to prise out the subtle distinctions between such acts in scriptural tradition and their relationship to other social values, including manliness, honour precedence/virtue and the like.

'It's Reigning Men!' Masculinity and Honour Precedence

If anthropology's sphere is 'the study of man' it is surprising that until very recently studying 'men as men' was never really part of its agenda. Gutmann has identified four recent ways in which anthropologists now classify and employ the ideas of masculinity in their work. First, 'anything that men think and do'; second 'anything men think and do to be men'; third, what makes some men 'inherently or by ascription ... "more manly" by other men'; finally, 'anything that women are not' (Gutmann 1997: 386). Three of these interests link with what could be called 'the social construction of manhood'. Such projects recognise that masculinity, like femininity, is not a biologically determined fact, but rather constitutes a nexus of cultural performances and is socially constructed. Suzanne Hatty's recent book, *Masculinities, Violence, and Culture* (2000) conducts what she terms a 'project of historicizing masculinity'. She agrees that a notion of masculinity is neither monolithic, nor all encompassing (Hatty 2000: 131). However, she also feels at base all conceptions of masculinity have to variously deal with what Clare Lees terms the 'Four Ps': power, potency, patriarchy and politics (Hatty 2000: 130–31).

Bruce Malina's definitions of the value of honour (1981: 47) are largely dependent on what Pitt-Rivers has identified as *honour precedence* (Pitt Rivers 1968–79: 510). Honour in this sense can be correlated with notable 'masculine' traits and correlates to the above 'Ps' (men must wield power, be virile, protect their line and seed, and be involved in decision-making). Precedence, constituting honour that validates itself before an evaluating public, is based on power and other status indicators and is often symbolic of the group. Indeed honour precedence maintains that the individual group member's behaviour affects the honour of the entire group. Honour is to be aggressively pursued and competitively safeguarded. The agonistic defence of precedence often leads to physical violence.

This picture is witnessed in constructions of Mediterranean masculinity. Herzfeld notes that in the Mediterranean region he studied there is a distinction between 'being a good man' and 'being good at being a man' (1985: 16). This underlines 'the performative excellence' involved in being a man and hints at the importance in honour/shame cultures of one's public appearance and perception. In Mediterranean anthropology, David Gilmore has also provided a picture of the exemplary man and his moral imperatives 'first, impregnating one's wife; second, provisioning dependants; third, protecting the family' (Gilmore cited in Gutmann

1997: 389). Gilmore expounds on these features in his celebrated, *Manhood in the Making* (1990), as follows. Men must operate in the public (male) sphere and occupy the dominating and penetrating role in sex. Men must avoid all things feminine and engage in competitions of manliness, displaying feats of courage, defending and increasing the wealth and status of kin and in-group. Men must also respond to insults; and display virility in word and deed (Gilmore 1990). Similar facets are attested in Fisher's contribution to Foxhall and Salmon's edited book, *When Men Were Men: Masculinity, Power and Identity in Classical Antiquity* entitled 'Violence, Masculinity and the Law in Classical Athens' (1998: 68–97). Fisher notes the symbolic importance of cock fighting in Athenian culture. He argues 'in affording the excitement of sport and gambling and providing powerful, if ambivalent images of masculine, aggressive and phallocentric assertiveness' (1998: 69). Fischler's essay 'Imperial Cult: Engendering the Cosmos' (1998: 165–183) also cites Nicole Loraux's link between manliness, violence and honour. In her terms 'in the Greek world of war [and politics] power is in essence virility' (1998: 165). In short, for such cultures masculinity is, as Peteet observed in her ethnography,

> verified and played out in the brave deed, in risk-taking, and in expressions
> of fearlessness and assertiveness ... is attained by constant vigilance and
> willingness to defend honour, face, kin, and community from external
> aggression and to uphold and protect cultural definitions of gender-specific
> propriety.
>
> Peteet 1994: 34

Bourdieu was one of the earliest theorists to catalogue agonistic responses to challenges. Such ripostes allowed males to establish their credibility and legitimacy as representatives of the world of masculinity (Bourdieu discussed in Peteet 1994: 34). Abu-Lughod similarly has seen the defining characteristic of manhood in the Awad 'Ali Bedouin tribe she studied as 'control'. This is defined as the 'lack of fear of anyone or anything'. In her opinion, 'Real men are able to exact respect and command obedience from others while they themselves resist submitting to others' control' (Abu-Lughod cited in Peteet 1994: 34). Of course there are counter-voices that show the transformation of masculine ideals into more peaceable avenues. For example, the Ghiyarti of Eastern Morocco have given up traditional ways of displaying manhood such as the feud and have developed more supportive means of showing their precedence, such as competitive wealth-seeking, generosity and supporting friends and clients (Marcus 1987). These ideals, however, also show an interest in what Marcus terms 'independent manhood' and the display of reputation.

In general terms though, a link between aggressive nationalistic pride and its nurturing of ideals of masculinity is well documented (Gutmann 1997: 399; on the anthropology of war, see Haas 1990). In the ancient Mediterranean (particularly in Roman ideals) 'death with honour' as has been seen, could be gained on the battlefield or in face-to-face duels. Paul Cartledge in his essay 'The Maschismo of the Athenian Empire or the Reign of the Phallus' (1998) suggests that 'war was seen as a field for the display precisely of *andreia*, that is virility or manliness in general, and specifically the peculiarly masculine, cardinal virtue of martial courage and pugnacity' (Cartledge 1998: 54). In short, physical violence and political power were the stuff both of history and men (Cartledge 1998: 54). Similarly, Esler links honour to war, for 'a war represents the game of challenge and response played out at the largest scale' (Esler 1995b: 243).

In biblical studies, David Clines has, in an unpublished paper (1995) attempted to use a social construction of masculinity (and war) in his reading of the Psalms. He sees the psalmists identifying with Yahweh, the prototype of masculinity, emphasised in metaphors of strength and height. He argues, 'the Psalmists need their God strong, for that is the quality they most desire in themselves' (1995). (Stephen Moore's construction of Yahweh as the masculine body-builder par excellence (1996) is also comparable). Clines categorises the masculinity of the Psalms' assumptions along the following lines.

- *The Ideology of Honour and Shame* is apparent. This is frequently cited as a dominant cultural backdrop of scriptural worlds. The now familiar facets of this value, particularly associated with manhood and group status are well rehearsed, not least the competitive nature of honour and its public ascription. Furthermore, Clines argues persuasively that the maleness of honour within the Psalter is constructed to the exclusion of female facets. For 'anyone who makes a fuss about honour is a man ... the Psalms, so full of anxiety about honour, represent male interests' (Clines 1995).

- *The Rhetoric of War* is apparent throughout the Psalms. The Psalmist is variously implied as a warrior. Furthermore, the Psalmist's God takes on characteristics of a violent 'arch killer' (Clines 1995). Mario Aguilar in his paper, 'Symbolic Wars, Age-Sets, and the

Anthropology of War in 1 Maccabees' likewise notes that 'war and warfare occur ... when a society decides to defend itself from socially constructed and symbolically defined outsiders labelled enemies' (Aguilar 2004a). He corroborates Clines's point when he asserts, 'throughout the Old Testament men were recruited in order to guard Israel from her enemies that in turn became Yahweh's enemies as well. Within the construction of Israel's history, war served a purpose and holy wars were considered of divine origin because they protected the monarchy, the land and much later the Temple where the God of Israel dwelt' (Aguilar 2004a).

- *The Construction of Enemies* in the Psalms is seen to be important vis-à-vis masculine ideals. Related to the above ideology of honour in particular, typical agonistic responses to social shame find resonance in the denunciations, even willed extermination, of opponents portrayed in the Psalter. Given that the semantic field of conflict language is rooted in the battlefield, once again a masculine arena is our backdrop. Clines declares 'the fundamental construction of masculinity in ancient Israel is of the male as warrior' (Clines 1995).

On account of the above, Clines submits that the Psalms are 'unmistakably male' (1995). Aguilar in another paper, 'Marcel Mauss, La Priere, and the First Book of the Maccabees' (2004b), similarly cites links made between war and male-initiation rites in pre-industrial societies and the transformation of cultic rites into the arena of the battlefield. In his words,

> As the colonial occupiers forbid the practice of circumcision and the practice of the law, social and *ritual initiations into manhood and war become the public signs of the covenant* ... warfare becomes temporarily a sacred occupation because it incorporates those males initiated into a military organisation and into a temporal symbolic system of belonging to Israel and to Israel's god within a society under colonial occupation.
>
> my italicisation, Aguilar 2004b

It is probably not unrelated that many cross-cultural rites of male initiation involve some form of violence. In Bowie's terms this 'violence is not merely gratuitous but can serve a psychological and social purpose ... cementing group loyalty, implanting esoteric knowledge, and initiating transformatory experiences' (Bowie 2000: 183). Such group bonding seems to be what is lying behind Aguilar's construction of war as a 'ceremonious' and 'religious' activity.

It is my contention that the features of 'willing deaths' in scripture marked by honour precedence and manliness can at times be symbolically represented as sacred occupations and rituals of initiation into another identity. In other instances a particular character's death can be rejected on account of their contravention of these ideals. I now turn to exploration of these diverse perspectives.

'Dying to be Men': Honour Precedence and Scriptural Willing Deaths

The motives of Samson share features with the cultural construction outlined above. To celebrate the honour precedence of the deeds, the author theatrically exaggerates Samson's heroic deeds. He kills a young lion with his bare hands (Judg. 14:6) and catches three hundred foxes (Judg. 15:4) to name just a couple. However, through treachery, Delilah weakens her husband's God-given strength by cutting off his hair (Judg. 16:19). He in response, we are told 'did not know the Lord had left him' (Judg. 16:20). The text then goes on to recount various projects of demasculinisation of Samson by his enemies and oppressors, the Philistines. Samson is captured, shackled and his eyes are gouged out. After praying to God for one last burst of power, Samson has the final word. He pushes down Dagon's sacred precincts, killing more than three thousand Philistine worshippers within its walls (Judg. 16:26–31). He also died in the last terrible destruction he brought upon his enemy group (Judg. 16:28–30).

Samson's mode of death, while aggressive (as he involves others in it), is nevertheless praised because those who die are enemies. The deed thus scores highly on all three of Clines's 'masculine' ranges: honour and shame, rhetoric of war and the construction of enemies. Brettler sees Samson's death in martyrological-like terms. He writes, 'there certainly is a vicarious benefit from his death: he killed many Philistines as he committed suicide, bringing down the Temple of Dagon on himself and the assembled celebrants' (Brettler 2002: 5). Moreover, in this story, confrontation with enemies becomes a sacred, ritualised occupation. Samson fights for Yahweh who is with him. Samson prefaces his mighty deed with prayer (Judg. 16:28) and entreats Yahweh to 'Let me die with the Philistines' (Judg. 16:30). The text therefore portrays Samson in a wholly positive manner. While his death is not a ritual of initiation into an afterlife (such thought patterns are anachronistic for this time) nevertheless a 'symbolic' resistance to the supremacy of the enemies is powerfully portrayed. His actions at death reinstituted his masculinity, strength and status, in spite of the efforts of his captors to humiliate and overcome his will. But this resistance was not only symbolic, but also physical, for 'those he killed at his death were more than those he had killed during his life' (Judg. 16:30). His kin bury him with status in the tomb of his father: patriarchy, power and politics coalesce in a neat end to this story.

'Men Behaving Badly': Shameful Scriptural Willing Deaths

One particularly revealing aspect of honour precedence and manliness is the protection and defence of kin, dependants or in-group. It is before these others (or in scripture before God) that status can be displayed and affirmed. Those men acting individualistically, against the will of God, or for selfish ends are in essence 'men behaving badly'. Saul, Abimelech, Ahithophel, Zimri and Judas are all foils to the positive construction of manliness exhibited in Samson's story.

Saul, at first sight, dies a death commonly celebrated in collective 'masculinised' environments, namely, war and the battlefield. However, the explicit link with death as a sacred enterprise is not evident here at all. Saul works against divine purposes and on account of this is rejected in the narrative. Samuel, via the sorcery of the witch of Endor, warns Saul that the kingdom has been taken from him because of disobedience and that he and his sons will die in battle with the Philistines (Judg. 28:19).

Saul fears being killed by his enemies, and thus opts for one last deed of precedence: falling on his own sword. He evades the dishonour of falling into enemy hands and being humiliated and the way in which the battle's death toll is summarised is significant: 'Thus Saul died, his three sons, his armour bearer and all his men on the same day together' (1 Sam. 31:6). As Droge and Tabor perceptively note, the author makes no distinction between those slain in battle and Saul and his armour bearer, who take their own lives. They conclude, 'He and his sons are subsequently mourned by David and given a proper burial which was a sign of honour in Hebrew culture … 1 Samuel presents Saul's death as tragic but wholly noble' (1992: 54). But is this really true? The text seems to have a number of interrelated themes that question the 'honour precedence' of Saul's demise.

While Saul has overcome Philistine oppression in the past, his disobedience to Yahweh is shown as instrumental to his sticky end. He may evade being killed at his enemies' hands in conflict, but he does not escape their defamation and assaults on his corpse. According to 1 Samuel, 'they cut off his head, stripped his armour and sent messengers throughout the land of the Philistines to carry the good news to the houses of their idols and to the people. They put his armour in the temple of Astarte and they fastened his body to the wall of Beth-shan' (1 Sam. 31:9–10). This is not to say, however, that these oppressors fare any better in the opinion of the author. The text portrays the Philistines' depravity as idol worshippers and decapitators, all actions that serve to question their 'victory' in the text. Throughout 1 Samuel the Philistines' triumph is questioned not on account of them being good warriors but on account of Israel's downfalls in faith. For example, taking the Ark in 1 Samuel 4 – 6 and placing it in their own temple next to the statue of Dagon is seen as a vile act of wickedness and idolatry. However, Yahweh resists: Dagon's limbs are severed, 'only the trunk of Dagon was left to him. This is why the priests of Dagon and all who enter the house of Dagon do not step on the threshold of Dagon in Ashdod to this day' (1 Sam. 5:4–5).

Saul, the monarch is not featured exercising kingly duties beyond his military exploits. Yet even here on the battlefield, his death is not kingly. The 'unconquered will' of one who defies death at the hands of an enemy is displayed; however this is no sacred, ritualised death. Assaults on Saul's manhood evaded in life are just performed by his enemies after death instead. Saul forsook true honour, because he forsook God. He dies at war; his choice in one sense is heroic; he embraces death but this is not a ritual of manhood, rather it is the demise of one who forsook God. He symbolises the Israelites' immorality and identity as 'a race behaving badly', one from which their God could disassociate with grave consequences.

The narrative of Abimelech's attempt to establish a kingship in his mother's town of Shechem in Judges is one of the most valuable accounts of the struggle for supremacy between the Israelites and Canaanites. The relationship established between Abimelech and his mother's people is underscored by use of kinship language: 'their hearts inclined to follow Abimelech; for they said, He *is* our brother' (Judg. 9:3). After persuading the Canaanite residents to support him, the narrative tells that Abimelech hired assistants to murder his brothers, the seventy sons of Gideon. Abimelech ruled only three years and eventually brought destruction to himself and the people. He was injured in battle when a woman dropped a millstone upon his head from a tower. The picture is almost comical. Fearing the embarrassment of being killed by a woman, Abimelech persuaded his armour bearer to kill him with his sword (Judg. 9:50–57). Ultimately the writer sees this as divine punishment (Droge & Tabor 1992: 54). Battle space is male space, and yet here a female (almost) gets the upper hand.

Little of Abimelech's behaviour reflects a concern for his natural kin group. He commits murder, acts for his own ends and reflects low social integration into the rest of the group. In short, he lives and dies for his own ends. His brand of leadership is the opposite of the kind of ruler the author of Judges promotes. Once more the battlefield is sacred and God is involved: 'God repaid Abimelech for the crime he committed in killing his seventy brothers'. Moreover, Ahithophel, like Saul, is representative of the immorality of his people: 'God also made all the wickedness of the peoples of Shechem fall back on their heads, and on them came the curse of Jotham son of Jerubbaal' (Judg. 9:57).

A similar pattern is observable in relation to Ahithophel (literally meaning traitor) who was one of David's counsellors (2 Sam. 15:12; 1 Chr. 27:33) but joins Absalom (2 Sam. 15:31, 34; 16:15, 20–23; 17:1–23) and, at the time of Absalom's revolt, deserts David (Ps. 41:9; 55:12–14). He turns against his in-group and acts individualistically. As a result David pleads 'O Lord, I pray you, turn the counsel of Ahithophel into foolishness' (2 Sam. 15:31). This end was accomplished and Ahithophel seeing he no longer had any influence, after arranging his worldly affairs, hanged himself and was buried in the sepulchre of his fathers (2 Sam. 17:1–23).

Likewise, Zimri is cast as a selfish individualist from the start: '... as soon as he had seated himself on the throne, he killed his entire house and did not leave a single male or kindred' (1 Kgs. 16:11). He reigned only seven days, when Omri, whom the army elected as king, laid siege to Tirzah, whereupon Zimri set fire to the palace and perished in the flames (1 Kgs. 16:11–20). This again is a willing death, undertaken by an individualistic self-grasping figure. Once more Yahweh plays a part in his destruction, and the text underlines the severe crime of leading Israel astray: 'because of the sins that he committed, doing evil in the sight of the Lord, walking in the way of Jeroboam, and for the sin that he committed, causing Israel to sin' (1 Kgs. 16:19).

Our last instance of a 'man behaving badly' and enacting a willed death is Judas in Matthew's Gospel (27:4–5). According to the account Judas regrets his actions, repents, returns his blood money to the Jewish authorities and goes out and hangs himself. All the evangelists show that it is Judas's act of betrayal that sets him apart from the other disciples and members of his in-group. Indeed his actions in 'Passion Week' define his personality throughout all the gospel narratives: 'Judas the betrayer', 'the one who betrayed him' (Mt. 10:4; 26:25; 27:3; Mk. 3:19; Lk. 6:16; Jn. 6:71, 12:4, 13:2; 18:5).

Matthew gives the reason for Judas's suicidal actions as the guilt of betraying innocent blood (27:4). Van Unnik has shown that the expression 'innocent blood' is not widely used; however, it was deemed a despicable crime in Hebrew thought. On account of this, many interpreters have since seen Judas's suicide as a death of despair. In a collective environment people particularly despised those who would betray a tie of loyalty for the sake of a bribe. However, Judas's suicide should not be viewed in isolation from his repentance (Mt. 27:3) (Whelan 1993). The word translated here 'repented' (*metamelomai*) is not the regular word for an unreserved turning to God. It seems more like penitence, being remorseful and thinking differently in hindsight. The term is also used in Matthew 21:29 in the parable of the two sons asked to work in the vineyard. The son who initially refused to go and work, later changes his mind. Judas similarly after a change of mind returns the money and does not profit.

C. F. Whelan in her analysis of Judas's death notes that the suicide may come closest to that of a Roman soldier shamed by false accusation (1993). The soldier's suicide was an attempt to restore honour by proving his worth to his comrades. She argues that the story of Judas's suicide serves to transfer the guilt for the death of Jesus from Judas to those ultimately responsible, the chief priests and elders. While it is true that the anti-Jewish rhetoric of the Matthean narrative wants to point the finger of blame on the religious leaders (Mt. 26:59; 27:20), Judas's own repentant motivations, as portrayed by Matthew, seem less interested in transferral of blame and more to do with personal remorse and regret. Further, unlike other honour precedence motivated deaths, this one is not performed publicly.

Ultimately Judas's act seems more like a fatalistic suicide. He realises the magnitude of his selfish, individualistic actions and thus dies at his own hands because he has contravened the ideals and trust of his collective grouping. Having isolated himself from his social centre of meaning in the group, he finds himself in an intolerable situation. It is interesting to note that various parallels have been suggested between Ahithophel's and Judas's suicide (hanging) and the nature of their respective crimes (betrayal of a superior). Davies and Allison's listing of these parallels are presented in Table 5.1 (Davies & Allison 1997: 565–66).

Table 5.1. Comparison of Ahithophel and Judas

Ahithophel	Judas
Betrays David (2 Sam. 15 – 17)	Judas betrays Son of David (Mk. 14:17–21)
David after being betrayed by Absalom and Ahithophel crosses Kidron (2 Sam. 15:23)	Jesus crosses the Kidron valley (Jn. 18:1)
David prays on the Mount of Olives that God 'might turn the council of Ahithophel into foolishness' (2 Sam. 15:31)	Jesus prays on the Mount of Olives that God might let the hour and cup pass (Mk. 14:32–42). The language of Jesus' prayer echoes Psalm 41:5 and 11, which Jewish tradition assigned to David and referred to the incident with Absalom and Ahithophel.
While the king is weary and discouraged Ahithophel plans to take David at night and make all the people that are with him flee (2 Sam. 17:1–2).	After the agony of Gethsemane, Judas comes upon Jesus at night with a crowd with swords and clubs and all the disciples flee (Mk. 14:43–50).
In Psalm 41:9 (attributed to David) we read 'Even my bosom friend in whom I trusted, who ate of my bread, has lifted his heel against me'.	Mark 14:18 alludes to Psalm 41:10, in connection with Judas while John 13:18 explicitly cites it in the same connection.
In 2 Samuel 18:28 we read, according to the failure of Absalom and Ahithophel 'Blessed be the Lord your God who has delivered up the men who raised their hand against my lord and king'.	John 13:18 inserts language from 2 Samuel 18:28, into its quotation of Psalm 41:10
	'I am not speaking of all of you; I know whom I have chosen. But it is to fulfil scripture. "The one who ate my bread has lifted his heel against me"'

Despite these parallels there are also significant differences. In the Ahithophel narrative there is no explicit, direct betrayal. Ahithophel commits suicide because his treachery was discovered and he wants to escape humiliation and punishment (Klassen 1997: 70). Also, from trying to tap into the logic of these acts, the motivations of the two are quite different. Judas's death, as was established previously, can be understood as a case of fatalistic death, a result of remorse for betraying his centre of meaning. In contrast to collective reasoning, Judas's actions in betraying his master were individualistic. Ahithophel by contrast seems to be an egoistic, individualistic suicide. He does not regret betraying his master but only the fact that he is found out.

Saul, Abimelech, Ahithophel, Zimri and Judas all variously provide a foil for manly and sacred 'deaths with honour precedence' such as that exemplified by Samson. They exhibit no anxiety for the shielding or protection of one's kin or dependants. Each of these figures acts individualistically and accordingly is negatively judged by the respective biblical authors.

'Rituals of Resistance': Masculinity and Honour Virtue

I have argued above that social constructions of masculinity in honour cultures involve the agonistic defence of one's reputation and freedom of living. Ethnography also witnesses to situations in which an agonistic response to crises need not physically hurt the oppressor but rather 'symbolically' strengthen and rebuild the self-reputation of the oppressed.

It is unsurprising then that foreign, oppressive, imperial regimes often try and pinpoint 'hot spots' of concern to the dominated and strategically attack these. In programmes of colonisation and imperialism, for example, it has been recognised that occupiers often engage in a project of *demasculinisation* of the colonised (Stoller discussed in Gutmann 1997: 389). In short, oppressors pursue strategic shaming. Violence is of course a particularly important vehicle of such project. As David Riches noted in his study of *The Anthropology of Violence* (1986), violence as a social act would be nothing without witnesses to understand the messages concerning the power encoded in it.

D. Montserrat in his essay, 'Experiencing the Male Body in Roman Egypt' (1998) provides evidence for such perspectives when he argues that the 'seen' male body provided a symbolic yardstick of power, identity and social rank (Montserrat 1998: 153). In his words, 'the ways that ancient people inhabited and experienced their bodies were inseparable from their social and economic position. Slaves were no more than bodies, the passive property of their owners; 'the most common Greek terms for slaves underscore this powerlessness and passivity: *soma*, literally body, and *pais*, infant' (Montserrat 1998: 153).

The body has of course been seen by many social scientists as a site for inscription and description of power networks. Foucault most prominently saw how the corporeal was involved in the political. 'Power relations have an immediate hold upon it [the body]; they invest it, mark it, train it, torture it, force it to carry out tasks, to perform ceremonies, to emit signs' (Foucault 1979: 25). One's movements, routines, and more importantly choices and freedom are out of one's control when under the jurisdiction of an alien or foreign body. As such 'the bodies of those under occupation are continuously called forth to present themselves to outsiders' (Peteet 1994: 37).

How can a suitable riposte be given by the oppressed or colonised in such a situation? The honour code demands public demonstrations against the challenger/enemy, however this is often not an option for those in situations of imposed displacement, colonisation or abuse. What is more viable and important for such groups is to reassert their own honour to themselves. They need to enhance their self-reputation, strengthen broken spirits and rise from the ashes of humiliation.

Peteet offers a particularly interesting example of this in her study of Palestinian young men who have been subjected to beatings in the West Bank. She investigates how they convert this violence into a positive experience to their in-group by interpreting their abuse as initiations into manhood:

> Palestinians as participants in and as audience to the public spectacle of beatings have consciously and creatively taken a coherent set of signs and practices of domination and construed them to buttress an agency designed to overthrow political hierarchies.
>
> Peteet 1994: 40

The aggressions themselves are construed by the Palestinians as 'cowardly and immoral, rather than a challenge' (Peteet 1994: 41). These young men in effect affirm their moral superiority over their oppressors and also affirm their cultural and national identity to their own people. Peteet concludes:

> What has all this to do with manhood? Palestinians have changed the cultural categories of the encounter so that manhood comes from a 'riposte' not to a challenge but to what Bourdieu distinguished as 'mere aggression'. And thus is constituted the national backdrop against which Palestinians are re-constructing defining elements of their culture and society.
>
> Peteet 1994: 41

In such situations the minority deem the estimation of the prevailing culture as insignificant. They see assessments made about themselves by others as misguided and seek honour 'virtue' in a heavenly court of standing rather than public forums. Rituals of resistance in this sense obliterate and delegitimise the activities of the tormentor by symbolic means. They also serve to question the principles of the perpetrators of violence. Such moves are surely what Erving Goffman was to characterise as 'cutting off the nose to destroy the other's face' (Goffman cited in Barton 2002: 30). Peteet concludes,

> A representation created with the intent of humiliating has been reversed into one of honour, manhood and moral superiority ... displaying physical marks of violence, that one is usually powerless to avoid, stands as a commentary on suffering but also I would suggest a commentary on sacrifice.
>
> Peteet 1994: 38

In such situations, the oppressed are raised from the ashes of shame and abuse, to once again assert the honour virtue of themselves, and in religious contexts, their God.

Cultural resistance to domination in the form Peteet describes is still dependent on male gender characteristics, but it is a symbolic as opposed to physical means, 'a dynamic act of resistance, a trick, if you will' (Peteet 1994: 31). While the violence was construed as a vehicle to weaken the oppressed, the oppressed through their experiences of abuse set about humiliating their oppressors as immoral. As such humiliation is transformed to glory, demasculinisation is transformed into a rite of true manhood. Peteet's argument deserves lengthy citation on this point:

> To return to Bourdieu's mapping of the relationship between masculinity and honour, we can now pose the question, what happens to the cultural categories and concepts around which honour is organised and expressed when challenge and riposte take place not between members of the same social group, but between a colonial entity, and its apparatus of force, and a subjugated, indigenous population? A man dishonours himself when he challenges a man considered incapable of 'taking up the challenge' (Bourdieu 1977: 11). When Israelis pursue and engage Palestinian youths, the cultural interpretation available to Palestinians is to consider the Israelis as lacking in the emotional qualities of manhood. Only men of little honour and thus dubious masculinity would beat unarmed youths while they themselves are armed with and trained in the use of modern implements of warfare. Because little or no effective riposte is possible at the instant –

there is no challenge – and the encounter degenerates into mere aggression (Bourdieu 1977: 12). Such aggression deprives its practitioners of claims to honour and morality.

Peteet 1994: 41

Of course in Peteet's study the victims survive, and it is through their verbal accounts of their ordeals that their newly initiated manhood is confirmed. As my study concerns willing deaths, it is up to the respective authors of the scriptural texts to bestow characteristics of the dying ordeals as rites into manhood or initiations into a transformed identity.

Rituals of Resistance: Self-Inflicted Deaths in Scriptural Tradition

The figures chosen to represent the enactment of passive 'rituals of resistance', of the type identified by Peteet, are all subjects of alien tyranny. The Maccabean martyrs lived through the evil reign of Antiochus IV Epiphanes, and Jesus of Nazareth and the martyrs of the Book of Revelation all died under Roman imperial rule. Anthropological definitions of 'empire' differ in accent – topographical, political, ideological or military dimensions are variously emphasised – all broadly agree, however, that empire is 'a territorially expansive and incorporative kind of state, involving relationships in which one state exercises control over other socio-political entities and of imperialism as the process of creating and maintaining empires' (Sinpoli 1994: 160). The bodies and lives of the subjugated, as outlined above, were prime places for inscription of domination. Interesting also is the fact that imperial rule often inscribes manhood on itself. Fischler notes how 'masculine power lay at the core of imperial ideology and hence notions of masculinity were fundamental to the way in which the emperor was understood' (Fischler 1998: 165). Alston also noted the complex of relationships between soldiers, masculinity and power in Imperial Rome. Soldiers were often seen to reflect qualities of masculinity associated with the emperor and carry out his purposes (Alston 1998).

In the Hellenistic period different responses to death were made in Jewish circles. The finality of death was remodelled through the lens of apocalyptic eschatology that offered hope of resurrection from the dead. This was a significant development towards the conception of what we now term martyrdom, namely, the role of vindication after death. The Wisdom of Solomon places the souls of the righteous in the hands of God where they are free from torment (Wis. 3:1). From such a perspective it is easy to see how ideas of exoneration after death were promoted. The idea of willing death as religiously motivated appears in the so-called suffering servant of Isaiah and in the Maccabees texts. Here we get models of sacrificial, altruistic deaths characteristic of collective environments. Once again the needs of the wider community take precedence over the individual who, as masculinity requires, displays virility and effective defence of his own and others' reputations.

Aguilar has revealed how collective prayers within 1 Maccabees intimate that armed forces fighting against evil power such as imposed colonisation congregate to recreate the feelings that have been obliterated by the oppressive foreign system (Aguilar 2004b). Read in this light, 2 Maccabees 7, which presents the narrative about the deaths of the seven brothers and their mother, consists of speeches in which the characters express the conviction that God is punishing Israel for its sins, but will vindicate innocent deaths in battle through resurrection. A parallel of this account in 4 *Maccabees* also praises altruistic concerns typical of collective environments. The author even refers to the mother with the accolade 'mother of the nation, vindicator of the law and champion of religion' (4 *Macc.* 15:29), a defiant rhetoric of resistance, which asserts the power of sociability against the fragmentation wreaked on the nation by the oppressor.

The suicide of Razis in 2 Maccabees 14:37–46 reflects this strong group environment. It states Razis was a 'man who loved his compatriots and was very well thought of and for his goodwill was called Father of the Jews' (v. 37). He falls on his sword in order to die nobly rather than fall into the hands of sinners. However, he does not hit exactly and the crowd continues to run towards him, upon which he extracts his innards and hurls them at the crowd while petitioning to the Lord to give them back to him (2 Macc. 14:42). This is not the death of someone who is in despair but one assured of some sort of transformation. Razis' death embodies a graphic ritual of resistance. His innards torn from his body serve to illustrate that nothing (not even death) can displace his link to his kinsmen and nation.

The gospel traditions all portray Jesus referring to his forthcoming death (Mt. 10:39; Lk. 9:24; 17:33) and the willing embrace of that fate. The passion predictions (Mt. 20:18; Mk. 10:33; Jn. 12:33) show the self-conscious knowledge of his own death, as does the agony in Gethsemane

(Mt. 26:39). Jesus was explicit in stating that his life was not being taken but that he was voluntarily choosing death: 'No one takes it from me, but I lay it down of my own accord' (Jn. 10:18). It is also not insignificant that in John, the Jews understand Jesus' reference to going away as a death threat (Jn. 8:21–22).

The Jesus of the gospels, however, also shows the profoundly self-sacrificing nature of his death. It is this aspect, commonly praised in collective environments, that is central to understanding how this 'self-inflicted death' is celebrated (for it seems that Jesus could have pleaded on his own behalf (Mt. 27:11; Mk. 15:5) or rescued himself from his torture (Mt. 26:53, 28:42; Mk. 15:32; Jn. 19:12). The son of man comes to give his life as a ransom for many (Mk. 10:45; Mt. 20:28), to lay down his life not only for his friends (Jn. 15:13) but also for the world (Jn. 6:15). Unlike the great praise given in collectivist cultures throughout the world, to those inferiors who lay their lives down in allegiance or respect for their superiors, in the New Testament it is the good shepherd who lays his life down for his sheep (Jn. 10:11–17).

Seeley has recently investigated the parallels between the death of Jesus and the martyrs' deaths in *4 Maccabees*. He lists the five components of a 'Noble Death' as (1) obedience; (2) the overcoming of physical vulnerability; (3) a military setting; (4) vicariousness; and (5) sacrificial metaphors (Seeley 1990: 13). Seeley plots the noble death onto Paul's understanding of Jesus' death. The importance of obedience for this is shown in Philippians 2:8 and Romans 5:19. The notion of overcoming physical vulnerability is raised in Romans 7 where Paul addresses the effects of sin; he overcame physical vulnerability and was obedient to death on a cross (2 Cor. 5:21). This obedient death broke the power of the old aeon ruled by sin and death (Rom. 6:16–22). The vicarious benefit of Jesus' death is imparted to Christians by re-enactment. In Romans 6 the re-enactment is shown in baptism – the believer, through this rite, effectively becomes a participant in Christ's willing death (Seeley 1990: 14–15). Paul explains, 'For if we have been united with him in death we will certainly be united with him in a resurrection like his' (Rom. 6:5). Similarly, Grayston believes that for Paul, Christ's willing death accomplishes two exceptional tasks: liberation and delivery from powers at work in the present evil age, and the gift of a new covenant (Rom. 3:24; 1 Cor. 2:6–9) (Grayston 1996: 257). One important difference, however, is that unlike Maccabean martyrs, Christ has accomplished once and for all atonement with God. Hebrews likewise speaks of Jesus as a perfect sacrifice that was prefigured by the animal sacrifices in the temple. He is the sacrificial Lamb of God 'crowned with glory and honour' who by the grace of God should 'taste death for every man' (Heb. 2:9). Also, in John's Apocalypse, Jesus is the slain lamb whose blood has purchased people of every nation (Rev. 7:14). Therefore, any willing death after Christ would not be sacrificial in the same sense and could even be motivated by an individualistic quest to experience life in a new realm.

Like the change of focus from this world to a world after death in Jewish apocalyptic, so Jesus also turned the attention of his followers to a kingdom not of this world (Jn. 18:36) and in turn relativised the importance of life on earth. Much of the rhetoric of his teaching demonstrates this. He warns his followers that taking up their cross may well involve death and persecution (Mt. 23:34; Lk. 21:16) and that saving one's life will originally involve losing it (Mt. 16:25; Mk. 8:35; Lk. 9:24). He also hints that death is the necessary precursor to transformation (Jn. 5:24) for 'unless a grain of wheat falls into the ground and dies, it remains just a single grain; but if it dies it bears much fruit' (Jn. 12:24). The resistance featured here is most profoundly seen in the rhetoric of reversal that is implicit in the picture of discipleship. Now ideals of strength and masculinity are replaced by the humility and the image of a child (Mk. 9:37). Now status in this world is irrelevant, for his kingdom is not of this domain (Jn. 18:36).

Those literally embracing death in this way are also celebrated in John's Apocalypse. The Book of Revelation glorifies those martyrs suffering violent deaths under the Roman Emperor, probably Domitian (81–96 CE) (Rev. 5:9–11; 16:6; 17:6). The discourse surrounding the martyrs of Revelation, however, shows that while pain and death were meant to disassemble the world of the Christians, in fact, the rhetoric of triumph constitutes a rebuff of this position. It delegitimises the assumed power of the empire and empowers the victims (for more on this general theme and the subjugated 'body in pain', see Scarry 1985).

Well-trodden paths of interpretation have plotted the Christian counter-narrative to Rome in the Apocalypse. Revelation is often read allegorically, the lamb (Rev. 5:6, 8, 12–13; 6:1, 16; 7:9–10, 14, 17; 8:1; 12:11; 13:8, 11; 14:1–4, 10; 15:3; 17:14; 19:7; 21:9, 14, 22–23) referring to Jesus; the beasts (Rev. 6:8; 13:1) as Caesar and Satan; the sea as the realm of chaos (4:6; 5:13; 7:1–3; 8:8–9; 10:2–8; 12:12, 17; 14:7; 15:21; 16:3; 18:17, 19, 21; 20:8, 13, 21:1); Babylon as an encoded word for the oppressive regime of Rome (Rev. 14:8; 16:9; 17:5; 18:2, 10, 21). It is shown that God protects those who 'have washed their robes in the blood of the lamb', that is those who in some measure by painful ordeal or death have shared Christ's suffering. Their vindication must wait until the required number of martyrs is complete (Rev. 6:11) (Droge & Tabor 1992: 260). They are singled out for special reward during the millennial reign of Christ (Rev. 20:4–6). Further, 'they who did not cling to life even in the face of death' (Rev. 12:11) and are accordingly rewarded and praised (Rev. 16:6). A similar strategy to the glorification of Jesus through death is accomplished here. By not resisting death at the hands of an oppressor, these martyrs, like the Maccabean martyrs before them, in fact affected a profound symbolic and spiritual riposte. They asserted their masculinity through death and vindication. What the oppressors could have seen as a shameful 'demasculinising' actually becomes an avenue for a ritual of transformation into true manhood for the oppressed. Through their tribulations, as the scriptural authors reveal, such individuals were publicly glorified, and realised authentic, spiritual modes of identity.

Esler outlines a symbolic strategy of resistance that seems to parallel Peteet's ethnography of rituals of resistance. Peteet would recognise in her Palestinian subjects, 'the development by subjugates of a discourse to counter that of the subjugators' (Esler 1995b: 240). Howard-Brook and Gwyther's *Unveiling Empire: Reading Revelation Then and Now* (2001) illustrates just this. They see the author of the apocalypse constructing a counter-mythology to Rome. Rome's empire and rule is set against the kingdom of God; the so-called Pax Romana is subverted by the image of murderous Babylon becoming drunk on martyr's blood (Rev. 17:6); Rome's victory is challenged through the myth for conquering through death (Rev. 12:11) and Rome's eternity is countered by the promise in Revelation that those willingly giving up their lives and suffering 'will reign forever' (Rev. 22:5). 'This engagement between Rome's legitimating stories and God's truth is what is called "the war of myths"' (Howard-Brook & Gwyther 2001:223). One could also say it constituted a mythology of resistance, which combined with the rituals of resistance enacted in the deaths of the martyrs, showed that the afflictions set before them were nothing more than a rite of initiation into glory.

Masculinity, Honour and Rituals of Resistance

It has been argued that manliness and honour precedence underlie collective, defensive deaths with honour precedence in battle or conflict. The death of Samson was shown to be exemplary of this. Those deaths that were deemed 'shameful' (Saul, Ahithophel, Abimelech, Zimri and Judas) served as a foil to ideals of masculinity and precedence.

Those deaths under imperial rule were compared with sentiments underlining 'rituals of resistance' as identified by Peteet. In such situations non-aggressive ripostes (in the form of rhetoric or symbolism) are often issued. The authors of 2 and 4 Maccabees, the gospel accounts of Jesus' death and Revelation submit to this mode. In these writings the violent oppression and extermination of the bodies of the righteous is converted into a rhetoric that shows these experiences as a ritual of initiation into another mode of existence. As such, the accounts of these self-inflicted and imperially inflicted deaths constitute dynamic acts of resistance and affirmation of the moral superiority of the oppressed. As Peteet notes, such strategies deal a powerful blow to what Scott termed 'the public transcript … the open interaction between subordinates and those who dominate' (Scott cited in Peteet 1994: 45). It perhaps also helps us realise why the thirst for 'willing death' grew in the early Christian centuries. Indeed Alvarez has concluded that 'martyrdom was a Christian creation as much as a Roman persecution' (1990: 58). Similarly, Fox submits,

> A religion of compromise would not, however, have been a Christian religion. Behind each martyrdom, whether or not the texts chose to dwell on it, lay the self-sacrifice of Jesus himself. To be a Christian, baptised or not, was to recognise the supreme value of this selfless death at the hands of misguided authorities. At its heart, Christianity glorified suffering and passive endurance; did this ideal and its rewards perhaps encourage Christians to seek arrest in the first place?
>
> Fox 1987: 441

In such instances the performers themselves transformed meanings that the dominant party imposed. Their rites of passage into the afterlife could be seen as 'trickery', a reversal of social order, and a strategic political and social action. For as Peteet warns,

> to let violence stand as constitutive of an inferior and submitting social position and subjectivity without interpretation and challenge would be to submit to the dominant performer's meaning. For the anthropologist, to interpret it otherwise would leave it as a textual rather than an agential problematic.
>
> Peteet 1994: 45

The 'performative' dimensions of scriptural accounts of willing death have been brought to the fore by exhibiting them alongside instances of the sort of events to which Peteet refers. For the biblical scholar to interpret these events otherwise would be to ignore the social agency and values that link both physical experiences of individuals and groups, and their intellectual and symbolic reflection on them.

6

Exhibit 4. Reading with Women's Religions

Procreation, Suffering and the Domestication of Religion

Curator's Notes

This exhibit displays cross-cultural studies of twelve religious traditions in which women play a prominent role alongside aspects of early Christianity. A process of 'domestication' of religion is then documented in reference to social 'development' and gradual assimilation of religious traditions to a patriarchal status quo.

If one wishes to understand why there are certain traits that characterise almost all women's religion ... It is helpful to look at the human experience that most clearly impacts on women differently than on men.

S. Sered

By exploring the different aspects, metaphoric, metonymic, linguistic or ritual of procreation I have been able to refer to a wider and more open version of identity ... to the folk ontology, the little tradition.

T. Paradellis

Anthropologists, like feminist readers of the Bible, have focused attention on 'woman' and started to try and gauge her vision of life apart from the dominant 'male-stream'. Some anthropology of the past, to cite Ardner's provocative metaphor, could be blamed for viewing women 'in the same way as the Nuer's cows': they were 'observed but also did not speak' (Ardner cited in Rapport & Overing 2000: 141). Now, however, it is increasingly realised that in not listening to women an important dimension of the cultural fabric of life was omitted in ethnography. For as Dubisch points out, 'women in particular may have different ideas about themselves, about their relationships with men, about the structuring of society and the nature of the world and about the symbolism and significance of sex and gender categories' (Dubisch 1986: 32). This is not an insignificant realisation in the realm of religion either, for while religious sensitivities are not dependent on combinations of X and Y chromosomes, it is nonetheless an interesting question to ask if sex-specific experiences differently impact religious ideas.

Studies of women and religion have often bemoaned the female's marginal status in male symbolic schemes: 'religious concepts generally reflect men's and not women's priorities and life-experiences' (Sered 1994: 3). However, Susan Sered's ethnographic study investigated features of those 'religions' in which women take a pivotal role or constitute the majority of members. Her 1994 book, *Priestess, Mother, Sacred Sister: Religions Dominated by Women* took as its starting point a comparison of those traditions catalogued in anthropology, where women were prominent. 'Dominated' may have been an unfortunately loaded term for her subtitle, for her project does not look at traditions in which men are marginalised but rather only those in which women play a significant role.

Discussion here will first introduce Sered's cross-cultural analysis of the twelve religions. The shared characteristics of these will then be brought to bear on selected aspects of early Christianity presented in Jesus' ministry in the gospels. Themes of women-dominated religions including rituals of solidarity, health, healing and maternity as symbolic constructions will be explored.

While I concede that early Christianity could never be described as a women-centred religion, it does nonetheless have some interesting resonance with such traditions that is brought into sharper relief by exhibiting them together. A comparison of early Christianity and characteristics of women's religions offers a different way in to considering the character of earliest Christianity, and of women's place within it. So many previous studies have been preoccupied with exegesis of women-related New Testament texts and arguing one way or the other for women's place within fledgling Christianity. Others have compared the position of women in Graeco-Roman and/or Jewish society alongside the treatment of women in the New Testament. In contrast to such projects, this exhibit offers a way to assess various characteristics of the ministry of Jesus in the light of a much broader anthropological study of women's religions in different cultures.

Cross-Cultural Aspects of Women's Religions

Sered selected for examination traditions united neither by geography nor shared history, but rather by their status as 'religions' and the prominence of women within them. Sered saw the study of religion to be profoundly important because in her opinion,

> It is so often via religious rituals and ideologies that women and men express their deepest concerns, their truest selves, their fears, hopes and passions. Studies of women's religious lives – whether utilizing textual, archaeological, ethnographic, historical, sociological, or psychological techniques – seek to discover how women construct reality.
>
> Sered 1994: 4

The twelve traditions selected were ancestral cults among Black Baribs in Belize, indigenous religion of the Ryukyu Islands, the *zar* cult of North Africa, Shamanism in Korea, Afro-Brazilian religions, *nat* cults of Burma, Christian Science, Shakerism, nineteenth-century Spiritualism and the twentieth-century feminist spiritual movement in the United States. Sered is swift to acknowledge the profoundly different social natures of each respective tradition. Some are 'self-consciously independent religions that exist in a society where the dominant religion is male dominated' (feminist spirituality and Afro-Brazilian religion). Others co-exist alongside male-dominated streams (the Ryukyu Islands, Black Caribs of Belize) and others are sectarian in nature, derived from otherwise male-dominated religions (Christian Science and Shakerism) (see Sered 1994: 11–13). She is also candid that the terminology she uses – 'women's religions' – could risk masking and reducing key sociological differences between the groups (respectively sects, cults, indigenous religions, socially dominant religions, etc.).

These caveats aside, Sered introduces the twelve religions with a typology based on three main regional categories: 'East and South-East Asia'; 'North America'; 'African and African-American Religions'. She speculates that those religions represented based in East and South-East Asia find roots in indigenous and ancient religions (with no account of a historical founder). She also notes that women were primary in many Japanese ancient religions. It is not altogether unexpected, therefore, to find that Ryukyu religion holds that women are spiritually predominant. In these islands, Sered notes, 'women dominated the religious life of the family, community, and (in the past) state. Only women can officially mediate between the supernatural and human beings' (1994: 14). Likewise, in Burma, *nat* religion (indigenous tradition) holds women as the primary specialists; this is in marked contrast to the co-existent Buddhist religion that sees men as main religious wielders. The relationship between these two religious perspectives in Burma was explored in Spiro's ethnography. He came to the conclusion that when people enter into *nat* rituals they can also be expressing misgivings with Buddhism: 'It is significant that *nat* myths often involve anti-Buddhist themes: disobeying Buddhist monks, honoring sensuality' (Spiro discussed in Sered 1994: 17). Rather than Buddhist themes of asceticism and detachment from material possessions and the body, *nat* religion is much more concerned with this-worldly issues.

Korean Shamanism is also identified as a women-centred religion. It constitutes in Sered's opinion a derivative of Korean household religion, where shamans are religious experts (Sered 1994: 18). She notes that Korean Shamanism co-exists with Buddhism, like the *nat* cults in Burma. However, rather than conceiving of each as opposed to the other, in Korean Shamanism, 'the prayers women make at Buddhist temples and shaman's shrines are the same: for the children, health and a peaceful family life' (Sered 1994: 19). Similarly, in Northern Thai matrilineal spirit cults, the woman is seen as custodian of the spirit of the house. Moreover, spirits themselves reside in female bodies and are passed from mother to daughter.

The second geographical/cultural cluster of women's religions identified by Sered is nineteenth- to twentieth-century North America. Unlike in Asia, individuals in the Western world are less communally orientated and more likely to live alone, with opportunities to explore religious traditions undeterred by a strictly controlled family/extended group. Sered notes how the growth of feminism as a political movement in the West undoubtedly contributed to the construction of women's religions there. She tells of Christian Science, founded by a woman Mary Eddy Baker and currently dominated by women (in 1989 the ratio of female to male practitioners within the group was 8–1). Christian Science sees 'the world as we see it with our physical senses is illusory. Therefore sickness and suffering are illusory. Once the individual understands that this is so, his or her sickness and suffering will disappear' (Sered 1994: 23). For Christian Science the world is whole and perfect and does not cry out for salvation. Christ, though healer and example of perfection par excellence, was not uniquely or exclusively equipped to attain this status. The opportunity is offered for all to take and embrace.

In a somewhat different vein, Shakers, responding to the socio-economic crises and developments of the late eighteenth century believed, on the basis of revelations of Ann Lea, that Christ's second coming was imminent. They reorganised themselves as fictive kin, brother and sisters in family/administrative units of around thirty to a hundred people overseen by four elders: two men and two women (Sered 1994: 25), illustrating their ideal of gender equality. While the movement attracted both sexes, more women remained within it than men did; so much so, that by the twentieth century 'Shaker women began to dominate nearly every aspect of the society's life' (Stein cited in Sered 1994: 225). Unlike Christian Science, Shakers preached pacifism and celibacy; they set themselves apart from the world and breathed a millennial ethos as opposed to Christian Science's primary emphasis on healing.

Spiritualism is also introduced as a women-centred tradition founded by two young sisters in 1848 in New York. Sered defines its two main beliefs as 'the human personality survives the death of the body, and it is possible to communicate with the spirits of the dead' (Sered 1994: 28). While women could be forbidden from preaching and teaching in church, in seances women found an authentic voice. Moreover, Sered reveals, 'Spiritualism does not demand that its members forgo membership in other religions ... [indeed] Spiritualist groups often choose not to meet on a Sunday in order to allow their members to attend church with more conventional Christian denominations' (Sered 1994: 29).

The North American based feminist spirituality movement is also discussed. This tradition, perhaps out of all the religions featured in Sered's book, is the only one self-consciously to put feminism and womanhood at its centre. Dreams, visions, experiences of individuals as opposed to dogma, rituals and official sacred texts are celebrated. The female life cycle is marked ritually and the seasons of nature are also hailed as significant. Non-materialistic values are central; openness to ongoing revelation and resistance to centralised power and authority structures are also hallmarks of the movement.

The third cluster of religions is centred on the regional focus of African and African-American religion. While not homogenising an entire continent and its cultural influence, Sered does note that indigenous religion in Africa tends to value both the male and female in different but complementary ways. Moreover the family, living and dead, is central. With the spread of Islam, however, women were constructed in different, often subordinate, religious roles. As a response to this development, some women formed 'new Islamic religious groups....

Religious practices involving *zar* possession' (Sered 1994: 30). The *zar* cult of North Africa and the Middle East is one in which 'capricious spirits known as *zar* are prone to attack and possess women, especially married women, who then turn to cult leaders in order to be cured' (Sered 1994: 36). Building on Boddy's famed ethnography of a North Sudanese village, Sered notes that most participants in *zar* religious events tend to be of 'secondary status within their cultural settings' (Sered 1994: 36). The *zar* cult, co-exists with Islamic thinking, and in common with other women cults within Islamic society, tends to be marked by ecstasy and non-formalised religious rites.

Similarly, the Sande secret society of West Africa is seen as a movement that is women-centred and based on fertility and reproduction. 'Adolescent girls are taught about childbirth, trained in household tasks' (Sered 1994: 31). At initiations, masked figures represent spirits; 'representations of spiritual and mythological symbols translated into wood and designed to express a spiritual message so complete that future generations can do no more than learn from its mysteries' (Richards discussed in Sered 1994: 31). Sande religion also serves as a power base for women, for example, they organised protests against unfair tax demands (Sered 1994: 32).

Afro-Brazilian religions are also identified as cults primarily appealing to women and the socially marginal. The most public religious spectacle for this group is possession of an individual by a spirit. Sered reveals that the appeal of spirits is particularly important in a world where conventional medicine and facilities are not widely available. Sered also speculates that Brazilian construction of manhood as 'impenetrable' makes them resist exposure to spirit possession. For 'in Brazil all religion is seen as a feminine activity – even the Catholic Church has trouble recruiting enough priests' (Sered 1994: 34).

Finally, in Black Carib (*Garifuna*) religion the leaders are old women. Kinship structures are based on matrifocal lines, and households typically revolve around women. It is not insignificant then that religion is primarily attached to kinship in this tradition: 'the greater part of Black Carib religion consists of rituals aimed at honouring, caring for or appeasing the ancestors. The good will of ancestors is deemed as necessary to the well being of descendants' (Sered 1994: 34). Sered further notes differences between this tradition and Catholicism, which dominates the surrounding culture:

Catholicism and Black Carib religion differs in terms of leadership (male v. female), literacy (ancestor worship, unlike Catholicism does not involve sacred texts), atmosphere at rituals (formal vs. informal) and organisational structure (Roman Catholicism is centralised, hierarchical world religion whereas Black Carib ancestor worship is a non-hierarchical, decentralised religion).

Sered 1994: 36

Sered was all too aware that the twelve traditions cited are artificially connected within her work. While she does seem to have faith in a general continuum from male- to female-centred traditions, she also realises that absolute categories are a misnomer, for 'in all known cultures both men and women are religious – my twelve examples are not pure types' (Sered 1994: 40). Sered is also not setting up women's religion as an anti-type to men's religion (if such a distinction could ever be legitimately sustained anyway). She writes,

> There is no such thing as an archetypical 'women's' or 'men's' religion; I do not believe that religiosity is a biologically determined sexual characteristic … [rather] I am comparing specific religions to other religions … Among the questions I ask are: What is the status of this religion – is it the official state religion, a new religion, a persecuted cult? In what way is this religion female dominated?
>
> Sered 1994: 12

These caveats notwithstanding, Sered proposed that the twelve religions outlined above were united by three main characteristics, many of which at first sight do not seem to easily dovetail with known features of early Christianity.

First, all religious traditions studied were predominantly 'female' either in terms of leadership or membership (1994: 3) or practised no discrimination whatsoever on account of sex and gender. Early Christianity undoubtedly appealed to members of both sexes and a variety of social positions. Women seemed to have exercised a variety of roles (including leadership) in early times. However, it would be wrong to submit that it was a predominantly female movement. Jesus after all is pictured calling twelve male disciples as his companions.

Second, in all twelve religions Sered noted that there was self-consciousness that each was a woman's as opposed to a man's religion (1994: 3). This again is not on the face of it a characteristic that can be validated in early Christianity. However, in many ways the discipleship ethos promoted by early Christianity, including love of neighbour, servitude and humility was embodied and imaged in those deemed subordinate in hierarchical society, the pauper, the leper, the child, the woman. While the self-consciousness of the movement may not have been sex-specific (indeed it seems such distinctions are deemed irrelevant in early Christianity) the disciples' faith consciousness could find ready parallels in the behaviour and self-countenance of those deemed inferior on worldly scales.

Third, each of the religions conceived of themselves as independent of a male-dominated institutional context (Sered 1994: 4). If the sectarian constitution of early Christianity is considered, in many ways this tradition does set itself up as the true interpreter and fulfilment of existing traditions. Symbols of Judaism were re-imagined and personalised in Christianity. 'Jesus refused to define holiness of God's elected people in cultic terms with reference to the Temple or the Torah, but redefined it instead as the wholeness of creation' (Schüssler Fiorenza cited and discussed in Ng 2002: 128–29). The temple now could refer to Christ's body (Jn. 2:19, 21), which is ritually ingested by believers. The socially mixed community of faith could in turn be called 'the temple of God' (1 Cor. 3:16, 17), the 'holy temple in the Lord' (Eph. 2:21). Purity concerns were also predominantly conceived in internal as opposed to external ways (a deviation from Pharisaic interpretations). In the gospels, it is that which comes from the heart that defiles (Mt. 15:11, 18; Lk. 6:45) not other factors.

In light of some of the obvious characteristics shared with female-centred traditions studied by Sered, it does not seem too unreasonable an exercise to see if structural features shared between the twelve religions she discussed are also mirrored or present in early Christianity. I will consider the following features in this task: the social contexts of women's religions, suffering and healing, rituals and relationships, maternity and meaning.

The Social Contexts of Women's Religions

Sered noted three main features of the environments in which women's religions rise and flourish. The first of these is *gender dissonance*, situations in which socially conventional thinking on gender is either extremely incongruous or quickly developing. She notes that Shakerism, Spiritualism and Christian Science all arose in a time of urbanisation and industrialisation, which in turn opened up new avenues of experience for women. She also notes that industrialisation led to opportunities of employment and prestige for women in the Sande secret society in West Africa.

Many have argued that the eschatological perspective of early Christianity would have constituted such a situation. The imminent end of the world would relativise family ties and change perspectives. In alignment with this, Kraemer has stated that it was through such re-envisioning of family that certain females gained autonomy and prominence within the fledgling movement (Kraemer 1992: 139). However, while eschatological fervour may well have produced the social circumstances necessary for a rise of female prominence within religion, it is also true to say that family life and women's roles provided symbolic sources for early Christianity, the physical presents the spiritual. Even Jesus' more questionable attitudes (even seeming rejection of his biological kin [Mk. 3:35; Mt. 12:50; Lk. 8:21]), allow 'the possibility of the physical family finding a place within the spiritual one' (Witherington 1984: 98). Jesus re-emphasises the commandment to honour one's father and mother and reunites biological kin, raising a widow's son (Lk. 7:11–17) and the brother of his friends (Jn. 11:44). Discussing John's picture of Jesus on the cross addressing his mother as 'woman', Witherington, for example, argues, 'She does not cease to be his mother; however, at Jesus' hour she becomes a mother of a different sort and joins with the family of faith' (1984: 95). Indeed it seems that the evangelists' respective presentations of Jesus show him trying to foster a balance between biological and spiritual notions of kin, presumably also illustrating a balance between the 'now and not yet' of the forthcoming kingdom.

This is also a relevant consideration given the second main feature that Sered notes in contexts leading to the rise of women's influence in religion, namely, a cultural prominence on the maternal position (1994: 43). Sered defines matrifocality, following feminist anthropologist Yanagisako, rather broadly. 'Matrifocal does not necessarily mean that a husband is absent from the house' rather 'it is sufficient for the mother to be the focus of the household' (Sered 1994: 46). She cites spirit cults of Northern Thailand where women are to a certain extent independent and play clear roles in household organisations (1994: 49). Similarly, in Korea, women's shamanism is focused in the female space of the house: 'while dramatically acknowledging a woman's affective ties to her own dead kin, a *kut* also reaffirms bonds between a woman and her living kin' (1994: 56). The Luvale of Zambia also associate kinship arrangements with women's religion. Quoting Spring, Sered submits, 'in matrilineal societies it often seems to be the case that even when the formal religion is male dominated, women gather in the context of female-dominated cult groups or ritual constellations' (Sered 1994: 60). This affirms that family and house are two domains that are intimately related to the predominance of women's religions and spirituality.

This, at first sight, is not easily squared with the context of the church; however, features of family preservation including love, nurture, servitude and education of children are part and parcel of early Christianity's vision. What is more, the 'ritual space' of the church, being the house, also maximised the potential for women to participate in the religious life of early Christianity. Schüssler Fiorenza has notably argued that the fact that the early Christian communities met in houses as significant vis-à-vis their status in the movement. The 'private' space of the house was traditionally women's space and they therefore could not be censored or banned from taking key roles in activities there. The fact that Christianity's ritual space was domestic did in this sense serve to inform 'the democratic vision of the movement' (Ng 2002: 17).

It is not insignificant either that in positing a primitive sexual equality in the Jesus mission Schüssler Fiorenza holds kingdom, the *basileia* of God, as a localised symbol of this egalitarian ethos. This plays directly into Sered's third main feature of social contexts that result in women's religions, namely, women feature greatly in religions that recruit from disprivileged sectors of society. Such people 'are drawn to religions that assure fair compensation – reward from one's own good deeds and punishment from the bad deeds of others' (1994: 5). Celsus' famed, though admittedly biased, characterisation of Christianity as a movement comprised of 'the foolish, dishonourable and stupid, and only slaves, *women* and little children' (my italicisation, Celsus quoted in Origen, *Contra Celsum* 3.44) expresses such sentiments.

Sered also argued that a *relationship ethos* led to greater participation by women in religion. In her words, 'there is greater female participation and influence in religions that teach brotherly love and love for one's enemies ... women's religious lives are often closely linked to their interpersonal concerns. The network of relationships that seems the most relevant to the understanding of women's religiosity is the family' (1994: 5–6). This feature is certainly evident in the practice and ethos of Jesus as presented in the gospels. He epitomises the law as love for God and one another, he teaches and enacts love for enemies and characterises the community of faith as brothers and sisters in faith.

Misfortune, Suffering and Healing

Sered identified a strong focus on misfortune, suffering and healing in the women's religions she studied. It has been proposed that childbirth itself may have confronted women with their own mortality in the ancient world. It was a physically hazardous venture. 'Puerperal infections, malaria, tuberculosis can all be traced in Hippocratic literature as significant threats to parturient women' (Demand 1994: 152). But in Sered's opinion it is not only primarily the physical but also the emotional insight that motherhood brings that leads to women's focus on the easing of pain. This is testified to by other ethnography. Caraveli-Chaves, for example, in her essay 'Bridge Between Two Worlds: The Greek Women's Lament as Communicative Event' sees bereavement as an event which provides resources for women to 'think with' suffering. She writes,

> It is a woman's capacity for reproduction that also gives her first hand access to the realm of the dead, as she becomes more vulnerable to pain and loss than men. As a mother, a woman has taken the first step in the hierarchy of understanding pain, an understanding that is the privileged territory of women and which increases with age and experience.
>
> Caraveli-Chaves 1980: 146

The alleviation of suffering in all its forms is a key factor in women's characterisations in the gospels. They petition Jesus on behalf of their loved ones (Mt. 15:22; Mk. 7:25) and seek healing for others and themselves. Furthermore, their intimate association with death rituals and mourning also serves to associate their lot with suffering and the positive task of emotional healing. In such contexts, Sered suggests, women can often serve as leaders: 'the feminization of suffering is used to justify women's religious leadership in societies in which leadership is perceived to be a male prerogative. Pain, a female prerogative, explains why women can be religious leaders' (1994: 216). Sered accordingly summarised the message of women's religions as 'suffering is not inevitable, individuals can and should seek means of alleviating suffering' (Sered 1994: 114). Jesus in his ministry alleviates suffering of countless people who are sick, bereaved and isolated. Furthermore, he himself does not shy away from suffering, and makes it a veritable virtue of the call of discipleship.

Women's natural association with birth and death leads to an ethos of interpersonal caring and responsibility (Sered 1994: 121) similar to the compassion shown by Jesus in situations in which he perceived social and physical hurts. The communicative vision of women's religions, which see relationships as the most important arenas in which social ills can be addressed is one shared in common with early Christianity, and leads us into the next of Sered's categories, 'Rituals and Relationships'.

Rituals and Relationships

Sered has identified relational aspects as central in women's religions' rituals. She discusses anthropological categorisations of rituals (rites of passage, rites of affliction and rites of solidarity) and concludes that solidarity rites are the most important in women's religions. Such rites are central because they serve to strengthen interpersonal bonds between people. She concludes, 'women's religions are characterised by concern with social ties, not biological facts' (Sered 1994: 138–39). This marks such traditions out from patrilineal lines, which 'develop various means, including religious means, to control women's fertility and thus to ensure that the patriline is true. Among the most common means are virginity tests, modesty rules and sexual taboos' (Sered 1994: 62).

One of Sered's most interesting insights in this respect is that in female-dominated religions there is virtually no emphasis on physiological changes. In short, 'social cohesion, communality and solidarity are more cherished than individual and personal change' (Korte 2003: 175). Female blood rituals are very uncommon and, perhaps related to this, sacrificial or bloodletting rituals are also very rare (Korte 2003: 166). Sered follows other feminist anthropologists in seeing a link between sacrifice and patriarchal ordered religions, which for a variety of reasons (including preservation of descent lines) are focused on blood ties. In contrast, for women, 'no sacrificial blood is needed to strengthen, prove, or dramatise that bond' (Korte 2003: 172). Perhaps here the correlation between the mission of Jesus as presented in the gospels and women's religions are at their weakest. While it is true that Jesus' attitude vis-à-vis the law is one that, following Hosea (Mt. 9:13; 12:17), focuses on mercy as opposed to sacrifice, and sees servitude as characteristic of a true disciple, it is also true that Jesus' death is presented within the gospels in partly sacrificial terms. Mark's Jesus gives his life as a ransom for many (Mk.10:45); Matthew's Jesus saves people from their sins through obediently shedding his blood (Mt. 20:24–28); Luke's Jesus reinstated a new covenant in his blood (Lk. 22:19–20); John's Jesus manifests glory in his death and lays down his life for his friends (Jn.15:13). In all cases, Jesus' blood initiates a new relationship between God and his people.

Sered explains that ritual systems in women's religion are often centred on feasting and serving. She first discusses food rituals/preparation as central arenas in which women enact solidarity. It is relevant that Jesus characterises his ministry and the coming kingdom as feasting and promotes open table-fellowship with all people, regardless of their station in life. It is this 'festive table-sharing at a wedding feast, and not the *askesis* of the holy man that characterises Jesus and his movement' (Schüssler Fiorenza 1992: 119). Furthermore, the fact that the Eucharist became one of the most prominent rites in early Christianity is significant, for it in itself is a rite of solidarity centred on food. Christ's body is ingested by the individual bodies of believers, and consequently as Paul says, though many, the community is one body through partaking of one bread (1 Cor. 10:17). The crucial ethos is that the Christian group is united in spite of their difference. This is particularly important given the stress put on relationships in early Christianity. In Ehrensperger's words:

> The relational power of the Christian community constitutes a redemptive reality over against conflict and struggle…. To be able to recognise difference and diversity and live with them is part of the vision of healing and redeeming relationships.
>
> Ehrensperger 2004: 118

Second, Sered discusses mourning rituals as rites of solidarity. Olyan in his impressive study of biblical mourning (2004) is instructive here. He utilises social anthropological perspectives to elucidate both ritual and social dimensions of mourning (in both death and non-death related contexts). Such rites in his opinion provide 'a context for the creation and recreation of social order and for its potential transformation' (2004: 4). Sered also identifies relational aspects of mourning to include social support for the bereaved, but also the easing of the passage of the departed. Thus women are intimately involved with both the living and the dead and as such outline the 'existential meaning of death and separation' (Sered 1994: 130). Olyan cites Hertz's conclusions that there is a striking similarity forged between the corpse and mourner in mourning rites, leading to the mourners being as 'socially dead individuals, cut off from communal life' (Olyan 2004: 7). 'Just as the corpse is polluted and repellent according to the beliefs of some Indonesian cultures, so is the mourner, with mourning lasting until the corpse has disintegrated, leaving only the bones' (Olyan 2004: 7). Moreover, mourning practices are often shameful and self-debasing (Olyan 2004: 34), but it is through such self-identification with the dead that a new relationship can be initiated:

> The old relationship, between two living persons, has been sundered by death. The enactment of identification by means of self-debasing rites re-established a social connection between the mourner and the spirit of the dead during the mourning period, a period of transition between the death and the mourner's return to day to day life.
>
> Olyan 2004: 44–45

In the gospels, Mary anointing Jesus' feet with her hair (Jn. 11:2), an act that is given theological meaning by Jesus, is seen by many commentators as an act of mourning (Van Tilborg 2000: 200). The women who come to attend Jesus' corpse and by virtue of this are placed in the right place at the right time to be first witnesses of his resurrection are also important boundary crossers. By ritually identifying themselves with the death, they are also incorporated symbolically into his new life. Furthermore, we witness Jesus himself 'mourning' over Jerusalem (Mt. 23:37–39; Lk. 13:34–35). Witherington comments on this with characteristic perception:

> It should not be overlooked that Jesus takes on a role normally performed by a Jewish woman of publicly and proleptically mourning for Jerusalem.... Jesus chooses here one of the most proverbially gender distinctive and instinctive roles a woman or female animal takes when he described his desires in terms of a mother's care and protection.
>
> Witherington 1984: 47

What is even more striking is the parallel importance in both women's religion and early Christianity of nurturing relationships and interpersonal bonds based not on blood, race or social status but rather something else – in Christianity, faith in Christ. Jesus conducts an inclusive mission where rituals of solidarity are central. As such sins are forgiven and those excluded or marginal in society (including women) are given a prominent place.

Sered noted that in women's religions, the public and private spheres are bridged and homes become prominent ritual spaces where food, life and death become central symbolic elements. Echoing this interpersonal aspect, the gospels' key metaphor for the community was not cultic but domestic, the family and household of God (Mt. 5:45). Believers were united in relationships of faith, not blood, as children of God.

Maternity and Meaning

Radcliffe-Brown touched on something of existential significance when he stated 'in primitive societies, whether they have matrilineal institutions it is normally recognised that the closest of all kinship bonds is that between mother and child' (Radcliffe-Brown 1950: 77). Sered confirms that religions with a strong sense of female roles address women primarily as mothers (1994: 5) rather than wives, and maternity is accorded a sacred status (1994: 61).

Childbirth and motherhood had not featured in any significant way in anthropology until twenty years ago. Johnson's study of obstetrics and midwifery in the Yucatan was a significant advance in the area. She notes that the secondary sources available to her were sketchy, and limited to Human Area Files and a survey article by Mead and Newton who themselves bemoaned the lack of interest in mothering in cross-cultural study. Now there is a growing field of interest in the subject as part of cultural systems. Davis-Floyd and Sargent's 1997 work, *Childbirth and Authoritative Knowledge: Cross-Cultural Perspectives*, looked at the construction of these in diverse situations from non-industrialised settings, to the Western world's bio-medical hegemony and assisted technologies. However, Sered is keen to stress that it is the social rather than biological aspects of motherhood that are celebrated in women's religions. Nurturing qualities in particular are prominent. For example, in the Black Carib 'motherhood connotes strength, the capacity and duty to protect others' (1994: 78). Even Shakers, a religion that requires celibacy, talks about spiritual growth in mothering terms.

In the New Testament the physical image of birth is used to represent the coming kingdom and in John's Gospel, Jesus' death and glory (Jn. 16:21). Darr has investigated the woman in travail image in biblical tradition and concludes that the image is often used to incite a particular reaction in times of crises (like the pain felt in childbirth) (Darr cited in Rushton 2003: 80–81). The travail image's evocation of pain is shown in eschatology, but the productive end of labour seems to be what is driving the image in John 16:21 (Rushton 2003: 82). Rushton submits that the Johannine parallel between birth, the quintessential woman's activity, and the divine is important in defining the meaning of the death and glory of Jesus as logos (Rushton 2003: 79). She submits that John 16:21 evokes Isaiah's 'daughter of Zion' idea (Rushton 2003: 90). In her words:

> There is a continuity with their religious matrix through the blessing of birth: the birth of a son through Sarah/the birth of a people through the 'daughter of Zion'/the new birth through Jesus' death and resurrection. Thus the image evoked through the parable of the woman in childbirth not only explains the death-glory of Jesus as linked to biblical history, but its recurring pattern of childbirth metaphors and their meaning is replicated in Johannine discipleship.
>
> 2003: 91

While all this could be conceived (no pun intended) positively, the physical aspects of birth when used in images could be used to serve patriarchal ends. Rushton makes a similar point in her study of childbirth images in the Bible,

> At the divine level, the role of God as birth giver was not only masculine but also bloodless ... blood and birth pain, so integral to women's experience of childbirth, are absent from these biblical constructions at both divine and human levels. In contrast, flowing blood and childbirth subject woman to the stipulations of pure and impure codes that function to protect male holiness and purity.
>
> Rushton 2003: 89–90

This is perhaps why, as Sered points out, women's religions focus more on the social rather than physical capabilities and experiences of mothers. Sered also claims that motherhood for women's religions is conceived from the woman's as opposed to the father's or son's perspective (Sered discussed in Korte 2003: 169). Sered cites the example of the travail images used by the founder of the Shaker religion, Lee. To illustrate this point she cites Lee's words,

> 'I felt as sensible as ever a woman did a child when she was delivered of it. Then I felt an unspeakable joy in God, and my flesh came upon me, like the flesh of an infant.'
>
> Sered 1994: 75

This adoption of the idea of spiritual motherhood, from the specific perspective of the mother, places high importance on these particular traits and experiences. The adoption of a mother's perspective by Jesus in the various Wisdom passages is relevant in this respect. The view that a link with Wisdom and the social and sexual equality of the movement can be forged has been popularised by Schüssler Fiorenza. In her words, 'The Jesus movement integrates prophetic-apocalyptic and wisdom theology insofar as it fuses eschatological hope with the belief that the God of Israel is the creator of all human beings' (Schüssler Fiorenza 1983: 120). The imaging of Jesus as a mother hen concerned for her chicks (Mt. 23:37–39; Lk. 13:34–35) and bewailing the failings of this generation like the failures of one's own children (Mt. 11:16–19; Lk. 7:31–35) all characterise situations from the perspective of mothering. Related to this, Van Aarde's interesting essay on 'Jesus as Fatherless Child' (2002) tentatively suggests that Jesus' ministry as a whole has far more qualities associated with motherhood than fatherhood. In his words,

> The fatherless Jesus seemingly behaved in a motherlike manner as an adult (see Jacobs-Malina 1993: 2). It can be seen in his saying and deeds in which he advocated the last place at table, serving others, forgiving wrongs, having compassion, and healing wounds. Such a conflict-laden performance caused spontaneous if not intentional anti-patriarchal behaviour.
>
> Van Aarde 2002: 81

It is also not insignificant when focusing on maternity and meaning that the symbol of the child became the pre-eminent symbol for the true believer in Jesus' ministry. Children exhibit the acceptance and humility required of faith (Mt. 19:13–15; Mk. 10:13–16; Lk. 18:15–17).

For both Jewish and pagan homes, the mother played a key educational role. In Jewish houses the children were brought up in women's domestic space and it was here that religion was inculcated and taught. 'The family constituted the key arena for the socialisation of each new generation, which would be equipped to raise the following generation in turn as Jews' (Barclay 1997: 69). Kirshenblatt-Gimblett et al. bolster the point that it is in the home that the mother is most important as an educator. 'She is often the one who tells stories to the children when they are very young [children would be weaned at about four years old] and later to the daughters in particular, since as soon as the boys are old enough they go to the synagogue with their father' (2002: 29).

Dixon's characterisation of the *Roman Mother* (1988) as a protector of cultural tradition, 'the transmitter of traditional morality – ideally a firm disciplinarian' (1988: 233) also bears hallmarks of motherly education. If such associations were conjured up for pagan converts to Christianity and they saw the central heart of their religion as the home and their identity as children of God, then presumably women's roles in these areas would also have been called to mind.

Procreation and the Parables: Nurturing the Kingdom

But can the pertinence of maternity and meaning cast light on any other aspects of the gospels? I want to ask if it is at least possible that some parables (even if not explicitly featuring women) can be symbolically associated with nurturing maternal metaphors (albeit through exhibiting ethnographic data beside the texts, rather than the texts themselves generating such associations). It is in the parables that stock images of everyday life are brought into play most explicitly to illustrate aspects of the kingdom. The movement's primary context was agrarian and it should come as no surprise that this world provides stock images for a number of metaphors for the good news and kingdom. For example, the sowing of seed is used to represent the spread of the gospel (Mt. 13:19; 25:24; Mk. 4:15–32) and the harvest characterises the time of judgement at the eschaton (Mt. 13:39; Mk. 4:29; Lk. 10:2; Jn. 4:35). It is also important for present purposes that a number of the parables feature women's spheres and roles as providers/mothers.

Within scripture there are a number of 'domestic' tasks incumbent on them. These include preparation of food (Gen. 18:6; 2 Sam. 13:8), spinning (Ex. 35:26; Prov. 31:19), making clothes (1 Sam. 2:19; Prov. 31:21), collecting water from the well (Gen. 24:15; 1 Sam. 9:11) and caring for flocks (Gen. 29:6; Ex. 2:16). However, it is the birthing process that provides the dominant backdrop for exclusively female experience. Barrenness was a curse for women (Gen. 30:22, 23; 1 Sam. 1:6, 7; 2:1–11; Is. 4:1; Lk. 1:25) and it was through procreation, especially the bringing forth of a son, that they fully realised their potential. Campbell has argued that identity is rooted in gender, particularly notions of household, marriage and family (discussed in Paradellis 1999: 216). A man must ensure his woman does not shame him by straying, as he must ensure the ascription of his honour to his sons. Women in turn gain 'positive' shame (their equivalent of respect) through childbearing and being sexually exclusive and true to their husbands. A division between public and private space ensured women's primary sphere of influence and activity was the home.

The parables associated with women witness to the above picture. They can be divided into: first, those that explicitly feature women – the wise and foolish virgins (Mt. 25:1–13), the lost coin (Lk. 15:8–10), the leaven (Mt. 13:33; Lk. 13:2–21), the persistent widow (Lk. 18:2–5); and second, those parables referring to traditional women's activities of sewing (Mt. 9:16; Mk. 2:21; Lk. 5:36), filling wineskins (Mk. 2:22; Mt. 9:17; Lk. 5:37–39) and spinning (Mt. 6:28–30; Lk. 12:27–28).

If, however, the pre-eminent characteristic of women's symbolic input in religions is often associated with the social aspects of motherhood, at first glance none of the above refers to this aspect whatsoever. However, one ethnographic study in rural Greece could make us reconsider. In his study of 'Procreation Metaphors in Rural Greece' (1999), Paradellis notes that there procreation is viewed as the sowing of a male seed (which contains the identity and essence of the person) into a female soil that nourishes, develops and protects the unborn child.

Thoughts about conception vary enormously among cultures. The ovum is a relatively new scientific discovery, and ancient world sources seem in part to echo Paradellis's findings regarding views on the sexual division of labour in reproduction. Harlow submits, however, that 'whatever school of thought one followed, there was an overriding concept that the child was a product of the father's semen' (Harlow 1998: 157). She cites the Hippocratic Corpus (fifth and fourth century BCE), which saw both parents producing seed but of unequal status. 'Some seed is strong [male] and some weak [female] … the child's sex is determined by whichever sperm prevails in quantity' (Harlow 1998: 157–58). Aristotle (fourth century BCE) also saw the male semen as the cause, while the female was passive and 'acted upon by the male seed' (Harlow 1998: 158). Soranus of Ephesus, a Greek working in Rome, explained that 'female seminal ducts passed from the ovaries to the bladder bypassing the womb. This meant that the female seed could not be used in the reproductive process' (Harlow 1998: 160). Harlow submits that the various 'conceptions of conception' played a part in subordinating women and were, 'translated into both Greek and Roman social and legal practice, where … legitimacy and inheritance pass primarily and preferably through the paternal line' (Harlow 1998: 159). Returning to Paradellis, he identifies root metaphors used to illustrate 'procreation' in Greece including bread-making and cultivation. It is interesting to note how these metaphors also play important roles in the gospels' portrayal of the kingdom, featuring female characters. Paradellis notes symbolic links between bread-making and women's fertility. For example, a barren woman is not allowed to plant or tend a wheat crop 'for fear that the wheat will also become barren. And no one takes yeast from a childless woman to make bread' (1999: 212). However, wheat and bread-making are also used in rituals to combat infertility, thus illustrating the dual-edged profane and sacred nature of the substance.

In scriptural tradition bread-making is a female activity, involving kneading the dough (Gen. 18:6; Ex. 12:34; Jer. 7:18) and baking in public ovens (Hos. 7:4; Jer. 37:21). However, whether this can be linked with biological aspects of mothering in the New Testament is questionable. What is true is that the social aspect of mothering, including the nourishing aspect of staple food, can be linked with similar nourishing effects of Jesus' message and work. This is shown both in the feeding miracles and the giving of his own body for nourishment (Mt. 15:33; 26:6; Mk. 3:20; Lk. 11:3; Jn. 6:7, 35).

The only example of actual bread-making in the gospels is in the parable of the leaven, which itself makes a direct link between women's work and Jesus' work of preaching: 'leavening the whole world with the leaven of the Gospel' (Witherington 1984: 40). Witherington notes that the amount of meal used is surprising, half a bushel, 'which would probably feed one hundred people' (Witherington 1984: 40). Hearon and Wire (2002) submit that the woman could be providing bread for the entire household for a week from the measurements produced here. Either way, the amount of meal and the woman preparing it conveys something of the nature of the kingdom.

Moving to Paradellis's second procreation metaphor of cultivation, we find that none of the parables explicitly featuring women refer to cultivation. However, symbolically the appeal of female imagery may extend into other parables. Most of the essays in Loizos and Heady's celebrated volume, *Conceiving Persons* (documenting cross-cultural beliefs surrounding procreation) make some parallelism between human reproduction and plant growth (1999: 10) and metaphors related to cultivation and vegetation (1999: 205).

In the Bible, plant fertility metaphors are common. A good example would be the phrase 'fruit of the womb' used in relation to human birth (Gen. 30:2; Deut. 7:13; Lk. 1:42; Ps. 21:10; 132:11) and the offspring of beasts (Deut. 28:51; Isa. 14:29). The link between humanity and earth is not only symbolic but also linguistic in scripture. The verb *tiktō*, literally meaning 'bear, give birth to, bring forth' (children) (Mt. 1:21), is used metaphorically of the earth 'producing yield' (Heb. 6:7). In the Hebrew Bible *adamah'* is translated as earth, soil or ground. The creation narratives designate Adam as such, for he came from the dust. Similarly, in Genesis 9:20, Noah is referred to as 'man of the soil'. Also the frequency of the term 'seed' for descendants of patriarchs etc. (Gen. 9:9; 12:7; 15:8; 46:6; Num. 16:40) could be placed in the same semantic range.

Following along this line of thinking, it is interesting to note how many parables feature images of soil. These include the parable of the soils (Mk. 4:1–20, Mt. 13:1–23, Lk. 8:4–18); the parable of the seed growing in secret (Mk. 4:26–29); the mustard seed (Mk. 4:30–32, Mt. 13:31–32, Lk. 13:18–19) and the wheat and tares (Mt. 13:24–30, 36–43). Furthermore, all the images about good and bad trees and solemn warnings about those trees not bearing fruit and being axed and cast into the fire (Mt. 3:10; Lk. 3:9) could have some resonance with Mediterranean fertility schemes outlined above. According to Paradellis, this metaphor is 'rich in creative vitality' and in his opinion, 'goes back a long way in the Greek and wider Mediterranean region' (1999: 210).

Carol Delaney, in her magnum opus, *The Seed and the Soil: Gender and Cosmology in Turkish Village Society* (1991) suggests, in alignment with Paradellis, that in the village she studied, it was believed that the male sperm contained the child. The female was merely a receptacle and nurturer for the new life. This so-called 'monogenetic theory of procreation' correlated in her view with 'the theological doctrine of monotheism. Both are concerned with genesis ... the principle of creation at both levels comes only from one source, and that is symbolically masculine' (1991: 3). Delaney noted that 'seed and soil, seemingly such innocent images, condense powerful meanings: although they appear to go together naturally, they are categorically different, hierarchically ordered, and differentially valued ... men appear to provide the spark of life, the essential identity of the child; while women, like soil, contribute the nurturing material that sustains it' (1991: 8).

Every time a field (*agros*) is mentioned in the parables it is the field belonging to God. In the metaphorical field of God (the world) the lilies do not grow, toil or spin but flourish. As Matthew explains, 'The field is the world; the good seed are the children of the kingdom; but the tares are the children of the wicked one' (Mt. 13:38). The kingdom is as a mustard seed sown, or treasure hidden, in a field (Mt. 13: 31). In short, the field as the world belongs to God. However, while Delaney would see such metaphors as representative of an oppressive patriarchal notion of creation, I would ask whether there is any clue that the parables may accord a more important role to the soil (womanly aspects of nurturing) than that of a purely passive recipient of seed.

It is in the parable of the sower that the importance of the fertility of the earth is shown. In line with Delaney's argument, this parable features the message of the gospel as a male seed planted in the female earth. The

Son of Man is the one who sows good seed, the kingdom message, in his field (Mt. 13:24). However, the crucial message of the parable lies in the fact that while the seed is good when planted, it is the soil/environment in which the seed is planted that in the end dictates its fruitfulness. Those seeds falling on 'good ground' brought forth fruit (Mt.13:8; Mk. 4:20). This represents the one hearing the word and understanding it (Mt. 13:23), or in Luke's terms, the one who 'in an honest and good heart' hears the word 'and bears fruit with patient endurance' (Lk. 8:15). In contrast, the one lacking fertile soil has no root 'and endures only for a while' (Mt. 13:21). This certainly would stand in contradistinction to a theory of procreation that saw the seed as the essence. Here nurture, not nature is seen as paramount. Other seed/soil parables also place primary importance on the environment and nourishment of the seed for eventual fruition. The kingdom itself is the smallest of seeds, though when nurtured by believers it will grow into the greatest of trees. The environment in which the seed is placed makes a difference to faith. This realisation perhaps takes us full circle to return to those other aspects of importance in women's religions, rituals of solidarity, food preparation, nurturing and education – all nurture as opposed to nature elements. If indeed the ideas of procreation placed primary importance on the male seed, then these parables would make arresting reading for many. Obviously I realise that agricultural imagery is not exclusive to women's religions but reflects broader agrarian social contexts. Nonetheless, overlaps in imagery used between Jesus' parables and reproduction beliefs as outlined by Paradellis are certainly worth noting and offer new and engaging perspectives from which to view the material.

I have not had to try too hard to find parallels between the characteristics associated with the twelve women's religious traditions outlined by Sered (social contexts; misfortune, suffering and healing; rituals and relationships; maternity) and features of the Jesus movement reflected in the gospels. This leads me to a brief exploration of another of Sered's projects: documenting the results of fieldwork conducted among oriental Jewish women (originally from Kurdistan and Yemen) in Jerusalem (1996; 1999). Unlike the twelve examples of women's religions she investigated in her earlier book, the Judaism of the elderly women's experience was not a tradition in which they dominated or indeed participated fully. On the contrary, it is a male-dominated tradition in which females are subordinated and excluded from key religious activities. However, even in this patriarchal environment, women made important adaptations of the tradition in their own lives, in a process that Sered coined a 'domestication of religion'.

The Domestication of Religion

The Oxford English Dictionary defines the domestic sphere as that 'of the home or household or family affairs' and sees the process of domestication as to 'accustom to home life and management'. Sered adopted the term 'domestication' from Fusel de Coulanges' ideas of domestic religion to denote a process whereby individuals acknowledge a religious tradition, but, being censored from full participation in its rites and rituals, at the same time transform and adopt its institutions and even theology in the contexts of their personal lives. Such adaptation is used to ensure the health and happiness of those with whom the women were closely linked (1999: 96–97).

In many ways 'domestication' is what seems to define that stage of 'institutionalised Christianity' where thoughts regarding women returned to the cultural status quo. Schüssler Fiorenza proposes that the early missionary days of Christianity were marked by an egalitarian ethos, which was gradually curbed in a second period marked by patriarchalisation. She believes female submission and emphasis on the maleness of Christ in titles and the restriction of behaviour on women found their genesis as early as Paul's mission. The post-Pauline and post-Petrine churches developed further still in this direction until there was a wholehearted shift from authority based on charisma to that of local ecclesiastical hierarchies. Such sentiments are shown in the Pastorals and texts such as 1 Clement (see Ng 2002: 19ff.), which censored the participation of women in the central religious activities (cult) and reverted to the status quo.

Although an organic process of development (akin to institutionalisation) between religions in which women play a prominent role and those in which they are forced to subordinate to male prominence is not explicitly spelled out in Sered's work, she does implicitly attest to such dynamics in the following statement:

Women often serve as shamans and charismatic preachers. Among the factors that encourage women's attainment of authority roles are emphasis on personality or supernatural powers rather than on hierarchy or the training of cult/church leaders, and spiritual identity predominating over social categories.... *These factors are particularly significant in new religious movements, where women often function as founders/leaders, losing their leadership roles as the religion becomes more institutionalised.*

My italicisation, Sered 1994: 4–5

A development can be plotted between Sered's work on female-dominated religions and female roles in male-dominated religions. This development is called 'domestication of religion'. She defines it thus:

> Domestication of religion is a process in which people who profess their allegiance to a wider religious tradition personalise the rituals, institutions, symbols and theology of that wider system ... individuals who have a great deal invested in interpersonal relationships, and who are excluded from formal power within an institutionalised religious framework, tend to be associated with a personally-orientated religious mode.
>
> Sered 1999: 96

While Sered uses the term 'domestication' in reference to female adaptations of male-dominated traditions, an evolutionary/developmental framework between her two projects is not explicitly cited. However implicitly, I think a link between domestication and institutionalisation within Sered's research can be defended.

Sered noted in her essay 'The Domestication of Religion: The Spiritual Guardianship of Elderly Jewish Women' (1999) based on her book *Women as Ritual Experts: The Religious Lives of Elderly Jewish Women in Jerusalem* (1996) how the women she observed in Jerusalem were poor and illiterate. Moreover, they did not have any say in the power structures or dominant religious traditions of society, but nevertheless lived profoundly spiritual lives within their personally orientated environments. They embodied the maxim that life is interdependent, sustained for and cared by relationships (1999: 98). Sered noted how these women were enmeshed in a number of relationships that they 'sacralised' in their domestic religion. They participated in 'the holy by caring for their kin and, by extension, the entire Jewish people' (1999: 99). In contrast to feeling isolated from the great tradition, as matriarchal guardians of the hearth, their religious life centred on their families and domestic duties such as food preparation.

The women fostered a religious world that focused on relationships with ancestors, kin and descendants; the dead, the living and the unborn. They saw themselves playing the role of spiritual guardians of their family, calling on the aid of ancestors for their kin and in turn teaching kin to honour their forbears (Sered 1999: 99). Women focused attention on the tombs of the dead in the hope that the deceased person would intercede on their behalf. Often the subjects of their petitions were a child, grandchild or great-grandchild suffering illness, infertility or singleness (Sered 1999: 101). The women's focus on bearing children seems at root, in Sered's opinion, to be a concern for the continuance of the Jewish people as a whole (Sered 1999: 103). Witnessing to this is the fact that the women often shifted from reference to 'my own children' to 'soldiers all of whom are like my children' (Sered 1999: 107). This shows that the women symbolically conceived their motherhood extending from the immediate blood family to the entire race.

According to Geertz, life, death and suffering are concerns central to religion, but they are also profoundly domestic as shown by Sered. The elderly women of Jerusalem played an integral part in the sacred realm, becoming ritual specialists, 'devotional virtuosi' (Sered 1999: 109), in their personal and domestic spheres. While they may not have been granted full participation in the main cultus, excluded from religious hierarchy on a number of grounds (purity, censored Torah study), they nonetheless practised and embodied in their day-to-day lives 'religious rituals, moral decisions and human interpretations of the holy' (1999: 109). In short, domesticity was not a feature of ritual or religion *per se* but rather a feature of their interpretations of ritual and religion.

It is interesting to note that those characteristics (focused on relationships; rites of solidarity; ritual space of the home) that characterised the traditions in which women were dominant also characterised the adoption of male-dominated traditions by women in their private lives. Parallels can be figuratively presented as in Table 6.1.

Table 6.1.   Comparing Traits of Female-dominated Religions with Female Behaviour in Male-dominated Religions

Female-dominated Religions	'Domestication' of Male-dominated Religions
Relationships with all are paramount	Relationships with ancestors, kin and unborn are paramount
Alleviation of suffering central	Focuses on caring for sick and petitioning for those suffering illness and infertility
Maternity central	Women conceive of themselves as mothers of kin and nation

———————▶   Domestication / Institutionalisation   ———————▶

The dynamics that Schüssler Fiorenza identifies regarding gradual assimilation to cultural norms are, I think, observable. However, whether the neat and rosy picture of total egalitarianism (an anachronistic ideological notion in reference to the New Testament) was gradually swallowed and eclipsed by encroaching patriarchalism is questionable. The process I have schematised from Sered's respective projects, entitled domestication, does not produce such a chasm between the earlier and later New Testament writings on this issue. It shows continuity in female experiences in both stages, something that Schüssler Fiorenza seems hard pushed to sustain.

While, therefore, in many ways the characteristics of the domestication of religion in Sered's study can be mirrored in the process of institutionalisation in early Christianity, it is at least plausible that emphases in women's practice of religion (shared by Jesus within the gospels) did hold to something constant throughout. However, due to the nature of our texts, a construction of such 'silent' perspectives is difficult. It is true to say that in contrast to motherhood, images of fatherhood became more frequent, and references to motherhood tended to be reserved for those instances and situations where authority was at issue. (Could this make some sense of the jarring assertion in 1 Timothy that woman will be saved through childbearing [1 Tim. 2:15]?) The household codes also reinforced patriarchal hierarchy as the norm. Botha, for example, in his discussion of Colossians 3:18–19, claims to perceive therein a rhetoric of authority and domination: '"In the Lord" in this text does not discriminate between kinds of behaviour, it affirms existing practice. Read together ... the instructions "submit", "obey", "work", "serve", "give thanks", "justice and fairness" and even " to love"' (Botha 2000: 27).

The importance of submitting to the status quo is also, Botha claims, inherent within the code in 1 Peter 3:1–7, a passage he believes could be a purposeful riposte to pagan accusations of immorality and attempts to subvert Roman power. In Botha's opinion the household code in 1 Peter is a defence: 'households are indeed in order', wives are properly 'submissive to their husbands' (Botha 2000: 29). However, Botha sees as the most important theological outcome the profound and loaded parallel drawn by 1 Peter between the suffering of women and slaves and the suffering of Jesus (1 Pet. 2:18 – 3:6). 'The author's sentiment is easily understood: suffering leads to positive outcome – here eternal life, the arrival of which is to be expediated by suffering' (Botha 2000: 30). Once more women and the concerns typical to them (suffering; healing; misfortune; motherhood) play central parts in a theology that has become 'domesticated' and 'institutionalised'.

Women's Religions and Early Christianity

Sered's work is a magnum opus of 'anthropological imagination' – in the very best sense of the term. She did not conduct face to face fieldwork within the 'religions' cited, but identified commonalties between different ethnographies on the subject of women and religion. This exhibit has also been anthropologically 'imaginative'. I have offered a different way of considering the character of earliest Christianity and women's role within it. I have displayed Sered's artefact against a broad picture of Jesus' ministry and teaching as portrayed in the gospels. I have argued that at least in some respects positive correlation can be drawn with features of those religions in which women play a prominent role. Jesus as a leader is a spiritual specialist and the movement itself is marked by an ethos of interpersonal relationships and solidarity. The axis of mothering, in its social and emotional, as opposed to biological aspects is present; the healing and empathetic sharing of suffering in this world is also held as key. The evangelists do not ideologically assert that the female sphere is better than the male. However, they do positively use typically female images to represent its message and ethos and consequently show that the female experiences as well as the male ones are legitimate avenues for presenting transcendental truth.

Furthermore, early Christianity seems to conceive of itself symbolically as the household/family of God. Procreation and kinship images serve to posit the Christian group as a family and promote interpersonal relationships with a variety of individuals, not related by blood, but faith (Mt. 12:49; Jn. 19:26). Petitioning the Christians to become as children promotes the importance of those educated in the domestic sphere, under women's supervision, for both the house and childbirth are typical arenas of women's experience (Mt. 18:4; Lk. 9:48). Suffering is embraced as theologically important by emphasising healing and the liberation from suffering. The collectivist and inclusive vision of the church and the rituals of solidarity it promoted consumed and overcame individualistic tendencies.

If metaphors used by communities reflect their own context and at times structure and reform reality, then it could be that women's capacities in mothering and the home were celebrated, and learned from, in early Christianity. Gill talks about a ministry of presence, 'a ministry that is orientated to individuals, not just problems ... personal relationships rather than with theology or organisation' (cited in Sered 1994: 237–38). This seems precisely to be the driving force behind many of the images and themes shared in common with women's religious traditions.

If a significant role can be defended for associations with women's religious traditions and Jesus' teaching about the kingdom, then presumably qualities held as central in such traditions are shown as crucial parts of Jesus' message. Social aspects of mothering, including nurture, were prized in both practice and ethos, and procreation ideas were informative of how people 'conceived' of each other as related participants in the 'Household of God'. As has been seen, the coming of the eschaton and the spreading of the good news could be pictured as the 'travail' of a woman giving birth. Each new Christian was initiated into the family of faith and the Christian ethos reflected social traits of motherhood. Moreover it shows that deprivation or oppression is not the primary stimulus for construction of women's religions, rather certain constructions of religion can empower people to re-imagine and at times change their perception.

As Christianity developed away from this 'domestic' sphere, sensibilities and ethics presumably also changed. In such circumstances it was not rituals of solidarity, the alleviation of suffering and maternity that provided the symbolic resources, but rather hierarchical patterns that produced an ethos of respect for authority. This development in turn led to what Sered pictures as 'the domestication of religion'. Subservience as opposed to nurturing became the norm. Crucially, however, women's interest in themes characteristic of these traditions could have continued after the process of domestication (as they did among the women personalising male-dominated traditions) but as our sources are written from an authoritarian/public/male perspective it is not easy to recover these sentiments from them.

Sered concluded her celebrated study of women's religious traditions with the following assertion:

> my argument here is not that the existence of a 'female sphere' characterises female-dominated religions; most known cultures have some sort of sexual division of labour. What does characterise female-dominated religions is an ideological assertion that the female sphere is as good or better than the male sphere, and the institutionalisation of autonomy for women operating in a female sphere.
>
> 1994: 211

A potentially damaging criticism of Sered's project is that it is of course hard to pinpoint her perspective on 'women's religions' as either solely in opposition to men's religions, or in naturalistic terms. In other words, are the features identified in these religions highlighted because they reveal characteristics in tension with male-dominated traditions? Or is it because 'natural' roles of women are celebrated therein? In the end any project that focuses on gender in exclusion to other status factors regarding race, age, position, etc. will be open to such criticisms. Her emphasis on the importance of relatedness and mutuality within women's religions, however, starkly illustrates that relatedness is necessary precisely because of difference. As Davaney, in a very different context wrote:

> Relatedness and dependency do not vitiate distinctiveness; on the contrary, they provide the bases out of which uniqueness emerges and upon which it depends. Distinctiveness and difference are not the corollary of autonomy and separation but of connectedness and the capacity for relation.
>
> Davaney cited in Ehrensperger 2004: 193

Even if Sered is liable to the charge of exclusion of other perspectives, her anthropological standpoint has nonetheless enlightened a number of future avenues of enquiry in relation to the position of women in the early church, hopefully – all tantalisingly 'pregnant' with promise and possibility.

7

Exhibit 5. Reading with Poetry

Modesty, Love and Desire

Curator's Notes

This exhibit displays characteristic elements of Indian and Bedouin poems and songs alongside features of the Song of Songs.

For why should I be like one who is veiled beside the flock of your companions?

Song of Songs 1:7

Though hegemonic discourses work to authorize a normal version of 'us', persons are not simply surfaces of inscription. They are also social workshops that forge new forms of association.... We are ourselves, renderings of possible social orders: imagined worlds to be.

W. Lachicotte

In her 1990 article 'The Romance of Resistance' Abu-Lughod outlined recent developments in the study of 'resistance' to power structures. She suggests that local opinions not tied to the overthrow of political or religious orders or even to ideologies of liberation (such as feminism) should be figured in any understanding of 'counter-' and 'sub-'cultural viewpoints (1990: 41). Her study revealed that poetry and song were avenues through which the lower status individuals in the Awad 'Ali (particularly women and young men) could legitimately express emotions that contradicted the dominant cultural model (1990: 47). By violating the honour code, but not seeking to overthrow it, the *ghinnawas* (oral lyric poetry) also implicitly witnessed to an individual's adherence to the moral order. Indeed the lyric forms acted as a pressure valve to ensure obedience to the status quo.

I want to judge whether a similar dynamic can be detected in the Song of Songs. If yes, then the cultural background posited may well negate attempts to attribute a feminist consciousness to the book. In contrast, it will reveal a viewpoint that actually serves to protect the prevailing duty/honour system, albeit at the same time testifying to the existence of different values within the culture, in this instance love and desire.

I place the Song of Songs, a text often claimed to bear hallmarks of female authorship, alongside two main ethnographic studies of 'marginal' poetry produced by *young* males and females, both drawn from cultures which value age above youth. These are Gloria Goodwin Raheja and Ann Grodzins Gold's, *Listen to the Heron's Words: Reimagining Gender and Kinship in North India* (1994) and Abu-Lughod's *Veiled Sentiments* (1986) a study of verse in the Bedouin Awad 'Ali tribe.

Listening to Muted Voices

Anthropology has long been in the business of understanding 'culture'. However, as critics have noted, one single discourse has often predominated and culture has been seen as something objectified, a unified way of thinking. As a result 'all human behaviour becomes either unambiguously "normative" or "non-normative" within a specific cultural system' (Raheja & Gold 1994: 2). This has never been truer than in respect to 'third world women'. Western interpreters often characterise such women as pure pawns of men's control, veiled, obedient and subservient. However as Raheja and Gold note, this is to deny such women the diversity we would not deny ourselves. In their words, such perspectives 'define and maintain postcolonial relations between the first and third worlds by positing, implicitly or explicitly, the moral superiority of the West and the moral degradation of the "patriarchal" third world' (1994: 8).

Both Raheja and Gold's and Abu-Lughod's ethnographies respectively involve some form of critical theory. They engage in projects taken up by many other anthropologists in trying to recover muted voices missing from the anthropological record. In constructing voices 'from below' they recover pictures of culture and cultural norms characterised as much by resistance as acceptance. Both works while celebrating the diversity of values presented in women and young people's genres also see that critiques of norms co-exist with the empirical reality of submission to those norms. As Knauft elucidates,

Women in Uttar Pradesh submit to male-controlled marriage even as they comment ironically upon it. Bedouin women perpetuate their domestic confinement and separation from political power even as their separation created a space for female dignity and meaning.

Knauft 1996: 231

In many ways both Raheja and Gold and Abu-Lughod are involved in uncovering what James Scott termed, 'hidden transcripts', 'everyday forms of resistance to ideological or material dominance' (Raheja & Gold 1994: 1). Their argument warrants lengthy citation:

> At least some of the speech genres used by women in Uttar Pradesh and Rajasthan tend more frequently than men's to stress the desirability of disrupting patrilineal unity in favour of a stress on conjugality; they speak of neutralizing hierarchical distinctions between bride givers and bride receivers, of the enduring nature of a woman's ties to her natal kin and the shifting evaluations of marriage that this entails, and of the moral obligation to reject sometimes a subordinate role vis-à-vis one's conjugal kin. From the vantage point of such a discourse, patriliny, hierarchy, female subordination, and so on are seen not as aspects of a fixed and reified cultural system but as strategically invoked idioms in an ongoing negotiation of personhood and relationship that, like proverbial utterances, may often be countered with other contrasting idioms that evaluate the situation at hand in quite different moral terms. Indeed, as Rena Lederman points out, women's acts of resistance to men's definitions of social order 'raise questions about the extent to which male ideology can be understood fully without appreciating how this ideology is an argument *against* women's ideas, rather than simply a positive, independent statement' (1980: 495–96).

Raheja & Gold 1994: 20

Similarly, Abu-Lughod sees poetry as 'social text'. She submits that the emotions contained within the poetry should not be seen as individualist or private but rather constitutive of social realities. The *ghinnawa* implicitly provides commentary on social hierarchy and power. She noticed that while these poems could be recited in public, the sentiments contained within them would often challenge elders and the official status quo. Nevertheless, poetry remained a culturally acceptable way of expressing such emotions, and people would not be disapproved of for reciting the lyrics.

The rejection of emotional talk in ordinary discourse and the acceptability of it in poetic genres seemed, to Abu-Lughod, to reflect a contrast of values in the Bedouin worldview: on the one hand, equality; and on the other hand, hierarchy. She saw the *ghinnawa* as a diversion from the honour code that puts premium importance on the sexual modesty of females and the centrality of the kin group. She reveals that a woman without modesty is seen as dangerous and offensive. For this reason 'the good woman or the good girl ... denies interest in men, love or sexual matters, and avoids members of the opposite sex except close relatives' (1986b: 161).

Instead of rooting this value in Islam, Abu-Lughod claims that the context against which such sentiments should be understood is social structure and patrilineal descent. She sees a potential threat to these bonds by love partnerships. Such liaisons threaten social order and risk upsetting family honour. To illustrate competition between love and social hierarchy she cites the following wedding song:

> When he shuts the door behind him
> He forgets the father who raised him.
>
> 1986a: 161

As a result, Abu-Lughod suggests that the love bond is undermined in a number of ways to preserve the Awad 'Ali tribe's agnatic bonds of power. These preservation techniques include women retaining close links to their paternal relatives; the possibility of multiple wives; marriage within the blood family being preferred to outside marriage. Finally, there is the modesty code, this 'assures that even individuals who do not have as much at stake in the system – especially women – will help perpetuate it because their virtue, or their standing as moral beings, depends on denying sexuality' (1986a: 162).

A similar dynamic is observable in Raheja and Gold's discussion of split images of women in Hindu South Asia, namely, the sexual potency of women as lovers and their nurturing qualities as mothers.

> Women as mothers contribute to the continuance of the male line, while women as sexual partners are seen to disrupt patrilineal solidarity among men. This ideological splitting has a number of practical and material consequences in women's lives. Because it is viewed as dangerous and volatile, female sexuality must be constantly controlled and brought under the surveillance of male kin; women must assume a posture of sexual reticence and shame and of withdrawal from any situations in which they might come into contact with men who are not close kin.
>
> 1994: 27

Both these ethnographic projects reveal that poems could not be categorised as feminist in the way Western interpreters would define such sentiments. The poems and songs may be 'subversive but [they are] not revolutionary' (Abu-Lughod 1986b: 164); they express subcultural sentiments but do not actively seek social change. On the contrary, they 'only declare, through their poetry, that they experience more than what their modest actions reveal' (Abu-Lughod 1986b: 164). In short, a genre of this sort 'celebrates the desires of individuals, against the demands of the system' (Abu-Lughod 1986b: 165). *Ghinnawa* and songs enforce intimacy instead of distance, because here people reveal themselves as vulnerable and passionate. Furthermore, intimate recitations serve a social purpose of uniting inferiors while at the same time ironically also protecting the status quo.

> Secrets function to exclude those who do not share them and closely bind those who do. Thus categories of equals gain cohesion and divisions between non-equals are intensified, reinforcing the structures of Bedouin society.
>
> Abu-Lughod 1986a: 235

Three purposes of *ghinnawa* and songs that can be drawn from Abu-Lughod's and Raheja and Gold's study therefore, are these. First, by expressing weakness in poetry and song, young men and women also show they voluntarily submit to the honour code. Second, by channelling sentiments into a particular medium, individuals demonstrate a measure of self-mastery and control. Third, by showing other sides to their experience they show cultural diversity from the duty/honour expectations (1986a: 245–46) of the wider society.

Anthropology of Emotions

Both the above projects are representative of the increasing attention paid to individuals' emotions in anthropology. The publication of Abu-Lughod and Lutz's, *Language and the Politics of Emotion* (1990) was monumental in this development. They focused on links between emotion and discourse and concluded:

> Emotion can be studied as embodied discourse only after its social and cultural – its discursive – character has been fully accepted. To take language as more than a transparent medium for the communication of

inner thoughts or experience, and to view speech as something essentially bound up with local power relations that is capable of socially constructing and contesting realities, even subjectivity, is not to deny non-linguistic 'realities'.... Emergent or constructed are both real and can have force in the world.

Abu-Lughod & Lutz 1990: 13

Crucial here is seeing the link between social discourse, emotion and power relations.

Discourse need not just reflect social relations; emotions expressed in various genres can be resistant or challenging. Moreover by reclaiming the importance of emotions, the social-scientific tendency to overlook the individual in grand schemes is overcome (Lutz & White 1986: 431). Lutz and White conclude,

Incorporating emotion into ethnography will entail presenting a fuller view of what is at stake for people in everyday life. In reintroducing pain and pleasure in all their complex forms into our picture of people's daily life in other societies, we might further humanize these others for the Western audience.... At issue are not only the humanity of our images, but also the adequacy of our own understanding of cultural and social forms.

Lutz & White 1986: 431

Raheja and Gold provide a lengthy discussion of language and discourse as one way in which cultural forms are created and recreated. They cite Sherzer's suggestion concerning 'artistic' forms of speech – including poetry, song, myth and verbal play – manifesting creative possibilities:

[Such forms] may constitute a tactical negotiation of status and identity (Sherzer 1987a: 300–302). This discourse-centred approach, like praxis theory, views societies not primarily in terms of structural fixities but in terms of the processes through which relationships are constructed, negotiated, and contested.

1994: 22

Like Abu-Lughod, Raheja and Gold term the North Indian songs they study as 'context restricted rituals of rebellion', 'enacted only in well-defined ritual contexts, allowing social unity and the dominant ideology otherwise to prevail in everyday life' (1994: 24). They tell an arresting story of how their picture of modest, shameful, sexually innocent Hindu women was shattered, when one night the women spoke of the pleasures of sex. The incident warrants full quotation:

> ... these women appeared to be singing about flirtation, enticement, erotic bites, exciting entanglements. They were also, as another verse performed that night demonstrates, imagining the pleasures of a less confined setting for their amours.... The women who enjoy singing such songs justly claim for themselves the same behavioral standards of modesty and shame required of the ideal Hindu wife as anthropological literature habitually depicts her. Yet clearly the songs express other powerful cultural motifs. For example, illicit liaisons evoked in wedding insult songs result, happily, in pregnancy. Singers themselves do not recognize a conflict between acting out the values of wifely devotion and lustily singing out such countervailing themes. They may describe the playful singing of such songs as making 'jokes', but the humor is grounded in positive attitudes toward reproduction and pleasure that coexist with more austere Hindu precepts.
>
> Raheja & Gold 1994: 40, 44

All the above testifies to the fact that as a discourse, creative and expressive genres can, at least in theory, be seen as an acceptable form in which to express subversive viewpoints. A similar dynamic is apparent in Foucault's suggestion that different types of discourse could subvert power relationships and play off norms against one another (see Rapport & Overing 2000: 121). In short, poetry and song give voice to 'love' as opposed to 'duty' and social hierarchy. They constitute socially acceptable media to express these viewpoints, because it is realised that by allowing expression of subaltern visions in these forms, the majority cultural position is actually protected.

The 'Textual Identity' of The Song of Songs

Berquist's questions regarding the genre and identity of the Song witness to the fact that simple meaning is not self-evident. 'Is it a love poem? Is it pornography? Is it an expression of political resistance against the oppressions that limit possibilities for life but do not take away the strength and beauty of sexual bodies?' (2002: 25). In reality it is variously all of the above.

Many interpreters, due to the Solomon connection, classified the Song as wisdom literature (Sadgrove 1978). Yet while it is true that wisdom theology, broadly conceived, finds echoes in the Song, it is also true that it presents something quite different in theme and form from other wisdom texts such as Proverbs. Others have attempted classification of each individual unit (though of course no consensus has been reached on where such divisions appear). Longman offers a generic classification as follows. First, those poems presented in monologue (Song 2:18–17; 7:12–14) as opposed to dialogue (Song 1:15–17; 2:1–17; 4:1 – 5:1; 8:13–14). Also what he terms admiration songs (Song 1:15–17; 2:1–13; 3:6–11) and songs of yearning (Song 3:1–15; 8:1–4; 8:13–14) as opposed to those cataloguing concrete experience (Song 2:4–17; 5:2–7; 6:11–12). Others are invitations (Song 2:10–14; 4:8–9; 7:12–14), teases (Song 1:7–8) and finally the *wasf* (Song 4:1–7, 12–14; 5:10–16; 6:4–6; 7:2–8) (Longman 2001: 49). *Wasf* is an Arabic word meaning 'description'. Such lyrics are often used as part of marriage celebrations (Fox 1984; Bergant 2004) and as a result some form critics posited the social context of the Song as a wedding. However, Robert Alter has warned of the folly of positing a single background to the text for 'we simply do not know' (1985: 186). Furthermore, given the composite nature of the Song it could well be that different parts should be apportioned to different settings, times, places and authors accordingly.

If genre classification has not been easy, the history of the book's canonisation and its 'afterlife' has not been any more straightforward. Rabbinic scholars accepted Solomonic authorship but felt uneasy with the sexual frankness of the Song. Rabbi Akiba's rejection of irreverent singing of the Song and his veneration of it as 'the Holy of Holies' (Mishnah *Yadaim* 3: 5) presumably based on a spiritual reading, witnesses to this. Religious understandings of the Song's message blazed the trail for both Jewish and Christian writers to read the book allegorically (as representing God's relationship with his people or with the soul). Others variously sought a dramatic backdrop, or a *Sitz im Leben* in cult and ritual (surrounding marriage, fertility and death) or a parabolic reading (based, for example, on Hosea's depiction of covenant with marital imagery).

Recently there has been a move to understand the Song literally as celebrating human sexuality and love. Many have seen parallels between love poetry from Egypt, Mesopotamia, North-West Semitic and other ancient literature (Longman 2001: 48–54). Jinbachian has also recognised some similarities between the Song and what he terms 'Pre-Islamic Arabian Odes' (1997) not only in subject but also form.

The Song undoubtedly shares characteristics with the lyric form of the *ghinnawa*. This consists of a formulaic and stylised genre, which helps to depersonalise the context of the lyrics, allowing people at one and the same time to identify with characters in the poetry but also disassociate themselves from them in public situations. Characteristics posited by Abu-Lughod as reflective of *ghinnawa* (1986a: 239–43) have correspondences with elements of the Song. First, she notes that the identity of the poet, addressee and subject of the lyrics are not revealed. The scholarly ink spilled across the centuries trying to figure out the provenance, purpose and message(s) of the Song would seem to adequately testify to this shared characteristic. The protagonists of the Song are shadowy figures. Furthermore, no concrete 'plot' or 'narrative' is apparent and the speakers' words are not always clearly delineated. Second, no names are offered and one gets a sense of the universality of the experiences presented. This can certainly be seen in the Song. In the words of Landy: 'The lovers are only images of the poet, his fictions, his reflections of experience. They have no existence outside the poem and its impression on the world' (1983: 62). Third, Abu-Lughod notes that *ghinnawa* can evoke dependency, both within the characters but also in their hearers and readers. In her words, 'poetic confessions of weakness disarm more powerful individuals' (1986a: 243). One could scarcely make up more appropriate lyrics to illustrate this point than the male's opinion in the Song that 'a king is held captive in the tresses' (Song 7:5) and 'you have ravished my heart with a glance of your eyes' (Song 4:9).

A 'Feminist Consciousness' in the Song of Songs?

Western feminist interpreters advocate equal rights for women and actively fight against patriarchal structures. As a result, Lerner has defined 'feminist consciousness' as follows:

> Women's awareness that they belong to a subordinate group, that they have suffered wrongs as a group … [and that they must] with other women remedy these wrongs.
>
> Cited in Rozen 2001

Among ideological critics, feminists have found the richest pickings in the Song. Some have claimed a woman wrote it. Brenner, for example, identifies 1:2–6; 3:1–4; 5:1–7, 10–16 as 'essentially feminine' (1993: 90–91).

At the very least, the Song is spoken for the most part by a woman (61½ verses out of 117). Furthermore, female sexuality is celebrated in itself with no reference to child bearing and no suggestion that a sexually eager woman should be seen as a temptress (for contrasting views see Pardes 1992: 118–43). Most revealing of all, the lovers share a mutual relationship, both find joy in the other and unlike the woman's relationship with her brothers, in her intimate relationship no oppressive, hierarchical or patriarchal structures are assumed.

Feminists have variously celebrated the fact that in the Jewish culture reflected in the Song physicality and spirituality is not sharply divided (Ostriker 2000: 40). In LaCocque's words 'its poetic power [is] so irresistible that no cover up has been able to put a conventional fig leaf on the controversial parts' (1998: 2). Trible has also spoken about the Song as sexuality redeemed or 'Paradise Regained' with the woman's sexual seeking of her man recalling a pre-fall Eden where humanity was unafraid of its nakedness (1993). Others have seen a political agenda of liberation within the Song. In the words of Landy, this female poet intended to 'cock a snook at all Puritans' (cited in LaCocque 1998: xi). It is not a text inscribed by obedience but rather by love and voluntary needs. Ostriker has also noted how the Song's metaphorical language is opposed to legalistic language (2000: 48). Even bonds of hierarchy in the world between humans and nature are overcome, with the humans themselves taking on characteristics of plants, animals and their environment. LaCocque accordingly submits that the Song is a critique of conformist societies and of the dualism between body and soul. He also criticises those who see it as a celebration of conjugal love when in fact marriage is never mentioned in the Song at all (1998: 7). The Song, for him, is thus more provocative than many interpretations allow. The lovers 'display their impetuous and passionate feelings, without regard for what society, not to mention sages, considers as propriety and poise' (1998: 8).

While all the above may warrant a veritable feast for feminism among the 'femi'-famine of most of the Bible, one must also beware of uncritically positing the Song as wholly 'feminist', not least because the culture it reflects is so entirely different from our own. Just as Abu-Lughod warns against positing the *ghinnawas* as representative of 'feminist consciousness', we must also be aware that we do not fall foul of anachronistic impositions onto the Song by reading our own liberating agendas onto the text. There is a cultural difference that cannot be uncritically sidestepped. We must also be careful not to propagate an Orientalist perspective that sees our own culture as progressive and empowering for women when compared with other cultures. For one, due to the more communally orientated environment of many 'collectivist' contexts, it often makes little sense to focus on gender or women's issues in isolation. Familial bonds link both men and women and the young and old in much more structured ways. To isolate one group's concerns from the whole unit is to misunderstand the complexity and interrelationships of such contexts.

For different reasons, Exum (2000) has also been careful to warn the feminist to keep his/her wits about them when reading the Song. Among the ten items Exum wants 'every feminist to know about the Song' are the following.

'This text can be hazardous to your critical faculties' (Exum 2000: 25)

Here, Exum refers to Clines's famous reading of the Song as a counter-balance to feminist readings. Clines provides a 'male fantasy' reading of the Song, which he constructs as a male wish dream about the ideal 'sensual' female. The man dreams of a woman who will take the initiative in sex, is strong, seductive, eager and immodest, the proverbial 'whore in the bedroom'. Clines thinks such a figure was so counter-cultural that it must be an imaginative creation of a male author.

However, Exum does not pose the question to Clines, why shouldn't a woman be allowed to have these sorts of fantasies as well? Abu-Lughod and Raheja and Gold document 'voices' of the young persons' (both female and male) desire and sexuality. While the modesty code vetoes such sentiments in public, in poetry women are presented as sexual beings who feel and want much more than their modest, outward behaviour would, at first sight, indicate.

'There are no real women in this text' (Exum 2000: 27) and 'the woman, or women, in this text may be the creations of male authors' (2000: 28)

Exum warns that, despite the presence of a dominant female voice in the Song, female authorship cannot be uncritically assumed. Marginal sentiments need not be less helpful to a feminist if a man, through a woman's voice, expresses them, particularly if a male speaking in a female voice is itself a challenge to cultural ideals. One thing is certain from the expression of subversive sentiments in poetry, namely, those who align themselves ideologically with the status quo do not write such lyrics.

Raheja, Gold and Abu-Lughod have not been lone voices among anthropologists who see poetry channelling other cultural sentiments into an acceptable medium (see Jihad Tracy 1996). Recently, Loya has investigated the work of a Syrian poet called Qabani. Qabani's social world was one used to the separation of the sexes, 'behavioural patterns especially towards the opposite sex were still governed by the traditional taboos of the past' (Loya 1975: 483). He reflected on young Arab males' opportunities for sexual relations with women, which seemed to be a stark choice between 'insipid relationships between the young strictly supervised by families' that led to marriage and 'carnal relations with prostitutes' (Loya 1975: 483). In contrast to this stark choice of sexual encounters, in a collection of poems entitled *My Beloved*, Qabani reflects on the importance of mutual love and desire between one man and one woman. The sentiments expressed illustrate an alternative value of love and the celebration of human sexuality and intimacy among young women *and* men. This love is 'greater than all words':

> I have for love
> Expressions
> Of which no inkpot has ever thought.

Qabani cited in Loya 1975: 490

'There is no gender equality' (Exum 2000: 30)

This is particularly important. Exum sees the man in the Song enjoying autonomy not shared by the woman. She is bound by social and cultural expectations. This is important in establishing that the Song does not reflect a 'feminism' that Western interpreters would recognise. Just as the Indian songs and Bedouin *ghinnawas* did not seek social change, so also the Song does not challenge patriarchy in a revolutionary way. The challenge of the Song is much more concealed; no radical reformation of the system itself is anticipated here.

'Bad things happen to sexually active, forward women' (2000: 30)

Exum focuses on the particular incident of the beating of the watchmen (Song 5:7) and the woman bemoaning the fact that she cannot openly kiss her lover in public (Song 8:1). She cites Brenner's speculation that 'in love poetry, perhaps also in premarital love relations in general, ancient Near Eastern women were allowed a freedom denied to them in other life situations' (cited in Exum 2000: 31). Exum, however, thinks that 'such freedom is difficult to reconcile with the circumscribed social position of women that we find in the rest of the Bible' (2000: 32). But this may be precisely the point. Poetry and song are generic arenas, unlike any other, in which women and young men can covertly express sentiments not normally acceptable in social discourse. Moreover, they are also forms that, while expressing different views, actually serve to reinforce the dominant system in the end. It is not surprising that social traditions and consequences are reflected (and accepted) in the Song, but are also set alongside other sentiments. The patriarchal order is not physically overthrown; indeed the status quo's power to regulate love bonds and its aim to preserve agnatic power is actually enforced.

A code of duty and modesty does not negate the existence of a cultural opposite such as romantic love and desire. Rowe, in a response to an earlier version of this exhibit that I had entitled 'The Joy of Text: Sanctified Subversions in the Song of Songs' has been particularly helpful in refining my thinking here. He notes how Ortner suggests that inherent contradictions in social orders mean that social actors are constantly faced with the decision of how cultural elements such as duty and desire can be reconciled. 'Ordinary praxis' may indeed constitute those behaviours expected by the dominant order. However, 'extraordinary praxis' constitutes something more in line with the young men and women's discourses discussed above. Rowe continues by making pertinent observations about the different statuses of both men and women involved in such practices:

I think it more plausible that the subversions you mentioned come from the young, male and female, rather than men and women generally. Although older women will not have had comparable status to men, they would normally have attained an interest in the cultural schema, i.e. support from appropriately married sons. I noticed in Pakistan how daughters-in-law who fiercely resented their treatment by their husband's mother, later became despotic mothers-in-law. Why? Original sin (?!); or because of the benefits to them of the cultural schema, which offered *one* way of resolving the conflict between duty and love that 'worked'. Perhaps it is always the young who see the clash of goods more clearly or, because they do not immediately benefit from the dominant cultural schema, envisage an alternative world where their concerns take precedence. So by rejecting the dominant 'honour-shame' cultural schema, the Song of Songs also reflects it: 'Joy of Text' is a 'Text of Joy', a vision of love unencumbered by duty.

Rowe 2004

All the above testifies to the fact that we need to get into the cultural skin of the text and see how it challenges, reforms or questions ideals held by those in power. Without trying to cultivate this cultural empathy, we risk, in Downing's words, 'laughing at what the other values, an obvious cultural imperialism' (2003: 143).

Modesty, Love and Desire: The Song of Songs

Jihad Tracy reveals that three general cultural values represented across a variety of Middle Eastern communities are: hospitality and chivalry, bravery and militancy, and honour and shame (1996). The anthropology of particular Middle Eastern communities has variously presented the control of women's sexuality on account of the honour system. Honour is primarily a male value, though it is related in some degree to the sexual behaviour of the female. Its basic measurement is the 'shame' of women, meaning female sexual chastity or, if married, faithfulness and exclusivity. In this way women become important 'capital goods' in the masculine quest for honour. Furthermore,

> Sexuality itself is perceived through a competitive idiom by which men jockey for control over women as objects to achieve narcissistic gratifications and dominance over other men. Sexuality is a form of social power.

> Gilmore 1987: 4

Bergant (1994a) produced a reading of the Song through the lens of the honour and shame model (Chance in his response to Bergant noted that a comparison with Abu-Lughod's work may be useful). Bergant notes certain features of the Song that would seem to dovetail with the model: the role of the brothers in their protection of their sister's honour (Song 1:6; 8:8); references to the mother and the daughters of Jerusalem implying the segregation of female space and interaction; the portrayal of the woman as seductive and in need of control. She also noted a number of deviations from the honour code: the woman evades her brothers' rules; she goes out into the streets alone; she and her lover both celebrate the other's sexual charms. Thus 'contrary to customs suggested by the honour/shame categories, this assertive woman independently preserves her own honour' (1994: 35). Bergant concludes that the Song does not sit easy with the honour code and asks whether 'the sexual relationship depicted here is more characteristic than previously believed?'(1994: 37).

To assume that this Song correlates in some way with an actual event, however, seems misguided. The sexual relationship presented here is one that the status quo would disapprove of; however, talking about such relationships within certain discourses is acceptable, not least because expression of weakness and desire in accepted mediums also shows that individuals submit to the social system.

With this in mind, I want to probe a number of elements of 'a hidden transcript' that are evident in the Song. These do not constitute a total undermining of the social system but rather a culturally legitimate avenue for showing how individuals have mastery and self-control in their day-to-day lives. These sentiments celebrate the desires of the individual and love relationships despite the demands of the modesty system, and show that people feel and express much more than dominant cultural models sometimes reveal. This will be discussed using the categories set out in Table 7.1.

Table 7.1. *Status Quo and Hidden Transcript*

Status Quo: Modesty/Duty	Hidden Transcript: Love and Desire
Male	Female
Father	Mother
Wife	Lover
Brother	Sister
Public	Concealed
Duty	Love

Male and Female

The honour code values modest, shy and quiet women. Al-Khayyat witnesses to a strong need to educate girls in modesty and control in order to avoid scandal. 'It is important to live up to expectations and they are conditioned to feel this way, in order to be good guardians of the family honour' (Al-Khayyat 1990: 22–23). Similarly, Abu-Lughod links female submission to the explicit denial of sexuality in women. Modesty in her opinion,

is a symbolic means of communicating deference to those in the hierarchy who more closely represent the cultural ideals and the social system itself.

This denial is necessary because the greatest threat to the social system and to the authority of those preferred by this system is sexuality itself.

1986a: 119

If the sexual modesty of the female is the centre of the honour code, then the Song certainly subverts cultural expectations. The woman is the protagonist and sexual predator in the Song: 'I am my beloved and his desire is for me' (Song 7:10). She arouses him (Song 8:5) and in many ways defines the male in contrast to cultural expectations. Indeed if anyone is 'objectified' in the text it seems to be the man. His characterisation depends entirely on the woman's description of him and his words to the woman (Song 4:1–7; 6:4–10; 7:2–10). In contrast, her description of the man is directed to the daughters of Jerusalem, thus a certain distancing occurs in the third person form (Song 5:10–16). Although she does acknowledge the existence of a modesty code (Song 1:5–6; 2:1), the woman does not play a submissive role or neglect her sexual desires. The love and mutual attraction between the woman and man is shown in the lengthy speeches characterising the respective delights of each. Their love and desire is mutual and they glory in the sights, scents and presence of the other (Song 2:18–24; 5:2–4).

Father and Mother

In the honour system blood is incredibly important in symbolising links between kin. Often cousin marriage is preferred in the Middle East because this keeps the family blood together. Kin bonds locate this blood in the father's line. Moreover, the father–son relationship provides the model for other hierarchical bonds, including between lineage elders and juniors and patrons and clients. It is interesting, therefore, that 'fathers' are never mentioned in the Song but 'mothers' are. The father's house is replaced by the mother's house (Song 3:4) and the brothers become 'the mother's sons' (Song 1:6).

Such transformations weaken the authority of the hierarchical order and establish an alternative matrifocality. There is also a role reversal, the invitation is from the female and the new kinship is with the mother's house: 'I brought him into my mother's house, and into the chamber of her that conceived me' (Song 3:4). Thus in Landy's opinion, 'love, the true maternal gift, infuses and gives birth to the poem, and is celebrated by it' (1983: 66).

Wife and Lover

Within the Song there are few references to a marital relationship. Notable exceptions are the references to a bride (Song 4:8–12; 5:1) and a wedding feast (Song 3:11). As noted earlier, LaCocque puts importance on the fact that the Song does not seem to state whether the lovers are married or not. However, according to the modesty code, this does not really matter, for whatever the formal union, love does provide a threat to social hierarchy. As shown in the wedding *ghinnawa* cited earlier 'love affairs bring great unrest and anxiety to the family' (1998: 65). The Song could well reflect courting young lovers, but equally it could refer to 'sexual' sentiments that would still need to be concealed from the world while the couple were married. In Abu-Lughod's words, 'By showing sexual modesty before these representatives of the moral system, those lower in the honour-based hierarchy express their respect for the social system' (1986a: 157).

Marriages in the Middle East were, and are, often arranged independently of the consent of those concerned. Love emerged after the wedding and there was no specific ruling against polygamy. What is certainly true is the fact that in agrarian societies the focus of marriage is reproduction. It is notable that this is not referred to at all in the Song, 'thus liberating the erotic from the economic' (LaCocque1998: 47). The woman's sexuality is not tied to motherhood. Her eroticism is celebrated on its own terms. Consequently, as LaCocque recognises 'in her power she magnifies luxury, nature, courtship, eroticism, all things the prophets and sages found objectionable' (1998: 56).

Brother and Sister

The brothers' role in the Song seems reflective of the honour code's protection of female chastity. Their cry illustrates this, 'we have a little sister and she has no breasts, what should we do for our sister, on the day that she is spoken for?' (Song 8:8). Females are defined by their reproduction but also the sexual threat they pose to the family's honour. Indeed the woman in the poem weeps: 'Oh that you were like a brother to me, who nursed at my mother's breast! If I met you outside I would kiss you and none despise me' (Song 8:1). The much-publicised phenomenon of honour killing (the murder of a woman caught in an illicit relationship) shows the extent of such monitoring and could well be reflected in the Song where the sentinels beat the woman and take away her mantle (Song 5:7). El Saadawi, an Iraqi female poet, expresses similar sentiments in her poem entitled 'Wiped Out in Blood':

> For us in the hand of father or brother
> And tomorrow, who knows which desert
> Swallows us, to wash off shame?
>
> cited in Al-Khayyat 1990: 36

In a sense marriage is a relief for the family who need to protect their daughter's or sister's virginity. Moreover, given the importance of blood ties, marriages are often 'a joining of two families, rather than two individuals' (Al-Khayyat 1990: 58). As noted earlier, Abu-Lughod revealed that one way that love is undermined in the Awad 'Ali to protect agnatic bonds of power is to promote cousin marriage and women's links to paternal relatives. It is important, therefore, that the Song puts premium emphasis on the joining of two individuals, one that is not like a brother (Song 8:1), rather than groups.

Public and Concealed

The complex interrelationship between public and concealed action is symptomatic of the modesty code. Lots of the imagery in the Song plays on this dynamic: The man declares 'Your eyes are doves' (Song 4:1) and 'your cheeks are like halves of pomegranate behind your veil' (Song 4:3). He petitions the woman to reveal herself in private:

> O my dove, in the clefts of the rock, in the covert of the cliff, let me see your face, let me hear your voice … Catch us the foxes, the little foxes, that ruin the vineyards for our vineyards are in blossom.
>
> Song 2:14–15

In the Song the couple leave town for their romantic trysts (Song 6:2). Through nature imagery the abandonment of sexual constraints is shown (LaCocque 1998: 23). Longman suggests 'the city, especially the street and the public square is a place teeming with people. Hardly conducive to romance' (2001:130). But this is to miss the main point shown by Abu-Lughod: that the street is connected with sexual immodesty. Du Boulay also witnesses that in honour contexts,

> The opposite of the house, which is the realm of cleanliness and order, is the street, a place of both dirt and immorality. Here, order and control are,

to some extent at least, absent.... The street and the fields that lie beyond
symbolise 'the wild' the outside, the realms of danger. In this outside world
are forces that threaten order and family life. A common euphemism for
adultery is to say that a woman deceived her husband in the street.

1986: 200

What is more, the couple themselves are symbolic of intimacy attained
when public constraints are overcome. They celebrate their relationship
as two individuals 'drunk with love' (Song 5:1) rather than as the honour
code would wish, the bonding of two family units.

Duty and Love

In a culture of arranged marriages love matches are opposed. They
violate the ideal of family control over marriage and represent individual
initiative and hence defiance of the system. Al-Khayyat shows in Iraq
that 'if a man loved a girl and this relationship became known publicly
the girl's family would never agree to marry her to him, as this might
seem to be public acknowledgement of their love affair' (1990: 65).

In her various warnings to the daughters of Jerusalem, the woman
likewise acknowledges the costly price of her love affair. She warns
the women that they have to be ready for love's emotional and social
challenges. Such obstacles however can be overcome if, as the woman
declares, 'his intention towards me was love' (Song 2:4). The Song thus
powerfully celebrates the triumph of love over the constraints of social
expectations: 'Love is strong as death, passion fierce as the grave ...
if one offered for love all the wealth of his house, it would be utterly
scorned' (Song 8:6, 7).

However, while the Song may tell a tale of 'male political power
enthralled by a woman' and a king falling 'in love with a country girl and
forsaking his kingdom' (Landy cited in LaCocque 1998: 19), it remains
only that: a tale. The Song's words are subversive, but they are not a
battle call to revolution. They inform us that cultural models held by
the powerful of society are not the whole story, but admit that theirs is
the hymn sheet from which everyone in the end must sing. Subversions
that are not sanctified will be physically excised.

Conclusions

In light of Abu-Lughod and Raheja and Gold's respective ethnographic
studies, I have argued that poetry and song in certain contexts provide

culturally acceptable avenues for expression of individual sentiments that often contradict the status quo. However, since such poetry does not seek social change, in many ways it is a channel that in the end diffuses concrete cultural subversion. '[Poetry's] message may be sanctified by the ritualised formality of its carrier. Those who benefit least from the system that the honour ideology maintains keep this vision alive' (Abu-Lughod 1986a: 259). In this respect the Song cannot be seen as a revolutionary text in feminist terms, and to label it as such is to ignore its cultural context.

As the Awad 'Ali preserved agnatic bonds from the divisive power of love by way of the modesty code and the Hindu women expressing 'split images', in the end played the public role of the 'obedient wife', so also the Song reflects a culture where human sexuality is closely monitored. What these poems show though is that the dignity of the individual's feelings and the intimate relationships they enjoyed are not totally abolished by the system. People experience and think more than their actions and public *persona* reveals. If this is correct, then the Song of Songs may be an instance where 'actions don't speak louder than words'. It is in words alone that those deemed marginal by dominant systems could find a voice. Downing may be nearer the purpose of the Song when he sees it promoting 'an aesthetics of abundance' (2003: 143).

> The poem imagines what might happen beyond the convention that puts a woman into a man's house and bed and expects them to get on well enough and even enjoy life a bit. And it is the 'beyond', the 'excess' ... [that] can only be expressed, constituted, in terms of the ... metaphorical world, which the Song evokes.
>
> 2003: 143

By both man and woman in the Song expressing sentiments of vulnerability and passion, both in essence become closer. Thus in glorifying love the Song also ameliorates social differences between the individuals. It is only 'in their poetry – these monuments built of words – that we find such evidence, and it speaks more eloquently than marble statues ever could' (Loya 1975: 481). It is perhaps an irony of history that the reception of the Song tried to 'sanctify' the overtly sexual elements by deeming the allegorical and spiritual meaning of the Song to be primary. The fact that contemporary readings of the Song have sought to reclaim its human and sexual nature pay witness to the fact that hidden transcripts always have a way of being heard (while muted, still potentially thunderous) no matter what the party line of the prevailing social or religious establishment.

8

Exhibit 6. Reading with Communities of Goods

Morals, Money and Virtuoso Religion

Curator's Notes

The early Christian 'community of goods' as portrayed in Acts is exhibited alongside similar practices among the community at Qumran and the Hutterites. An 'anthropology of virtue and virtuosity' is presented in reference to all three groups to show how bodily practice and attitudes to material possessions inculcate moral values and 'virtuoso' identity.

Where is Paradise? Where is Perfection? Where is Utopia? These questions have echoed through the folklore and imaginations of virtually all people in all moments of time and place.... They have sought that which could be improved upon, dreamt of what might be made better, and asked: Why not?

M. Stanton

we [must] pay attention to religious virtuosity both as a form of religious salvational orientation and as the nexus of a complex type of communal integrative processes.

I. Silber

If there will ever be a perfect culture it may not be exactly like the Hutterites – but it will be similar.

J. Hostetler and G. Huntington

Max Stanton sees *utopia* as something variously sought in the imaginations of people across the world. While utopia is literally an 'imagined perfect place or state of things', derived from the Greek *ou* ('not') and *topos* ('place') (*Oxford English Dictionary*), it has nonetheless been seen by some as a realisable goal in the present. In the pursuit of it, individuals and groups have variously looked to revelation remote from themselves or enlightenment from within themselves, or made a conscious choice to live differently. The latter often seek to embody an alternative social or economic pattern and cultivate more perfect, fulfilled lives. Among the revolutionaries, visionaries, rebels and religious founders the world over, there have been a select few that have opted to live in a communal manner. From the Amana Colony to the Dukhobors, the Kibbutzim to the Qumran community, the Hutterites to the early Christians, communal living has been used as an avenue to realise social and religious ideals.

In his essay 'All Things Common: A Comparison of Israeli, Hutterite and Latter-Day Saint Communalism' (1992), Stanton provides an important vista for opening discussion. He investigates the failure of communal living in the Latter-Day Saints when compared to the success of the secular Israeli Kibbutz communities and the religious Hutterites. While the Latter-Day Saints are not involved in communal living now, the attempt was made in the past, and the practice is still preserved as 'an expectation of ultimate commitment' (Stanton 1992). He cites the Mormon Book of Doctrine and Covenants, section 82 for evidence of the ideal of sharing 'all things in common':

> You are to be equal, or in other words, you are to have equal claims on the properties, for the benefit of managing the concerns of your stewardships, every man according to his wants and needs, inasmuch as his wants are just.... And all this for the benefit of the church of the living God, that every man may improve upon his talent ... yea, even a hundred fold, to be cast into the Lord's storehouse, to become the common property of the whole church.
>
> Doctrine and Covenants 82:17–19

It could well be true that the primitive stages of religious movements (often small-scale, face-to-face practices) are far more easily able to enact utopian ideals than later, more developed stages. However, like the case of the Mormons, this need not mean that utopian ideals are disregarded, but rather become part of a sacred tradition of ideals. Could this have any bearing on confirming the historicity of Acts' account of the community of goods, despite there being little evidence for the practice elsewhere in the New Testament?

In attempting to probe some of these questions, this exhibit displays the development of 'anthropology of virtue and virtuosity' as embodied in the Acts' account of the community of goods. I build on an earlier essay in which I looked at the social identity and virtuosity constructed in The Community Rule at Qumran (Lawrence 2005). Comparisons here will be drawn with reference to Qumran and Hutterites. Both these use attitudes to possessions as a tool for the development of group virtue, identity and the attainment of a 'perfect state of things'.

I will look at how ritual practices of sharing serve to construct, enforce or protect communal identity in these respective groups. I will also explore how the social complex of virtuosity enables one to see communal practices as constitutive of moral and ethical configuration, in essence serving to develop and sustain 'a ritualised life' (Levi 1987), and embody a 'utopian' state.

It is worth stating at the outset that I am not interested in affirming or denying possible historical connections between the groups surveyed; for example, the Christian tradition linking Acts and the Hutterites. Rather, I believe that studies of diverse groups can shed light on each other, by highlighting points shared in common (money, discipline, etc.). It is also true that study of 'living' groups could shed some light on less-accessible but comparable historical settings, such as the community of goods as presented by Luke in Acts.

Introducing Selected 'Communities of Goods'

Early Christians as Portrayed in Acts

All who believed were together and had all things in common; they would see their possessions and goods and distribute the proceeds to all, as any had need.

Acts 2:44

There was not a needy person among them, for as many as owned lands or houses sold them and brought the proceeds of what was sold. They laid it at the apostle's feet, and it was distributed to each as any had need.

Acts 4:34–35

In Acts, *koinonia* constitutes communion and fellowship that is embodied between believers (those baptised in the name of Jesus) and the Holy

Spirit. For example, directly preceding the first account of the community of goods, Luke tells us, 'and they devoted themselves to the apostles' teaching and fellowship, to the breaking of bread and the prayers ...' (Acts 2:42). The community must remember their common tradition and identity in the Spirit. One way in which this is concretely shown is through sharing of material possessions.

Acts' picture of believers sharing 'all things in common' and surrendering goods for community distribution has very often featured in scholarly discussions regarding the historicity of the practice. Ancient parallels with Greek philosophical utopian ideals and groups idealised and praised in Palestinian Judaism have variously been cited. Capper provides a helpful summary of scholarship in his essay, 'The Palestinian Cultural Context of Earliest Christian Community of Goods' (1995) in which he tries to defend the historicity of the practice in the early church, in the face of the following four main criticisms.

First, the account is seen by many to have too many similarities with Greek philosophical texts picturing a utopian ideal society. Luke is accordingly seen as positing the early Christian community as a realisation of the 'vaunted ideal of Greek Friendship'. The phrase 'all things in common', for example, is found in Plato's 'utopian' writings (*Republic* 4:424). Also friendship, or the idea of friends being of one soul, is a typically Aristotelian concept. Capper argues, though, that any formulation surrounding communal property was bound to have echoes of the philosophical texts idealising such a practice. However, that does not mean the practice itself should therefore be seen as pure fiction in reference to early Christianity.

Second, Peter's rhetorical questions to Ananias and Sapphira are suggested to indicate the voluntary nature of the donation of property: 'while it remained unsold, did it not remain your own? And after it was sold, were not the proceeds at your disposal?' (Acts 5:4). From this it is argued that there was no formally organised community of goods. Capper counters this objection by pointing out that a small group may well have practised the community of goods, and that participation was voluntary. Having willingly volunteered to join the group and surrender possessions, it would be a more serious crime to retract; hence, the stark examples made of Ananias and Sapphira's corruption.

Third, the widows' complaint in Acts 6:1–6 that they are being overlooked, is seen to be evidence that the community of goods was not an institution, but rather a badly run charity scheme. And last, the sharing of property is not testified to elsewhere in the New Testament. Indeed it does not appear again until the monastic patterns of life emerging in the third century. Both these criticisms can be read differently in Capper's opinion. Both assume wrongly that it was a practice uniting the whole church, when actually it could have been a minority practice. Capper suggests that selected members of Jesus' followers could have followed this celebrated form of Jewish piety, following in the tradition of Jesus' disciples sharing the common purse.

No matter what the historicity of the actual practice, however, what is certain is that Luke wanted to present the earliest Christian community acting and living in this manner, and presumably thought important lessons regarding virtue could be taught from its presentation. A community united in the spirit, eating, worshipping, praying and living as one marked this picture of the golden age of the Jerusalem church.

Essenes

The communal routine of the Essenes is described and praised by Philo and Josephus respectively:

> Thus having each day a common life and a common table they are content with the same conditions, lovers of frugality who shun expensive luxury as a disease of both body and soul.
>
> Philo, *Hypothetica* 11:10–11

> It is a law among them [the Essenes], that those who come to them must let what they have be common to the whole order – insomuch, that among them all there is no appearance of poverty or excess of riches, but every one's possessions are intermingled with every other's possessions.
>
> Josephus, *War* 2:122

Although the correlation between the Essenes and the community of Qumran is not absolutely unquestionable, most scholars believe a connection is nonetheless defensible. The Community Rule from Qumran (1QS) pictures the – most probably Essene – community as an embodiment of the new covenant (1QS 1:6 – 2:18). They strive for moral, physical and spiritual wholeness and perfection (1QS 2:2). This excellence is linked with their identity as the 'community of God' (1QS 1:12; 2:22), participants of God's divine congregation. They lived and walked in the 'perfection of the way' (1QS 8:21) and accordingly conformed to all his wishes (1QS 3:8–10).

… [The Rule is] to establish the spirit of holiness in truth eternal … in order to form a most holy community, and a house of the Community for Israel, those who walk in perfection.

1QS 9:3–6

The Dead Sea Scrolls themselves explain the lengthy initiation into the community. After the novice year, the Essene initiate would surrender his property to the common purse:

If it be his destiny, according to the judgment of the Congregation, to enter the Community then shall he be inscribed among his brethren in the order of his rank for the Law, and for justice, and for the pure Meal; his property shall be mixed and he shall offer his counsel and judgment to the Community.

1QS 6:21–23

The person initiated into the society envisioned in 1QS had to bequeath spiritual, material and moral independence, with possessions being bequeathed to the community. Capper also notes that once property had been surrendered, the individuals would be expected to hand over daily wages.

Craftsmen and day laborers pursue their own occupations during the day, but are required each evening to hand over their earnings to the community. Commentators have missed this 'double' structure in the Essene system of property sharing. It is also implied in the (otherwise quite curious) legislation of the *Rule of the Community*, where the novice's 'property and earnings shall be caused to approach into the hand of the man who has the oversight of the earnings of the Many' (1QS VI: 19f) and community members are exhorted to abandon wealth and earnings.

Capper 1995

A variety of activities, including physical movements and functions were subject to strict legislation. It was also necessary to endure episodic scrutiny in which one gave account of behaviour and beliefs, a process that established one's own standing within the group. In short, in a number of areas the initiate was individually limited and answerable to the code of behaviour of the many. Capper suggests that the community of goods was found in various parts of the Essene movement in Palestine (not just a monastic sector), though it was probably not a universal practice.

The Hutterites

John Hostetler's famous ethnography (1974) documents the biggest family-type communal group in the Western world, the Hutterites. The Hutterites are one of a trio of Anabaptist groups (Hutterites, Mennonites and Amish) originating in the Protestant Reformation. The Anabaptists rejected infant baptisms and withdrew to found voluntary church groups. Originally derived from the Austrian Tyrol and Moravia in the sixteenth century, by 1965 the Hutterites numbered 16,500 people in 170 colonies (Hostetler and Huntington 1967: 1). Troeltsch noted that the Hutterites were the only 'community of love' that successfully carried out communal living for any amount of time. Furthermore, while they are now more easily placed in an isolationist sectarian mode, in earlier times they were fiercely conversionist (Hostetler & Huntington 1967: 2).

The Hutterites' central assumptions are that the individual must die to carnal nature and are born spiritually in Christ. This is achieved 'by believing in the Word of God as interpreted by Hutterite sermons, by repentance of sin and by the continuous and daily surrender of self to the will of God in communal living' (Hostetler & Huntington 1967: 7). The colonies, through communal practice, wished to establish a colony of heaven.

> They do not have illusory ideas that their colony is perfect, but they have acquired some utopian-like characteristic in their social patterns: economy of human effort, elimination of extremely poor or wealthy members, a system of distribution that minimizes privileged position, motivation without the incentive of private gain, and a high degree of security for the individual.
>
> Hostetler & Huntington 1967: 1

Hostetler and Huntington note that 'living communally is believed to be the divine order of God' (1967: 11). The Hutterites name their pooling of possessions, *Gütergemeinschaft*, which literally translates 'community of goods'. Need and equality are two extremely important principles. 'Fellowship in holy things requires sharing of temporal goods … the physical existence of human life must be controlled in such a way that the divine pattern is reflected during life' (Hostetler & Huntington 1967: 47).

Anthropology of Virtue and 'Virtuoso Religion'

virtuoso n.—person skilled in technique of a fine art, esp. music
virtuous a.—possessing or showing moral rectitude; chaste

Oxford English Dictionary

Anthropology is a discipline that observes peoples. Its interests lie in embodiment and behaviour. In the sphere of moral questions 'professional anthropologists have tended to focus on "customs" phrased in terms of cultural traits and social institutions'. As a result, '"morals" have largely disappeared into the larger category of "ideology" or "ontology"' (Widlock 2004: 54). In most other disciplinary fields, studies of a more logocentric position have dominated. Theorists look for principles, laws or end results, often giving less attention to the actual practice of morality. It is here that anthropology can help to redress an imbalance.

Thomas Widlock, for example, in a stimulating article entitled 'Sharing by Default? Outline of An Anthropology of Virtue' (2004) sees himself outlining a theory of 'virtuous agency' as opposed to a theory of ethics (2004: 58). He argues that there are 'moral acts – virtues – that realize intrinsic goods' as opposed to viewing practices derived from a code or representative of something else (Widlock 2004: 60). In short, it is the attitudes and actions, as opposed to the ethical dogmas or laws that are primary. His approach is non-consequentialist and realist. In his words,

> It is non-consequentialist in that it accounts for the moral dimension of practices such as sharing and reciprocal exchange without relying on problematic presumptions about net results or ultimate consequences. It is realist in so far as it is based not on rationalist categories but on situated social practices.
>
> Widlock 2004: 53

It links with what Connerton, in his celebrated study of social memory, termed 'inscribed practices' or the 'mnemonics of the body' (Connerton 1989: 74). Connerton ascribes a central function to embodiment and as such in Battaglia's opinion 'profoundly challenge[d] the view that incorporated practices are merely settled for in societies lacking literacy' (Battaglia 1992: 3).

Widlock's position has many affinities with Aristotelian virtue ethics as popularised by MacIntrye and Hauerwas. Perhaps any anthropological ventures into ethics were bound to be attracted to this paradigm. The methods of anthropology are not suited to complex philosophical reflection of the order of Kantian ethics, but rather focus on the stories people treasure, their actions and community practice. Anthropologists would concur with the 'collective' convictions expressed by Aristotle when he noted,

For even if the good of the community coincides with that of the individual, it is clearly a greater and more perfect thing to achieve and preserve that of a community; for while it is desirable to secure what is good in the case of an individual, to do so in the case of a people or a state is something finer and more sublime.

Aristotle, *Nicomachean Ethics*, 64

Widlock was right to see a link between virtue and skill. Etymologically these two can be seen as intimately linked. The Latin *virtus* can refer to moral 'virtue' as well as 'skill', hence the term 'virtuoso', referring to specific skills gained through rigorous training. It was Weber who first used the word 'virtuoso' to refer to specific types of social and religious practice (Weber 1963 [1921]: 162–5). Often virtuoso religious communities see themselves embodying and realising in their life patterns, religious ideals – a utopia. Others building on his work have developed a picture of social and religious virtuosity. It is voluntary; it demands a greater religious commitment than normal; it seeks perfection in the present realm; it involves strict and structured forms of behaviour and action; it is not required of all members of a religion; crucially those embodying it need not do so on account of ascription but only personal choice (based on Silber 1995: 190–99; on virtuosity in reference to the Judaean social world and Sherpa Nepal see Ling 2004). This could be particularly relevant vis-à-vis Capper's argument for a certain section of the early church following communalistic living. It is for this reason that a virtuoso group, unlike a sect, concentrates on dissenters from the group itself, rather than dwelling on distinctions between itself and the rest of humanity. Virtuoso communities must believe that a more perfect life is attainable and that ideals can be met within the group that elsewhere may have been compromised.

No less important is the fact that virtuosity is attained through following a strictly structured life and routine. In this sense it is often connected with the needs and agendas of 'asceticism', a word derived from the Greek *askesis*, denoting training or a set of regulations frequently (though not solely) concerning the body (*Oxford English Dictionary*). Foucault, for example, saw that ascetic practices allowed the individual to be educated into their social environment and the identity assumptions that underlie it (Valantasis 1995: 546). Moxnes found his work particularly useful in understanding how a new social identity for an individual or group is formed:

I suggest that Foucault's perspective on ethics as the formation of self through askesis falls within a broad definition of asceticism, understood as performances within a dominant social environment intended to inaugurate a new subjectivity, different social relations, an alternative symbolic universe.

Valantasis discussed in Moxnes 2003: 14

The Holy Spirit becomes a major symbol in Acts for the purity and holiness of the community. Peter states 'Repent and be baptized every one of you in the name of Jesus Christ, so that your sins may be forgiven and you will receive the gift of the Holy Spirit' (Acts 2:38). The presence of the Holy Spirit is part of the common action of those believing and pooling possessions: 'Day by day they spent much time together in the temple, they broke bread at home and ate their food with glad and generous hearts praising God and having the goodwill of all the people' (Acts 2:46–47). The importance of being filled with the Holy Spirit as a prerequisite for unified life is also underlined in the second account of the community of goods: ' … they were all filled with the Holy Spirit and spoke the word of God with boldness. Now the whole group of those who believed were of one heart and soul, and no one claimed private ownership of any possessions, but everything they owned was held in common' (Acts 4:31–32).

A similar approach to the attainment of virtue is also observable in the Essene movement, where the strict regulations concerning the body are prescribed on account of the fact that the body is no longer the property of the individual alone. Rather, they are now part of the body of the community, 'a most holy community, a house of the community of Israel' (1QS 9:6). Davies agrees that 1QS envisions holiness primarily through the bodies of its members (Davies 1999). He sees collective eating and drinking as central to denoting the unity and integrity of the group. Furthermore, physical purification accompanying atonement rituals (1QS 3:4–6) and meals (1QS 5:13) preserves rigorous social boundaries.

Robert Kugler in his recent article 'Making all Experience Religious: The Hegemony of Ritual at Qumran' (2002) persuasively argues that ritual exercised measurable hegemony over the people at Qumran, making large portions of their experience religious. He limits his definition of ritual to Catherine Bell's typology; however, if the net is cast wider to define ritual in Geertzian terms as 'enacted faith' (Geertz 1957) or 'consecrated behaviour' (Geertz 1966: 28) every aspect of life presented in 1QS could legitimately be seen as ritualistic.

Similarly, Hostetler's ethnographic study of the Hutterites reveals that their form of group communalism saw communal property as a requisite for salvation and thus key to the success of the inculcation of the group's moral values. As a result the individual Hutterites' sense of self was barely distinguishable from communal identity that is given to frugality and deference to the power of the group (Hostetler 1974). The pooling of possessions in this respect is itself a transformative ritual and one that establishes a firm ideological link between the sharing of material goods and the cultivation of group values and ethics. In Hostetler's words,

> The adult Hutterite receives constant social reinforcement.... The constant 'pruning', which adapts each individual to the group, results in a minimizing of differences.... The elimination of extremes and the respect of the order enable members to find satisfaction in the 'narrow way' that leads to salvation. Adult responses to attitudinal questions reveal few doubts, a hardy ego structure, willingness to change for the good of the group, strong beliefs about sharing, and general agreement on questions of morality.
>
> 1974: 244–45

To conclude, identity in the early Jerusalem church presented in Acts, the Essenes and the Hutterites, is inscribed on mind and body through the strict regulation of thought and action. The group establishes and protects boundaries by their actions but also believes that these actions are constitutive of moral formation. All three groups embody what Widlock seemed to mean when he described 'anthropology of virtue' as involving action-based 'virtuous agency' as opposed to ethical theory (2004: 58).

Money and Morals: Virtuosity in Communal Practices of the Early Christians, Essenes and Hutterites

It is important to reiterate that virtuous groups are based on voluntary submission and thus strict censorship of defectors within the group is exercised. Interesting comparisons can be drawn between our three communal groups in this respect as well. It is interesting to note that defection is often seen to occur in situations where the individual will strays from collective control. Wanting more material goods or acclaim for the individual self is often symptomatic of this problem.

As the title of Oakman's recent essay, 'Money in the Moral Universe of the New Testament' (2002) suggests, money can be connected with the manners and virtues promoted in early Christianity. Moreover, it is often in actual actions rather than the citation of principles that virtue is recognised and praised. He notes that money in the ancient world was 'an elite political tool not a universal medium'. As such it inordinately served the powerful, and 'held captive values esteemed by common folk' (2002: 343). Oakman traces a transformation from Jesus' negative attitude to (even rejection of) money as presented in the gospels (Lk. 16:13), to the development of 'moralisms about the love of money' (2002: 347). Such 'moralising' is seen in Acts, the Catholic Epistles, Hebrews and the Pastorals, all of which reflect the urban spread of Christianity throughout the Eastern Empire. Moralising about one's attitude to money appealed to those reconciling their livelihoods and professed belief in Jesus Christ. Accordingly, in Oakman's opinion, these writings:

> show the need to reckon with moneyed interests. The interests displayed do not question the value or utility of money, only its moral place in the heart. Such sentiments speak out of an elite consciousness … [which] now strike[s] the dominant note in the movement.
>
> 2002: 346

In analysis of the moral and social implications of defection from 'religious virtuosity', I take as my starting point Davies' important work on attitudes to money as a medium of the Spirit in Acts. In his contribution to a collection of essays I co-edited (Lawrence & Aguilar 2004), Davies provides an intriguing analysis of elements of the Acts of the Apostles. He utilises anthropological perspectives to show how the Holy Spirit becomes the primary focus, symbol and value of the community of faith in Acts. In his opinion, the Holy Sprit can be linked with what Rappaport termed 'Ultimate Sacred Postulates' or central symbols: 'To act improperly towards these symbols … is to engage in ritual impurity as far as the majority population is concerned' (Davies 2004: 264). Davies speaks about 'moral impurity' (as opposed to ritual purity) being of primary significance in Acts. Purity rules that are connected to boundary maintenance have been transformed to focus on internal relationships in the church. 'Rules once serving to separate insider from outsider … became principles for intra-community life' (Davies 2002: 101). He cites the evidence of the Council of Jerusalem to show that Gentiles can be members of the church for they have, like other believers, been cleansed and given the Holy Spirit. He continues,

In the Acts of the Apostles the means by which grace takes effect and the conquest is achieved is through the Holy Spirit, the power that follows from Christ's resurrection. The old nature … grounded in reciprocity and described in terms of 'law', is replaced by a new nature symbolized by 'spirit'. In the new found power of 'spirit' the convert sets out to conquer the old nature wherever it may be found.

(Davies 2002: 72

Davies connects ideas of 'inalienable gifts' with the Holy Spirit. Citing Godlier's proposal regarding a 'fourth form of giving' (to add to Mauss's giving, receiving and giving again) Davies introduces 'inalienable gifts' that include giving to the gods. 'Such gifts, he [Godlier] argues, afford a kind of "anchorage in time", relating people to their origin, they also focus symbolic value and the power of the imagination' (Davies 2004: 268). Davies proposes that the Holy Spirit in Acts serves this function: linking believers to their origins in Jesus and his resurrection.

For Davies the Spirit replaces blood as a central 'moral purity'. Furthermore, money becomes one medium through which 'impurity' or assaults against the Spirit can be performed. He cites a number of instances in Acts where money seems to be connected with moral behaviour. These include Judas' betrayal (Acts 1:18); Joseph, Ananias and Sapphira's part in pooling possessions (Acts 4:36–37; 5:1–12); The distribution of money to the widows (Acts 6:1); Cornelius's alms-giving (Acts 10:2); converted magicians burning their books worth 50,000 pieces of silver (Acts 19:19); Paul's evasion of bribes (Acts 24:26) and his own subsistence (Acts 28:30).

This can be corroborated by reference to the proper use of money in Luke's Gospel. He is the evangelist who most explicitly links economics with belief, giving parables dealing with the proper use of money: Debtors (Lk. 7:41–43); the Rich Man (Lk. 12:16–21); the Unjust Steward (Lk. 16:1–8); the Rich Man and Lazarus (Lk. 16:19–31); and the Pounds (Lk. 19:11–27). Moreover narratives about the rich young man who cannot forsake his riches for Jesus (Lk. 18:18–23) and the poverty-stricken widow who gives the money she needs to live to God (Lk. 21:1–4) reflect similar interests. Davies seems correct in viewing unseemly use of wealth in relation to the Spirit as being 'virtuous' and other dealings less so. While the language of purity is not explicitly used in these passages, the sentiment of proper practices of faith vis-à-vis money can, I think, legitimately be cast in a 'purity' semantic range.

In the community of goods traditions, a positive example of giving is provided by Joseph, named Barnabas by the apostles in Acts 4:36. His future role in the mission is introduced at this point but his virtue and character is legitimised by his actions vis-à-vis money and possessions. He 'sold a field he owned and brought the money and put it at the apostles' feet' (Acts 4:37). The text seems to imply that this was an entirely free and voluntary action on Barnabas's part, but it serves as a positive foil to the episode that directly follows.

The failures and fate of Ananias and Sapphira need few introductions. They lied, not only to the community but also more grievously to the Holy Spirit (Acts 5:3), a sin that Jesus had characterised as unforgivable (Mt. 12:31–32). The text itself thus provides a link between money, morals and virtue. They exemplify a cleavage between external and internal disposition and as such constitute a threat to community cohesion and boundaries. Deception of the community is central to their crime. The voluntary nature of their contribution, like Barnabas's, is underlined in Peter's declaration 'While it remained unsold, did it not remain your own? And after it was sold, were not the proceeds at your disposal?' (Acts 5:4).

Ananias's crime does not seem to be one of not surrendering his property, he could have kept everything, and he was under no obligation. Rather, by professing one belief and not aligning his actions fully with that belief, he was guilty of hypocrisy (literally stage-playing). While appearing to have magnanimously denoted his wealth to the community and poor, he in fact withheld some for his own selfish benefit. Satan fills his heart (Acts 5: 3) in a similar manner to Judas in Luke 22: 3, another individual who offends and betrays by an association with money. The message is transparent – God punishes him for his betrayal of the Spirit.

Davies is instructive in his reading of this episode. He interprets the deception of Ananias and Sapphira as representative of moral impurity. Apostates, such as Ananias and Sapphira, 'embody' what Douglas termed 'internal contradictions' or 'autonomous pollutions' arising in situations where external behaviours and internal motivations contradict. Incorrect behaviour vis-à-vis the Spirit, constitutes 'pollution', defined by the *Encyclopedia of Social and Cultural Anthropology* as 'opposed to purity, disturbs equilibrium destroys or confuses desirable boundaries and states' (Barnard & Spencer 1996: 437). The maintenance of symmetry and protection of identity is particularly important in the famous account of the early Christian community pooling their resources. Davies accordingly notes,

> The case of Ananias and Sapphira ... makes greater sense if discussed in terms of 'blasphemy' against, lying to or tempting the Spirit, as in our

final chapter (Acts 5:3, 9). Blasphemy against the Spirit becomes a direct symbolic equivalent of ritual impurity involving blood or death.

Davies 2002: 106

Ananias does not trust in God's goodness and assaults the community; as a result fear is said to reverberate across the community (Acts 5:5). Sapphira, unaware of what has happened to her husband, echoes his lies and shares his fate (Acts 5:10). Their story would no doubt act as a powerful policing of deceit and offences against the Spirit. Relevant here also is the fact that many of the virtue/vice lists in the New Testament while seemingly focusing on internal/external boundaries, also implicitly attest to in-group maintenance. For example, in Galatians after listing vices and virtues Paul concludes, 'If we live by the Spirit, let us also be guided by the Spirit. Let us not become conceited, competing against one another, envying one another' (Gal. 5:25–26). Similar dynamics are apparent in 1 Corinthians 5 and 6, where the brother becomes an outsider; for while 'God will judge those outside' the community in-group must 'drive out the wicked person from among you' (1 Cor. 5:13).

A censorship of defectors from the communal living of the Essenes is also apparent in 1QS. Penalties for contravention of group principles are diverse – ranging from cutting food to permanent exclusion (1QS 6:24 – 7:25). Interesting here is the fact that the anti-model to group identity is not provided by out-groups alone, but also, as is characteristic of religious virtuosity, by in-group members who reject the way or do not complete initiation: '... his spirit will be obliterated, the dry with the moist, without mercy. May God's anger and the wrath of his verdicts consume him for everlasting destruction' (1QS 2:15). Those negatively identified are characterised as rejecting their relational identity and following their own wants and needs, and are accordingly sanctioned. Similar to Davies' argument about offences against the Holy Spirit in Acts constituting moral impurity, 1QS accordingly uses the idiom of impurity to symbolise those rejecting their calling while in the group:

> Anyone who declines to enter [the covenant of Go]d in order to walk in the stubbornness of his heart shall not [enter the Com]munity of his truth, since his soul loathes the disciplines of knowledge of just judgments. He has not the strength to convert his life and shall not be counted with the upright. His knowledge, his energy and his wealth shall not enter the council of the

Community because he ploughs in the mud of wickedness and there are stains on his conversion. He shall not be justified while he maintains the stubbornness of his heart, since he regards darkness as paths of light. In the source of the perfect, he shall not be counted. He will not become clean by acts of atonement, nor shall cleansing waters purify him.

1QS 2:25; 3:1–4

Concern over desertion and disloyalty can also be seen in the way these vices are negatively characterised. The community is called to believe that 'God will have no mercy for all those who deviate from the path' (1QS 10:20–21).

Similar dynamics are shown in Hartse's discussion of 'The Emotional Acculturation of Hutterite Defectors' (1994), which explores how certain members started to 'openly reject communal life as the only path to salvation; instead favoring personal relationship with Christ' (1994: 69). She cites Peter et al.'s 1992 article, which discusses defection in the group. These anthropologists see a competition in the mind of defectors between *Gelassenheit* (yielding individual will to God) and *Gütergemeinschaft*. Peter et al. argue that the rationale of many defectors is that Hutterite colonies no longer took *Gelassenheit* as their goal. Personal involvement was overridden by what they saw as forced submission to the collective. Peter et al. saw technological innovations leading to increased indivdualisation and privatisation. This in turn led to certain members wanting more for their individual selves. Hartse similarly argues,

> often the Hutterite defector's goals revolve around such concerns as obtaining a farm of his own or an automobile or money.... Emotional acculturation occurs through the adoption by defectors of the dominant society's concept of emotion and self ... these former Hutterites now emphasise the internal over the external, emotion over rational thought.

1994: 83

Hostetler and Huntingdon document that the causes of defection from a communal vision are twofold in the Hutterites' opinion. First, too much wealth has an adverse influence on the colony's spiritual vision: second, the temptations of individuals to illegitimately gain goods or withhold money from the community is a danger when individual wills stray from the community vision (Hostetler & Huntington 1967: 101). For this reason, Hostetler and Huntington explain, distrust of individual motives is acknowledged as a central part of the colony system. As one member elucidated, 'In the fear of God we observe and watch one another … telling each his faults, warning, and rebuking with all diligence' (Hostetler & Huntington 1967: 50). The Hutterites undoubtedly recognised that wealth was one means by which 'impurity' or dissension from community values could be fostered.

> Carnal men are viewed as living in perpetual covetousness by making property, food, land, and created things the object of private gain … God's gifts are not given to one member alone, but for the whole body with its members … privately owned material possessions lead human beings away from God.
>
> Hostetler & Huntington 1967: 12

The present existence must always be ultimately controlled by a spiritual order. If goods were central in one's life, then one's relationship with God would be under threat. Not only the giving of goods, but perhaps more importantly, *Gelassenheit* (self-giving or surrender) to the will of God was fundamental to the longevity of the Hutterites' communal living.

In essence, this practice itself shows that the community of faith is more important than the individual and 'the corporate group has the power to exclude and to punish, to forgive and to readmit' (Hostetler & Huntington 1967: 12). Moreover 'sin must be punished in proportion to its severity. Unconfessed sins will be held against the individual on the Day of Judgment and punishment will be meted out in the afterlife' (Hostetler & Huntington 1967: 12). This seems to strike more than a *pianissimo* chord with the ethos projected in the Ananias and Sapphira episode and the harsh warnings against revolt in 1QS. In such instances the community, as a collective, police and promote 'moral purity', and protect the spiritual identity of the group. This is specifically related to morality, of the order that Davies seemed to be referring to when he first noticed the potential association of impurity with selfish use of material goods as offences against the Spirit, in Acts.

Conclusion

Morals, money and virtuosity are profoundly interrelated. In the three communities of goods surveyed, collective control is enforced through supervision of individual bodies. Akin to the importance of embodied practice in anthropology of virtue and virtuoso religion, each community is a group not only of belief, but also worship, work, leisure, etc. The three groups fuse the economic with the religious, and in shaping patterns within respective contexts have sought to manage the problems of disintegration, of idiosyncratic goals and individual defection.

Stanton notes that one of the factors that have led to the success of the Hutterite communal living has been the relatively small size of their colonies (around a hundred members). In his opinion 'this allows for a high degree of daily face-to-face interaction. No person is very far removed physically or socially from the decision-makers in the group' (Stanton 1992). Presumably the same would be true for those Essenes that lived communally. However, in the rapid expansion of the early Christian movement, as communities grew larger and more dispersed, perhaps the utopian action of pooling possessions became 'utopian' ideal.

Moreover, Stanton notes that the Constitution of the Hutterian Brethren Church stipulates strict and specific rules about the giving of property, whereas the United Order of the Latter-Day Saints (a communal group that failed to sustain a community of goods practice) was far more vague. Acts also provides no specific rules, but rather two very idyllic clips of the early Jerusalem church living communally. Elsewhere in the New Testament, as Capper notes, we are offered no evidence of such a practice. However, maybe like the Latter-Day Saints, the utopian spirit-led 'primitive' Jerusalem Church became symbolic of a place apart from the world, but one that nonetheless provides a symbolic example for future generations.

This could offer an interesting slant on the historicity debate regarding the authenticity of the historical community of goods in the early Jerusalem church. By viewing this practice alongside living groups who practically lived in this manner, but after development, idealised the practice, the option is opened to not necessarily rejecting the historicity of the community of goods out of hand, despite it never being catalogued elsewhere in the New Testament.

Following this hypothetical 'development' from concrete practice to utopian ideal, Oakman is right that the more radical of Jesus' sayings regarding wealth were sieved out in favour of moralisms regarding love of money in the Catholic Epistles, Hebrews and the Pastorals. Some examples include:

> But those who desire to be rich fall into temptation, into a snare, into many senseless and hurtful desires that plunge men into ruin and destruction. For the love of money is the root of all evils; it is through this craving that

some have wandered away from the faith and pierced their hearts with many pangs.

1 Tim. 6:9–10

But understand this, that in the last days there will come times of stress. For men will be lovers of self, lovers of money, proud, arrogant, abusive, disobedient to their parents, ungrateful, unholy.

2 Tim. 3:1–2)

Keep your life free from love of money, and be content with what you have; for he has said, "I will never fail you nor forsake you".

Heb. 13:5

Perhaps this is an inevitable part of development and growth. Wesley's warning about the success of new movements makes salutary reading in this respect,

I do not see how it is possible, in the nature of things, for any true religion to continue long. For religion must necessarily produce industry and frugality … cannot but produce riches. But as riches increase, so will love of the world, in all its branches.

Wesley cited in Burns 1987: 100

It is perhaps this that is the greater lesson to be learnt from Acts. Giving up possessions was just one form of self-surrender required by the Spirit. Luke's presentation of the community as one in Spirit presumably informed and impressed on his readers not individual, but collective living. Tonkin notes that 'in framing collective interpretations of the past social memory also actively created the experience of commonality' (Tonkin 1992: 111–21). Social memory in this respect glosses over individual, personal memory and presents the world in more collective terms. If the practice was historical and had died out by the time Luke wrote, he could be following other groups in keeping alive the memory of primitive ideals that are increasingly unrealisable as a movement develops and grows. While a radical tradition can be embodied at the beginning of movements, spiritualising is one clear strategy of acknowledging the ideal's importance even if not physically practising it any more (somewhat like the developmental dynamics vis-à-vis communal living in the Latter-Day Saints).

It is perhaps a tragedy that inheritors of the Acts traditions today, are largely dismissive of Luke's picture of primitive ideals, often reinterpreting or questioning their historicity in some way. Coupling money and morals is perhaps too dangerous a cocktail (it shakes and stirs), only those pursuing virtuoso religions are willing to sip and taste a utopian elixir here in the present.

9

Exhibit 7. Reading with Food and Memory

Consuming at Corinth

Curator's Notes

This exhibit displays an ethnography of food and memory (the embedding of remembrance in eating's social and sensory aspects) alongside 1 Corinthians' account of the celebration of the Lord's Supper and the overcoming of social divisions that Paul effects through the use of an 'embodiment' metaphor.

Why would anyone want to remember what they had eaten?

D. Sutton

All sorts of ideological barriers exist between intellectual activity and the consumption of natural produce. The head and the stomach are at odds.... We have to choose whether to speak or to eat: we must not speak with our mouth full.

M. Jeanneret

We who are many are one body, for we all partake of the one bread.

1 Corinthians 10: 17

Food bestows interpreters with food for thought. It is, according to Pottier 'the primary gift and repository of condensed social meanings' (1996: 238). One does not need to delve too far into scripture to witness this. Food regulations establish and confirm relationships with the divine (Lev. 11; Deut. 14). Prescriptions regarding identity render all food consecrated to other gods as illegitimate, likewise diseased and torn flesh ravaged by wild beasts is rejected (Ex. 34:15). Expectations are laid down about who can eat with who (Gen. 43:32; Jn. 4:9; Mt. 9:11) and, as a central part of household life, food also acts as a medium of social relations. Hospitality (Gen. 18:7; 19:3; 2 Sam. 3:20; 2 Kgs. 6:23; Lk. 15:23), special occasions, birthdays (Gen. 40:20; Job 1:4; Mt. 14:6) and marriages (Judg. 14:10; Gen. 29:22) are all marked by feasting.

Theological truths are also expressed and imprinted on believers' minds through the medium and metaphor of food. God's abundance and provision (Gen. 1:29; Ps.104:14; Deut. 8:13) is displayed and his plan and order for creation is defined by food associations. Just as humanity's disobedience is portrayed through the act of eating (Gen. 2:17), so covenant obligations are also expressed in part through laws surrounding food. Within the New Testament, eating itself becomes symbolic of salvation (Rev. 9:9); Jesus eats with those normally deemed unworthy and enacts kingdom ethics in the present. Jesus himself even becomes the spiritual food of his followers, who in turn carry in their bodies Jesus' death 'so that the life of Jesus may be made visible in mortal flesh' (2 Cor. 4:11).

Robertson Smith was one of the first anthropologists to adopt food as an explicit focus in ethnography. Studying both Arab and Israelite sacrificial patterns he stated,

> The very act of eating and drinking with a man was a symbol and a con-
> firmation of fellowship and mutual social obligations.... Those who sit at
> meat together are united for all social effects; those who do not eat together
> are aliens to one another, without fellowship in religion and without
> reciprocal duties.
>
> Robertson Smith cited in Feeley-Harnik 1981: 11

Robertson Smith described how totemic group members ritually sacrificed an animal and ate it 'with a sense of joyous optimism and of union with their ancestor-gods' (Davies 2002: 81). In a similar vein, Radcliffe-Brown discussed food unions in the Andaman Islands (1948) and Richards (1939) looked at the various links between the agricultural environment and community feasting in the Bemba. Levi Strauss produced his magnum opus on mythology surrounding food – both raw and cooked (Lévi-Strauss 1970); and Mary Douglas analysed Hebrew food taboos grounded in thinking on ethnicity, boundaries and the protection of group identity, for 'holiness requires that different classes of things shall not be confused' (Douglas 1992 [1966]: 53).

If food has been 'good to think with' in anthropology, does it contribute in any way to social memory? It is this question that will preoccupy this exhibit. I draw on David Sutton's recent ethnography, *Remembrance of Repasts: An Anthropology of Food and Memory* (2001), to bring insights to bear on 1 Corinthians, a text that offers lots of material centred on embodiment, eating and social practice, most notably surrounding the transcendence of social division and conflict.

Food and Memory: An Anthropological Perspective

Douglas's 1971 work *Deciphering the Meal* explored relationships between different sorts of eating, particularly festive feasts and daily consumption. Douglas's use of food as a repository of memory, evoking and providing concrete links with other occasions provides the starting point for Sutton's own study (2001). Sutton conducted fieldwork on the Greek island of Kalymos, and soon became aware that food was a central part of the island people's identity. He writes, 'In telling me to use the transitory and repetitive act of eating as a medium for the more enduring act of remembering, they were, in fact, telling me to act like a Kalymnian' (Sutton 2001: 2).

Sutton noted how food and consumption was a powerful repository of social memories, concealing 'powerful meanings and structures under the cloak of the mundane and the quotidian' (Sutton 2001: 3). In establishing this, Sutton adopts Connerton's celebrated work on *How Societies Remember* (1989), which draws a pertinent distinction between 'inscribed' (written) forms of memories and 'incorporated' (embodied) memories. The latter are of course the most relevant in relation to food and feasting.

> An image of the past, even in the form of a master narrative, is conveyed and sustained by ritual performances. And this means that what is remembered in commemorative ceremonies is something in addition to a collectively organized variant of personal or cognitive memory. For if ceremonies are to work for their participants, if they are to be persuasive to them, then those participants must not be simply cognitively competent to execute the performance; *they must be habituated to those performances. This habituation is to be found ... in the bodily substrate of the performance.*
>
> My italicisation, Connerton cited in Sutton 2001: 12

Sutton explores three interrelated themes in his book. First, the ways in which ritual and everyday forms of eating are associated and affirm each other. He shows how seasonal cycles, births and deaths are all linked with food rituals. But it is not only 'loud' and prominent rituals, but also the commonplace forms of eating that can carry and convey powerful symbolisms. Thus 'the mundane and extraordinary eating are connected: mutually entailed in systems of meaning ... metaphors of each other' (Sutton 2001: 20).

Second, Sutton explores the creation of memories through narratives surrounding food and exchange (generosity, hospitality, or lack of these). He adopts Munn's 1986 work on the reciprocity of exchange to elucidate his thinking here. She looked at Gawan trading patterns, which 'act on the mind of the other', connected the present to the past and future and specifically linked gift-debt with remembering:

> The memory to be induced by the donor in the recipient ... projects the recipient's mind toward the future ... in this way extending the transaction (the past) and the particular media involved beyond themselves and holding them, as it were, in the form of an ongoing potentiality that is not finished.... By remembering, one keeps the objective medium or act from disappearing.
>
> Munn cited in Sutton 2001: 46

Sutton emphasises the 'future' possibilities of remembering in food, which is a particularly powerful 'embodied' medium precisely because it 'internalized the debt to the other' (Sutton 2001: 46). The donors of the food are themselves involved in this act of remembering as 'absent presence' (Battaglia's estimation cited by Sutton 2001: 47).

Third, Sutton explores the embodied practices of eating and the links of these to sensory experiences. Citing Tilley, Sutton underlines the fact that metaphors related to sensory experience are central to memory:

> '"They cooked the land" is likely to be remembered far longer than a state-ment such as "they burnt the forest". In so far as metaphors can evoke vivid mental images they facilitate memory' (Tilley 1999: 8).... Through metaphor, Kalymnians seem to be providing the powerful images that might facilitate recall.
>
> Sutton 2001: 97

Also, building on Fernandez's ethnographic description, Sutton argues that the performative dimension of eating, and the images it conveys, produces what could be called a 'cosmology of participation' that underlines and protects the unity of a community (Sutton 2001:

76). Sutton adopts the notion of *synesthesia*, which he defines as 'the crossing of experiences from different sensory registers' (2001: 17). These aid in what Fernadez described as 'returning to the whole' in contexts of religious revitalisation (Sutton 2001: 17). Sutton adds, 'unlike vision, which is divided up into developed categorical systems such as named colors, taste and smell have relatively few verbalized categories associated with them' and as such 'become evocative of social situations with which they are associated' (Sutton 2001: 17).

Anthropology, as an observing discipline, views memory less in terms of psychological mechanisms and more in terms of corporeal practices. In this respect Sutton is convincing in the associations he draws between food and memories, and shows how these concerns illustrate key interests, not only in anthropology but any social enquiry – not least in understanding Paul's advice to the church at Corinth.

The Consuming 'Body' at Corinth

Problems surrounding food, the body and sex were rife in Corinth. With good reason the Corinthian church has accordingly been referred to as a 'community divided' and 'church in crisis'. The social, ethnic and religious diversity that hallmarked the city as a whole also indelibly marked the group of Christ followers that met there. Such distinctions mixed a potentially explosive and deadly cocktail of opposing interests and expectations. Paul, the great apostle to the Gentiles, undoubtedly had his work cut out in trying to find a viable way through this fragmenting quagmire of immorality, divergence and strife that was 'Christianity at Corinth'.

From the outset, it is clear that Paul faces the hard task of damping down disputes on a number of fronts. In chapter 1, four main points of contention are outlined: first, in general terms, is the fermenting wound of conflict marring the community (1 Cor. 1:10–11); second, the boasting in a particular leader, which threatens a unified vision of the whole church (1 Cor. 1:12); third, an attachment to the wisdom of the world, presumably reflecting the world's value system, as opposed to the wisdom of Christ crucified (1 Cor. 1:17); fourth, glorying in one's spiritual status, which inevitably occurs to the exclusion of others who appear not to be blessed with such gifts (1 Cor. 1:26–29). As the epistle goes on, differing opinions on sexual immorality, idol meat, spiritual gifts and the form of the resurrection are among other ideological and social problems contributing to disunity.

One of Paul's basic tactics in overcoming these problems is the wielding of rhetoric focused on an 'embodiment' metaphor. Corinthian Christians are reminded that they are collectively 'the body of Christ and individually members of it' (1 Cor. 12:27). Moreover, each part of the body has an elemental part to play, so much so that 'if one member suffers, all suffer together with it; if one member is honoured, all rejoice together with it' (1 Cor. 12:24).

The monumental force of metaphorical embodiment in this epistle has been immeasurably enlightened by Martin's celebrated book, *The Corinthian Body* (1995). Martin asserts that all the various conflicts reflected in 1 Corinthians find their genesis in diverse and conflicting constructions of the ancient body. His argument is forceful and largely persuasive that those addressed as the 'Strong' in Corinth have a hierarchical view of the physical body, which in turn impacts and destabilises Paul's ideal of the unified, egalitarian body of faith. Martin explains,

> Paul and (probably) the majority of the Corinthian Christians saw the body as a dangerously permeable entity threatened by polluting agents. A minority in the Corinthian Church ('the Strong') stressed the hierarchical arrangement of the body and the proper balance of its constituents, without evincing much concern over body boundaries or pollution. The different stances taken by Paul and this minority group on various subjects – rhetoric and philosophy, eating meat that had been sacrificed to idols, prostitution, sexual desire, marriage, speaking in tongues, the resurrection of the body, and the veiling of women during prophecy – spring from different assumptions regarding both the individual human body and the social body – in this case, the church as the body of Christ. Furthermore these positions correlate with socio-economic status, the strong being the higher-status group, who enjoy a relatively secure economic position and high level of education, and Paul, like many members of the Corinthian Church, being among the less educated, less well-off inhabitants of the Roman Empire.
>
> 1995: xv

Graeco-Roman philosophical thought could have encouraged the idea that there was a soul/flesh hierarchical division of parts within the body. However, Paul makes it clear that all bodily facets are equally important: itself a subversive development from Graeco-Roman conceptions of the body in political discourse. In Martin's opinion, for Paul:

The higher elements of the body are called upon to yield to the lower elements. The spirit is to yield to the mind, the head to the genitals, the strong to the weak; and the higher-status Christians to those of lower status. In all cases, what Paul says of the human body, he expects to be applied in the church, the body of Christ 'in order that there be no schism in the body' (12:25; 1:10).

Martin 1995: 103

The fact that Paul utilises the physical body as a model for the social body is further explored in his rejection of sexual immorality within the community. He writes 'The body is not meant for immorality, but for the Lord, and the Lord for the body' (1 Cor. 6:13). To associate oneself with someone or something other than the Lord was to negate one's identity as Christian.

Food and consumption are also tellingly used as 'embodied practices' to make theological points within the epistle. Food appears with notable frequency in 1 Corinthians and serves as a powerful and evocative image for debate on other issues. Paul tells the immature Corinthian believers that they are given milk as opposed to solid food on account of their infantile spiritual status (1 Cor. 3:1–2). In chapter 5, Paul urges for the Christian 'not to even eat with' (1 Cor. 5:11) those who are drunkards, robbers, idolaters and the like. In chapter 10 he presents the spiritual rock from which food and drink comes throughout history as Christ (1 Cor. 10:3). Paul, it seems, uses food and food-related contexts to express central truths about the identity markers of Christianity – it would not be a complete overstatement to call him a *'gastropolitician'*, a term used by Appadurai (1981) to describe Hindus who use food to propose and protect certain social structures.

Food and consumption's metaphorical appeal in 1 Corinthians should come as no surprise, for as McGowan notes, food in many cultures 'provides a powerful medium for the expression of power relations, and one which invokes the legitimacy which the natural order so often brings with it' (McGowan 1999: 1). This is particularly true in the controversy regarding the eating of idol meat in 1 Corinthians 8 – 10. The problem at hand seems not just to be the consumption of idol meat per se (menu) but rather the social interaction within pagan temples (venue), which could range from club meetings to family celebrations. Paul appeals to the Christian believers' scruples and urges them to abstain from such environments in order to preserve, and affirm, their religious identity. Theissen further suggests that there would be discrepancies between the viewpoints of strong and weak vis-à-vis meat offered to idols. He argues that the poor would only have been able to eat meat at pagan religious events, whereas the rich would not think of that arena alone in connection with eating meat (1982: 121–43). In short, the ideological implications of eating meat and being within the temple varied according to the respective social status of each member. This seems to illustrate something of McGowan's broader point regarding sacrificial eating:

> Acceptance or rejection of the cuisine of sacrifice was not merely a symbolic enactment of social conflict but constituted conflict itself.... To eat or not to eat was not merely a question of signalling allegiance, but of acting that allegiance out in the most important and obvious way ... to eat it literally to internalize the reality of the gods whom one served.
>
> McGowan 1999: 226

The celebration of the Lord's Supper (1 Cor. 11) is another prominent food- and embodiment-centred discourse, which also reflects, via imitation of Graeco-Roman feasting protocol, a community divided, who eat in the shadow of social power structures, as opposed to the ethos of post-baptismal equality. It is often said that we would not have Paul's primitive account of the celebration of the Lord's Supper, if the Corinthians had celebrated it properly in the first place. This is implicitly strong grist to the mill that memory as 'incorporating practices' (embodied) rather than 'inscribing practices' (written) were primary in the earliest life of Christianity. Presumably this was even more important if recruitment to the fledgling movement included those illiterates for whom embodied practice was the primary means of education, initiation and remembrance of the key aspects of their new-found faith.

Interesting is the fact that the call to remembrance (*anamnēsis*) is absent from Mark and Matthew's version of the meal in the upper room; Luke mentions remembrance (Lk. 22:19) but only in reference to the bread, not the wine. It is only Paul in his correspondence with the Corinthian church whose version repetitively incorporates memory as a key notion throughout the meal and ritual (1 Cor. 11:23, 25). On account of this, here I will 'read with' Sutton's threefold discussion of food and memory (documenting links between ritual and everyday eating; narratives surrounding food exchange; embodied/sensory aspects of food and eating) in relation to Paul's advice regarding the celebration in Corinth of the Lord's Supper.

Food and Memory: The Lord's Supper

Ritual and Everyday Eating

For Sutton, food rituals and religious practice are to be related to more everyday eating through symbolic and ethical means. It is particularly interesting therefore that Paul seems to picture the rites of the Lord's Supper being celebrated within an ordinary meal, made up of food brought by various participants from home (1 Cor. 11:21). The breaking of the bread seems to have occurred first, then an intervening meal was eaten and finally the meal was concluded with the blessing and distribution of wine (1 Cor. 11:25). The ritual literally 'bracketed' the entire feast. Presumably the intervening meal would have followed social dining expectations of the day. Theissen suggests that the meal may have been perceived by some as an equivalent to a Roman festal or cultic meal. He accordingly surmises that the higher status Christians would act as benefactors of both venue and food, on such occasions (Theissen 1982: 147–63). As meat would usually have been served only to the elite, he hypothesises that different meals were eaten by the participants and that the elite were gorging themselves (in the intervening meal) while the poor went hungry. This inequality enforced by social convention (different food for respective levels, reticence to share food with those from different social levels, etc.) leads Paul to conclude that the mixing of ethos surrounding 'ritual and everyday' eating renders the Corinthian celebration of the Lord's Supper invalid (1 Cor. 11:20).

Sutton saw food rituals as key sites of memory linking the present with the past and future. This is relevant to the fact that Paul reinforces the idea of the 'incorporated' traditions being passed down through time: 'For I received (*parelabon*) from the Lord, what I also handed on (*paredōka*) to you' (1 Cor. 11:23). Sutton also notes how food can orientate people to future events: 'the idea of prospective abundance is most clearly expressed in people's attitudes toward fasting periods, and the feasts that follow them' (Sutton 2001: 29). Paul links the present with the future, through the assertion that the ritual feast itself acts to 'proclaim the Lord's death until he comes' (1 Cor. 11:26). In short, he sees ritual repetition as important in consolidating powerful feelings of unity through the passing of time and in awaiting the final eschatological consummation. The Lord's Supper itself also holds at its heart, the image of Passover. The bread and wine are evocative of this feast (Ex. 12; Deut. 16) and Jesus aligns himself with the sacrificial lamb and embodies, proclaims and promises future deliverance.

Also important is the link between food and the identity of the one in whose name feasting people meet. Sutton notes for example how in mortuary feasts, 'the dead participate in life again because their names are heard again' (Sutton 2001: 35). It is not insignificant in this respect that Connerton views the Eucharist as a rite of incorporation and commemoration par excellence, remembering the atoning, salvific death of Christ. Paul repeats, as noted above, the command of remembrance in relation to both bread and wine, which in Connerton's opinion constitutes:

> A special kind of actualisation, and it is in its sacramental aspect that liturgical language has its most evidently actualising quality. In repeating the words of the Last Supper, for instance, the celebrant is held to repeat once again that which Jesus Christ did, in giving again to the words which Christ used the same efficacy which Christ gave them, by conferring on those words again the power to do what they mean. There is, first of all, the primary performativity, by means of which Christ enabled certain words to do what they meant. And there is, in addition, what we may call a secondary or sacramental performativity, by virtue of which the celebrant, in repeating those words in the context of the prayer … is held to be restoring to them their primary performativity. In verbal re-enactment of this kind we have embodied, not indeed total repetition, but the idea of total repetition.
>
> Connerton 1989: 68

Paul further personalises the relationship between Jesus and those celebrating the meal in his name, by saying that this body is 'for you' (*huper humōn*, 1 Cor. 11:24) as opposed to Mark's more universal, 'poured out for many' (*ekchunnomenon huper pollōn*, Mk. 14:24). Often in remembrance feasts, Sutton notes a particular food-related generosity of the dead is celebrated and remembered (Sutton 2001: 39). By directly linking the giving of the body to the participants of the meal, Paul seems to be evoking an image of Jesus as profoundly munificent, and in turn providing an example of 'giving' to the living community. Moreover, the imperative command to repeat this rite – 'Do this in remembrance of me' (1 Cor. 11:24, 25) – shows that Paul looks further than the material food to the incorporation of the community into Christ's very identity through it.

Narratives Surrounding Food Exchange

Food can provide a key metaphorical resource for social well-being. For example, Sutton submits that on Kalymnos:

Those who are miserly and stingy are referred to as 'hungry' with the idea here being that they are more interested in putting their money in a bank than in enjoying the pleasures of life encapsulated in eating.... Always to have a full plate, then, and always to have enough to offer others, is seen as a sign of fulfilment by many.

Sutton 2001: 27

Gifts can also provide 'long-term bonds of reciprocity' (Sutton 2001: 45); moreover, these gifts need to be openly displayed before others in order to be authenticated. Food itself can form debts to the provider on the part of the consumer. It is a physical substance that 'internalises' debts owed to the other (Sutton 2001: 46).

The food … is strengthened by this attention to tradition by being made 'more like people' – that is, more the model of the memorably nurturant self one projects through giving.

Battaglia cited in Sutton 2001: 47

The symbolism of food for one's personality is, of course, at the centre of the logic of the Lord's Supper: Jesus gives his very flesh to be ingested by, and nourish his followers. More than that, however, within the narrative surrounding food exchange in Corinth, Paul also presents Jesus providing a foil to those who resist sharing their food with others and, as such, compromise the status of the rite in which they participate. Graeco-Roman social convention may well have proscribed different foods and who could legitimately eat with whom, but the notion of a wealthy sector not sharing their food with those of lower status within the church is anathema to the spirit of the feast. If the ethos of generosity revealed in Christ's giving of himself is not mirrored in the behaviour of those at his meal, then they, as Paul rightly states, are not really eating the Lord's Supper at all (1 Cor. 11:20).

Adopting Munn and Battaglia's work on personal exchange relationships, Sutton proposes what he terms 'memories of *Gemeinschaft*', a memory in Kalymnos where 'food was exchanged freely, and when communal rituals had a greater role in people's lives' (Sutton 2001: 54). Often endemic to these stories is the belief that in the past people were more neighbourly, more open and more willing to practise sharing; no one was treated as a stranger. Paul's remembrance of the Lord's giving of his own self in the feast at the upper room and on the cross is explicitly connected with the Corinthian celebration of the Lord's Supper. He rhetorically asks, the cup of blessing that we bless, is it not a sharing in the blood of Christ? The bread that we break, is it not a sharing in the body of Christ? Because there is one bread, we who are many are one body, for we all partake of the one bread.

1 Cor. 10:16–17

Sutton also discusses Hyde's theory that those who pass on gifts will be rewarded, whereas those who resist sharing or attempt to benefit from a gift will be punished. Paul's stark warning that those 'not discerning the body eat and drink judgment on themselves' (11:29) seems of one accord with this perspective.

Embodied/Sensory Aspects of Food and Eating

Western intellectual traditions, as the citation from Jeanneret at the opening of this exhibit witnesses, often ascribe 'vision to the more evolved cultures and taste and smell to the "primitive"' (Sutton 2001: 4). A Cartesian cleavage between mind and body may have informed this bias. However, a resistance to linking embodiment and thought is rejected in scripture. Moreover, divisions between spirit and body were unknown in Jewish thinking (even if they were alive in Hellenistic thinking).

Feeley-Harnik's study, *The Lord's Table: Eucharist and Passover in Early Christianity* (1981) persuasively argues that food became one medium of identity for the covenantal people: 'food was the embodiment of God's word, his wisdom, or a people who would have no graven images. The food God provided was his word' (Feeley-Harnik 1981: 107). As such it is an important avenue for exploring a number of themes, not least social divisions that seem to be at the heart of the problem that Paul addresses in Corinth. Feeley-Harnik makes this connection explicit when she writes 'Many Jews believed that the Messiah would repeat the miracle of the manna when he came back. Paul gives Jesus the name for manna, "God's Wisdom"' (1981: 114).

Food and eating involve powerful sensory experiences, most explicitly taste and smell. This, according to Sutton, adds to food's memorable appeal: 'a flower-pot of basil can symbolize the soul of a people better than a drama of Aeschylus' (Dragoumis, cited in Sutton 2001: 73). Sutton conceives the links of tangibility and taste in the formation of memory in three ways. First, he shows how the sensory can place a person in experiential terms right back to another place, or enable them to empathise with distant events. Second, a foodstuff, for instance basil (in the Eucharist, bread) can function and symbolise different things in different settings. Third, and most importantly, Sutton reveals how food can present what he terms 'a cultural site'. This, he asserts, is 'especially useful in understanding Kalymnian and Greek experiences of *displacement, fragmentation, and the reconstruction of wholeness*' (my italicisation, Sutton 2001: 74–75). He shows how food can play a part in restoring social concord, which might have been corrupted or compromised. He cites Fernandez's work on the Fang of Gabon, a tribe that had experienced profound disintegration under colonial power. In responding to these mass changes, these people recaptured and revitalised a sense of unity by fusing past and present in food rituals.

> Returning to the whole requires a 'mutual tuning in' based on shared sensory experiences that are explicitly synthetic (crossing sensory domains). Hearing, seeing, touching, tasting – in primary groups.... This is where revitalization comes in, the process by which a domain of experience that is experienced as fragmented or deprived is revalued by simply marking it for ritual participation: 'The performance of a sequence of images, revitalize, in effect, and by simple iteration, a universe of domains, an acceptable cosmology of participation, a compelling whole.'

> Sutton 2001: 76, citing Fernandez

Sutton continues by asserting that an emphasis on taste and smell provides an appeal of memory as 'symbolic rather than linguistic', 'recognition rather than recall', and as such 'does not simply symbolize social bonds, and division; it participates in their creation and recreation' (Sutton 2001: 101–102).

The Lord's Supper is of course a veritable 'feast' of sensory stimulations. Hearing, taste, touch and smell are crucial to its powers and efficacy. Paul need not elaborate much on the reasons why the rite should accomplish and embody unity in Christ, for it is plain for all to see. Indeed those acting 'differently/divisively' (not sharing food, eating and drinking to excess (1 Cor. 11:21) while others have nothing) are in effect fragmenting the community, and stand as the antithesis of the true purposes of the ritual. Doing and being must be profoundly related in the consumption and 'living out' of Christ's body. It has often been noted that Paul repeatedly uses a term *sunerchesthe* (1 Cor. 11:1, 7, 18, 20, 33–34) drawn from political concord discourses that aim to overcome factional disputes and achieve harmony. Indeed the conclusion of the Lord's Supper passage involves the plea for individual members to discern the body of the community and Christ. For without such reflection, without such solidarity and union, an individual will 'eat and drink judgment against themselves' (1 Cor. 11:29).

In short, it is the sensory, experiential elements of the rite that convey and affirm its effectiveness. The life-giving theological assertions can easily be nullified by ignoring the ritual's practical, unifying appeal. The importance of the advice given at the Lord's Supper concerning embodiment and memory is in this respect, also applicable to every cause of division within Corinthian Christianity. As Rappaport notes, emotion aroused within communal or bodily focused events can alter consciousness (1999: 258–59), the feelings 'remembered' and / or evoked within particular ritual contexts are strong and powerful precisely because they encourage people to feel, think and act in a new way:

> ... it is indubitable that emotions are regularly stimulated in many rituals, that these emotions may be strong and they may seem persuasive. It is not unreasonable, therefore, to take them to be a source of ritual's 'power' or of the participants' ability to bring about the states of affairs for which they strive, also a source of ritual's actual, as well as putative, efficacy.

> Rappaport 1999: 49

The force of embodiment and humanity as ceremonial animals is not lost on Paul and his advice to a church divided.

Conclusion

This exhibit has, following Sutton's recent ethnography, traced food and memory as two parts of a social dynamic that relates variously to rituals, exchange, embodiment and social fragmentation. It has been seen that, 'food memories work through mutual reinforcement of the cosmos and the mundane' (Sutton 2001: 159). The early Christian celebration of the Eucharist was primarily 'incorporated' (embodied) as opposed to 'inscribed' (written) as a ritual event. It was through its very actions and celebrations that meanings associated with it were conveyed. Christ's body, offered for each person, becomes a powerful symbol of the types of exchanges and sharing that should characterise and mark the memory of the community of faith. Moreover, unlike any other object, food can only be nourishing when ingested: thus it 'internalizes debt, once again calling for verbal and non-verbal acts of remembrance and reciprocity' (Sutton 2001: 160).

Often interpretations of the Lord's Supper passage in Corinthians concentrate on what the rite was meant to symbolise, as opposed to what the rite physically accomplished. By turning to the embodied aspects of the feast, including sensory stimulations, the exegete is able to reclaim the evocative nature of food as a tool of memory. 'Deprivation in the present created a space for the bubbling up of memories of hunger past' (Sutton 2001: 168). Those Corinthians feeling the pangs of hunger were no doubt conjuring up conflicting memories: their body wanted nourishment and their Lord claimed to have provided it; however, other members meeting in his name did not share their food. For Paul, new life in faith meant rich and poor united as one, mutually interdependent, one in the body of Christ.

Also important to Paul's strategy in addressing the church divided at Corinth was underlining the crime of forgetting. In many ways the Corinthians who did not share their food were guilty of forgetting their new identity in Christ by persisting in pre-baptismal social and religious conventions. Their behaviour vis-à-vis their food and resources in effect 'killed' and 'negated' the meaning of the Lord's Supper in which they participated.

All in all, it seems clear that feasting and other embodied practices are not to be seen solely in terms of a representation of something else, but rather are constructive of, and implicated in, networks, identities and social memories. Paul's retort to the opening quote of this exhibit 'Why would anyone want to remember what they had eaten?' would surely be, remembrance is crucial, for in Corinthian Christian terms, 'you are what you eat'!

10

Exiting an Exhibition

We can pretend that we are neutral scientists collecting unambiguous data and that the people we are studying are living amid various unconscious systems of determining forces of which they have no clue and to which only we have the key. But it is only pretence.

P. Rabinow

It has been a consistent theme that objects stir recollection, that they inspire stories whose retelling constitutes memory ... forever evolving, reshaped in order to make our sense of the present lead coherently towards a desired future.

N. Macgregor

This book was conceived on the premise that exhibitions are the innovations and sole 'preserve' of their curators. In one sense this is entirely true. However, if you are still reading at this point, then you also, as readers, are implicated in the act of meaning-making and evaluation of the 'exhibits' you have observed. For the very act of exhibiting pieces before others transfers the tenure of the objects from the custodian alone. If something is to be presented for public consumption then the public often want, and are to some extent entitled, to know 'Why?'

One need only think of the sensationalist responses to Professor von Hagen's infamous *Body Worlds Show* exhibited in London in 2002, to illustrate the above point. He claimed that displays of real corpses, preserved by his plasticising process, could help humans understand themselves. On a biological level, he was no doubt right. But faced with a skinned horseman, a chess player's divided brain and a bisected pregnant woman, some viewers asked what possible benefit average Joe/Josie Bloggs could gain from such a spectacle. Many even went so far as to say that those visiting the exhibition must have the same macabre streak in them that drew spectators to executions and freak shows in times long passed. Whatever one's response to that particular exhibition, it is an event that aptly illustrates how exhibitions and museums are not just places to retell facts, or events of the past, but can also stand as sites of contest, tension and creativity for the present and future.

The perspectives of the curators must also be considered. The myth of 'objectivity' has long been deconstructed. Curators (like anthropologists and biblical scholars) produce displays that may claim to tell 'how things are' and uncover certain truths but, in so doing, are inevitably involved in pretence. One must always acknowledge the 'perspectival' nature of all such endeavours. This is not to say, however, that the learning environments constructed by curators cannot strategically *inform* and *reform* people's thinking and opinions in particular ways.

This exhibition of selected aspects of scriptural religion has been openly opportunistic, hybrid and eclectic in its methods and comparisons. It began with a short review of work that has brought anthropology and biblical studies into dialogue and moved on to counter the commonly cited critique that anthropology and social-scientific enquiry is a priori reductive, vis-à-vis faith and the transcendent. Documenting both Charles Kraft's and Douglas Davies' use of anthropology in missionary work and theology respectively, I went on to outline two particular concepts that seemed to me important arenas for interaction between the two disciplines, namely, embodiment and humanity as ceremonial animals. Embodiment entailed seeing inscription of the sacred in learned ways of acting and living out faith and belief. A focus on the body involves a focus on individual, social and political aspects of existence. This aided in concentrating on situations in which flesh and faith, body and soul, context and *kerygma* fruitfully converged and mutually informed one another. Seeing humanity as ceremonial animals, ritualising 'deep into the bone', highlighted the fact that as individuals we are often socially and ritually fashioned throughout our lives. This is no less true in respect of faith, belief and ethics than it is in reference to social behaviour and everyday convention.

The exhibits proper were then displayed. Taking as my starting points main themes of interest in current anthropology (religious practitioners; religions and cosmology; power and violence; sex and gender; body and emotion; ritual; social memory), each exhibit displayed ethnography and selected scriptural passages in conjunction.

First, anthropological thinking on religious figures informed my 'Reading with Religious Practitioners', most explicitly shamans and shaman healers. The former are mostly associated with the primitive forms of altered states of consciousness and seemed to dovetail most naturally with Mark's presentation of the spirit-led Jesus. The latter are associated with more developed, communitarian forms and find comparison with Luke's Jesus who practises prayer, etc. While a spirit Christology can only take us part of the way in our understandings of Jesus, nonetheless it reclaims an important dimension of both his and early Christian believers' religious experiences, one that orthodox two-nature Christology often overlooks.

Second, religion and cosmology informed 'Reading with Tricksters', an exhibit that posited comparisons between John's picture of Jesus and the so-called trickster trope in anthropology. I also considered the imagination of worldviews and pictures of origins and creation by way of Preston's 'trickster imagination' dimensions (spatial, temporal, morphological and comprehensive). Trickery is often one avenue through which those who do not have a stake in power structures can comment on their position. How apt that communities like those addressed by John, who feel they do not belong to the world's value systems or assumptions, should turn to such dynamics to comment on their liminal place and identity.

Third, power and violence grounded my 'Reading with Rituals of Resistance'. This exhibited recent anthropological analysis of violence interpreted by the victims as rites into manhood, alongside biblical instances of deaths in war and imperial situations. Once more the reality and agential aspects of these events were stressed in interpretation. Moreover, the reflective theological accounts of such deaths as initiations into another realm of existence provided a powerful retort and ritual of resistance to oppression within the texts studied.

Fourth, sex and gender informed my 'Reading with Women's Religions'. This exhibit documented studies of religious traditions in which women played a prominent role. Interests in the alleviation of suffering through healing, rituals of solidarity and emphasis on maternal characteristics all seemed to dovetail nicely with aspects of the Jesus movement as presented in the gospels. A process of domestication (adaptation of a male-centred tradition by females) was also explored in reference to the development of religious movements and gradual assimilation to the status quo. I argued that 'domestication' was an important category in overcoming false dichotomies that often riddle accounts of institutionalisation in the early church; for example, Schüssler Fiorenza's rosy picture of primitive Christian egalitarianism eclipsed by encroaching patriarchal structures. Domestication showed a link between women's experiences as prime actors in religious traditions and those in which they were subordinated or marginalised from a male-centred cult or tradition and, as such, pictured their experiences on a developing, coherent tradition, as opposed to mutually exclusive eras.

Fifth, body and emotion were used to imagine my 'Reading with Poetry'. This exhibit presented anthropological studies of Indian and Bedouin poetry and song alongside features of The Song of Songs. I argued that poetry was a genre that often encapsulated and displayed values held in contradistinction from the status quo, in this case, young people's feelings of love and desire in distinction from duty and honour. In recapturing the importance of emotions, the exhibit showed that unitary scripts or conventional values are not the only ones to which people subscribe or feel, in scripture and social life.

Sixth, a broadly envisioned notion of ritual enlightened my 'Reading with Communities of Goods'. This compared the accounts of the pooling of possessions in Acts with similar practices amongst the Qumran community and Hutterites. By concentrating attention on the cultivation of 'virtuosity', aspects of group dynamics, especially the censorship of defectors, were brought into clearer focus. Additionally, it was speculated that the historicity of the Acts account of the community of goods should not be rejected on the basis that it is nowhere else attested in the New Testament. There are examples of communities (such as the Latter-Day Saints) for whom utopian practices marked the early stages of the movement, but as they grew and developed these values were held as an ideal to be aspired to, rather than a custom to be practically embodied.

Finally, the notion of social memory informed my 'Reading with Food and Memory', a comparative display of the Corinthian celebration of the Lord's Supper and ethnography of a Greek island community's meals and remembrances. By showing how the Eucharistic rite itself was an 'incorporated' (bodily) practice for the primitive Christian community, one was able to concentrate on what it actually achieved in itself (overcoming of division), rather than seeing it as a purely symbolic rite representative of something else. Meals are ceremoniously executed in many communities for purposes of remembrance and enforcing social unity. The earliest forms of Christianity were no exception.

All the exhibits variously touch on diverse themes including ethics, morality, gender and political protest. My interests in tales and histories of struggle 'from below' and trying to decipher oft-muted voices and perspectives buried in our texts are undoubtedly reflected in my displays, themes and conclusions. However, if I had to identify elements that marked my exhibits out as innovative in the context of current anthropological reflection on scripture, it would be their cumulative emphasis on the consciousness, agency and creativity of the individuals presented in the Bible.

Consciousness is important because, in acknowledging the embodied person (emotions and all), one is able to liberate scriptural characters from the straitjackets of cultural scripts. Human activity is of course ordered in social habits, but this does not eclipse the important role of individual feelings (even in more collectively focused societies). Agency is also related to this and illustrates how individual and collective decisions and morals are commentaries on present states of affairs. The ideal of community especially serves as a repository of action-centred belief and faith. Finally imagination is central, for this fosters creativity. As Rapport and Overing note 'rule breaking of inspired individuals leads to new social formations on which cultural vitality depends' (Rapport and Overing 2000: 6).

My exhibits suggest some ways in which anthropology and biblical studies can be viewed together. However, I have also implicitly tried to reclaim some of the radical and visionary formulations inherent in scriptural religion and its embodiment. Scripture does not just catalogue a religion of thought, but one of radical action, agency and experience. This should encourage us in the present to see how action, not only belief, is crucial. This, of course, links with social-scientific enquiry, which sees body and soul as intimately related, in distinction from those primarily preoccupied with theology and thought seemingly divorced from social reality.

While definitions of 'religion' have often focused on concepts such as belief in spiritual beings, holiness and relationship with God, it is also true to say that religion can also involve political, social and emotional experiences, family and community. These collectively can provide a purposeful narrative about one's relationships with others and the world. In this respect, religion should not be seen as a static institutionalised regime of dictated rites and practices, but also one where symbolism, fluidity and meaning can be interpreted differently by individuals according to their place in life (sex; socio-economic status; cultural tradition; social situation). Such diversity has been touched on in some of the exhibits displayed in this book. It is surprising that it is often in the unlikely 'bodily', 'ground level' experiences of particular people that powerful commentaries on religion and spirituality can be found.

Daniel Libeskind's architectural plans for New York's 'Ground Zero' embodied the 'horizontal' memory of events there, as opposed to those architects more obsessed with the 'vertical' stature of their building plans. Likewise, we as faithful readers and exegetes must see horizontal and vertical aspects of scriptural witness in tandem. We must reclaim embodied manifestations of religion as dialogical partners to more theologically orientated pursuits. Such sentiments help us to renew a communal and collectivist vision, which in our increasingly individualistic world is all the time more difficult to sustain. But perhaps the greatest lesson to be learnt from cross-cultural analysis is to show that scripture does not just reflect 'our' industrialised Western social context. On the contrary, often a responsible reading of other cultural situations finds more enlightening resonance with it. Such cultural 'defamiliarising' must play a part within our reading of scripture, for only then will we avoid 'domesticating' the texts we read within our own worldview.

A final word: objects in museums, if they are completely divorced from life, are static, useless and archaic (the proverbial use of 'museum' testifies to this). Exhibitions can only exert influence if people take what they have learnt from them into their own lives. 'Reading with Anthropology' can hopefully help to foster empathetic understandings and relationships with those from diverse traditions, social contexts and walks of life. Anthropology provides resources for us in the contemporary world to build bridges of respect and appreciation with those 'alien' to us in geographical, social, religious and political terms. It is only by such compassionate empathy that we, as biblical interpreters, will be truly enabled and liberated to learn and act upon the human experiences of the divine and his incarnate son, exhibited within the glass cabinets of scripture itself.

Bibliography

Abu-Lughod, L., *Veiled Sentiments: Honor and Poetry in a Bedouin Society* (Los Angeles: University of California Press, 1986a)

——, 'Modest Women, Subversive Poems: The Politics of Love in an Egyptian Bedouin Society', *Bulletin of British Society for Middle Eastern Studies* 13 (1986b), 159–68

——, 'The Romance of Resistance', *American Ethnologist* 17 (1990), 41–55

——, and C. Lutz (eds), *Language and the Politics of Emotions* (Cambridge: Cambridge University Press, 1990)

Aguilar, M. I., 'Symbolic Wars, Age-Sets and the Anthropology of War in 1 Maccabees', Unpublished Paper presented to Conference on Old Testament and Social Sciences, St Andrews University (2004a)

——, 'Marcel Mauss, La Priere, and the First Book of Maccabees', Unpublished Paper presented to the Symposium on Anthropology and the Old Testament, University of Glasgow (2004b)

——, 'Changing Models and the Death of Culture', in L. J. Lawrence and M. I. Aguilar (eds), *Anthropology and Biblical Studies: Avenues of Approach* (Leiden: Deo, 2004c), 299–313

Al-Khayyat, S., *Honour and Shame: Women in Modern Iraq* (London: Saqi Books, 1990)

Alston, R., 'Arms and the Man: Soldiers, Masculinity and Power in Republican and Imperial Rome', in L. Foxhall and J. Salmon (eds), *When Men Were Men: Masculinity, Power and Identity in Classical Antiquity* (London: Routledge, 1998), 205–23

Alter, R., *The Art of Biblical Poetry* (New York: Basic Books, 1985)

Alvarez, A., *Savage God: A Study of Suicide* (Norton: WW and Company, 1990)

Appadurai, A., 'Gastro-politics in Hindu South Asia', *American Ethnologist* 8 (1981), 494–511

Aristotle, Ethics, tr. J. A. K. Thomson, rev. H. Tredennick, intro. J. Barnes (Harmondsworth: Penguin, 1976 [1953])

Asad, T., *Anthropology and the Colonial Encounter* (London: Ithaca Press and Humanities Press, 1975)

Ashley, K. M., 'Interrogating Biblical Deception and Trickster Theories: Narratives of Patriarchy or Possibility', in C. Exum and J. W. H. Bos (eds), *Reasoning with Foxes: Female Wit in a World of Male Power* (Semeia 42, 1988), 103–16

Ashton, J. (ed.), *The Interpretation of John* (Fortress Press, 1986)

——, *Understanding the Fourth Gospel* (Oxford: Clarendon Press, 1991)

——, *The Religion of St Paul* (New Haven: Yale University Press, 2000)

——, 'William James Lecture 2002–03' *Harvard Divinity Bulletin*. Available online at <URL>http://www. hds. harvard. edu/news/bulletin/articles/ashton.html</URL> (accessed 6 April 2004)

Atkinson, P., *The Ethnographic Imagination: Textual Constructions of Reality* (London: Routledge, 1990)

Babcock-Abrahams, B., 'A Tolerated Margin of Mess: The Trickster and His Tales Reconsidered', *Journal of the Folklore Institute* 11 (1975), 147–86

Barclay, J., 'The Family as Bearer of Religion in Judaism and Early Christianity', in H. Moxnes (ed.), *Constructing Early Christian Families* (London: Routledge, 1997), 66–80

Barnard, A. and J. Spencer (eds), *Encyclopedia of Social and Cultural Anthropology* (London: Routledge, 1996)

Barton, C., 'Honor and Sacredness in the Roman and Christian Worlds', in M. Cormack (ed.), *Sacrificing the Self: Perspectives on Martyrdom and Religion* (Oxford: Oxford University Press, 2002), 23–38

Barton, S., *The Spirituality of the Gospels* (London: SPCK, 1992)

Battaglia, D., 'The Body in the Gift: Memory and Forgetting in Sabari Military Exchange', *American Ethnologist* 19 (1992), 3–18

Bauckham R. J., 'Jesus and the Wild Animals (Mk 1:13): A Christological Image for An Ecological Age', in J. B. Green and M. Turner (eds), *Jesus of Nazareth: Lord and Christ* (Grand Rapids, 1994), 3–21

Beavis, M. A. (ed.), *The Lost Coin: Parables of Women, Work and Wisdom* (Sheffield: Sheffield Academic Press, 2002)

Beidelman, T. O., 'The Moral Imagination of the Kagura: Some Thoughts on Tricksters, Translation and Comparative Analysis', *American Ethnologist* (1980), 27–42

Bennet, C., *In Search of the Sacred: Anthropology and the Study of Religions* (London: Cassell, 1996)

Bergant, D., 'An Anthropological Approach to Biblical Interpretation: The Passover Supper in Exodus 12:1–20 as a Case Study', *Semeia* 67 (1994), 43–62.

——, '"My Beloved is Mine and I Am His" (Song 2:16): The Song of Songs and Honor and Shame', *Semeia* 68 (1996), 23–40

——, 'Biblical Wasfs Beyond Song of Songs', *Journal for the Study of the Old Testament* 28 (2004), 327–49

Berger, P., *The Sacred Canopy* (Doubleday / Anchor Books, 1967)

Berghe, P. L. and K. Peter, 'Hutterites and Kibbutzniks: A Tale of Nepotistic Communism' *Man* 23 (1988), 522–39

Berquist, J. L., *Controlling Corporeality: The Body and the Household in Ancient Israel* (Rutgers University Press, 2002)

Blackler, C., 'Initiation in the Shugendo: The Passage Through the Ten States of Existence', in C. J. Bleeker (ed.), *Initiation* (Leiden: Brill, 1965), 96–111

Blasi, A. J., J. Duhaime and P. Turcotte (eds), *Handbook of Early Christianity: Social Science Approaches* (Walnut Creek, California: Altamira, 2002)

Borg, M. J., *Jesus a New Vision* (London: SPCK, 1993 [1987])

——, *Meeting Jesus Again for the First Time* (New York: HarperCollins, 1994)

Boring, M., K. Berger and C. Colpe (eds), *Hellenistic Commentary to the New Testament* (Nashville: Abingdon Press, 1995)

Botha, P. J. J., 'Paul and Gossip: A Social Mechanism in Early Christian Communities', *Neotestimentica* 32 (1998), 267–88

——, 'Submission and Violence: Exploring Gender Relations in the First-Century World', *Neotestamentica* 34 (2000), 1–38

Bourdieu, P., *Outline of a Theory of Practice* (Cambridge: Cambridge University Press, 1977)

Bourguignon, E. (ed.), *Religion, Altered States of Consciousness, and Social Change* (Columbus: Ohio State University Press, 1973)

Bowie, F., *Anthropology of Religion* (Oxford: Blackwells, 2000)

——, 'An Anthropology of Religious Experience: Spirituality, Gender and Cultural Transmission in the Focolare Movement', *Ethnos* 68 (2003), 49–72

Boyarin, J. and D. Boyarin, *Powers of Diaspora* (Minnesota: University of Minnesota Press, 2002)

Brenner, A., 'Woman Poets and Authors', in A. Brenner (ed.), *A Feminist Companion to the Song of Songs* (Sheffield: JSOT Press, 1993), 86–97

Brettler, M., 'Is There Martyrdom in the Hebrew Bible?', in M. Cormack (ed.), *Sacrificing the Self: Perspectives on Martyrdom and Religion* (Oxford: Oxford University Press, 2002) 3–22

Brickhouse T. C. and N. D. Smith, *The Trial and Execution of Socrates: Sources and Controversies* (Oxford: Oxford University Press, 2002)

Bultmann, R., *Die Geschichte des synoptischen Tradition* (Gottingen: Vanderhoeck and Ruprecht, 1921)

Burns, A. S., *The Shakers: Hands to Work, Hearts to God* (New York: Aperture Books, 1987)

Buss, M. J., 'An Anthropological Perspective on Prophetic Call Narratives', *Semeia* 21 (1981), 9–30

Camp, C. V., 'Wise and Strange: An interpretation of the Female Imagery in Proverbs in Light of Trickster Mythology', in C. J. Exum and J. W. H. Bos (eds), *Reasoning with the Foxes: Female Wit in a World of Male Power* (Semeia 42, 1988), 14–36

Capper, B., 'The Palestinian Cultural Context of Earliest Christian Community of Goods', in R. J. Bauckham (ed.), *The Book of Acts in Its Palestinian Setting Vol 4* (Grand Rapids, Eerdmans, 1995). Available online at <URL>http://216.239.59.104/search?q=cache:4RL8ev-FYuoJ:arts-humanities.cant.ac.uk/Religious-Studies/earliest.doc+capper+community+of+goods&hl=en</URL>

Caraveli-Chaves, A., 'Bridge Between Worlds: The Greek Women's Lament as Communicative Event', *Journal of American Folklore* 93 (1980), 129–57

Carroll, M. P., 'The Trickster as Selfish Buffoon and Culture Hero', *Ethos* 12 (1984), 105–31

Carter, T., *Beyond the Pale* (Cambridge: Cambridge University Press, 2003)

Cartledge, P., 'The Maschismo of the Athenian Empire or the Reign of the Phallus', in L. Foxhall and J. Salmon (eds), *When Men Were Men: Masculinity, Power and Identity in Classical Antiquity* (London: Routledge, 1998), 54–67

Chalcraft, D. J. (ed.), *Social-Scientific Old Testament Criticism* (Sheffield: Sheffield Academic Press, 1997)

Charity, A. C., *Events and their Afterlife* (Cambridge: Cambridge University Press, 1966)

Clines, D. J. A., 'The Book of Psalms, Where Men are Men On the Gender of Hebrew Piety' Unpublished Paper presented at Society of Biblical Literature Annual Meeting, Philadelphia (1995). Available online at <URL>http://www. shef. ac. uk/uni/academic/A-C/biblst/DJACcurres/GenderPiety. html</URL> (accessed 5 August 2004)

Connerton, P., *How Societies Remember* (Cambridge: Cambridge University Press, 1989)

Cormack, M. (ed.), *Sacrificing the Self: Perspectives on Martyrdom and Religion* (Oxford: Oxford University Press, 2002)

Craffert, P. F., 'The Anthropological Turn in New Testament Interpretation: Dialogue as Negotiation and Cultural Critique' *Neotestimentica* 29 (1995), 167–82

——, 'On New Testament Interpretation and Ethnocentrism', in M. G. Brett (ed.), *Ethnicity and the Bible* (Leiden: E. J. Brill, 1996), 449–68

——, 'Jesus and the Shamanic Complex: First Steps in Utilising a Social Type Model' *Neotestimentica* 33 (1999), 321–42

Crossan, J. D., *The Historical Jesus: The Life of a Mediterranean Jewish Peasant* (San Francisco: HarperCollins, 1991)

Csordas, T., 'Embodiment as a Paradigm for Anthropology', *Ethos* 18 (1990), 5–47

—— (ed.), *Embodiment and Experience: The Existential Ground of Culture and Self* (Cambridge: Cambridge University Press, 1994)

Csordas, T., 'The Body's Career in Anthropology', in H. Moore (ed.), *Anthropological Theory Today* (Cambridge: Polity Press, 1999), 172–205

Culley, R. C. (ed.), 'Anthropological Perspectives on Old Testament Prophecy' *Semeia* 21 (1981)

Culpepper, R. A., *Anatomy of the Fourth Gospel* (Philadelphia: Fortress Press, 1983)

D'Anglure, B. S., 'Shamanism', in A. Barnard and J. Spencer (eds), *Encyclopedia of Social and Cultural Anthropology* (London: Routledge, 1996), 504–8

Dalman, G., *Arbeit und Sitte in Palastina* (Gutersloh: C. Bertelsmann, 1928–39)

Danker, F., *Jesus and the New Age* (Philadelphia: Fortress Press, 1988)

Davies, W. D. and D. C. Allison, *A Critical and Exegetical Commentary on the Gospel According to St Matthew* Vol 3 (Edinburgh: T&T Clark, 1997)

Davies, D. J., 'An Interpretation of Sacrifice in Leviticus' *Zwitschrift fore die Alttestamentliche Wissenchaft und die Kunde des Nachbiblischen Judentums* 80 (1977), 388–98

——, *Anthropology and Theology* (Oxford: Berg, 2002)

——, 'Purity, Spirit and Reciprocity in the Acts of the Apostles', in L. J. Lawrence and M. I. Aguilar (eds), *Anthropology and Biblical Studies: Avenues of Approach* (Leiden: Deo Publishing, 2004), 259–80

Davies, P. R., 'Food, Drink and Sects: The Question of Ingestion in the Qumran Texts', *Semeia* 86 (1999), 151–63

Davies, S., *Jesus the Healer: Possession, Trance and Origins of Christianity* (New York: Continuum Press, 1995)

Davila, J., *Descenders to the Chariot: The People Behind the Hekhalot Literature* (Leiden: Brill, 2001)

Davis, J. (ed.), *Religious Organization and Religious Experience* (London: Academic Press, 1982)

Davis-Floyd, R. E. and C. F. Sargent (eds), *Childbirth and Authoritative Knowledge: Cross-Cultural Perspectives* (California: University of California Press, 1997)

De Troyer, K., J. A. Herbert, J. A. Johnson and A. Korte (eds), *Wholly Woman, Holy Blood: A Feminist Critique of Purity and Impurity* (Trinity Press International, 2003)

Delaney, C., *The Seed and the Soil: Gender and Cosmology in Turkish Village Society* (University of California Press, 1991)

Demand, N., *Birth, Death and Motherhood in Classical Greece* (London: John Hopkins Press, 1994)

DeMaris, R. E., 'The Baptism of Jesus: A Ritual-Critical Approach', in W. Stegemann, B. J. Malina and G. Theissen (eds), *The Social Setting of Jesus and the Gospels* (Minneapolis: Fortress Press, 2000)

Denzin, N., *Interpretive Ethnography: Ethnographic Practices for the 21st Century* (Thousand Oaks, CA: Sage, 1997)

Derrett, J., 'The Evil Eye in the New Testament', in P. F. Esler (ed.), *Modelling Early Christianity* (London: Routledge, 1995)

Destro, A. and M. Pesce, 'Kinship, Discipleship and Movement: An Anthropological Study of John's Gospel', *Biblical Interpretation* 3 (1995), 266–84

Dixon, S., *The Roman Mother* (London and Sydney: Croom Helm, 1988)

Dokka, S. T., 'Irony and Sectarianism in the Gospel of John', in J. Nissen and S. Pedersen (eds), *New Readings in John: Literary and Theological Perspectives* (JSNT Supp. Series 182, Sheffield: Sheffield Academic Press, 1999), 83–107

Doty, W. G. and W. J. Hynes, 'Historical Overview of Theoretical Issues: The Problem of the Trickster', in W. G. Doty and W. J. Hynes (eds), *Mythical Trickster Figures. Contours, Contexts, and Criticisms* (Tuscaloosa: University of Alabama Press, 1993), 13–32

Douglas, M. T., 'Deciphering a Meal', in C. Geertz (ed.), *Myth, Symbol and Culture* (New York: Norton, 1971), 61–82

——, *Implicit Meanings: Essays in Anthropology* (London: Routledge & Kegan Paul, 1975)

——, *Purity and Danger: An Analysis of Concepts of Pollution and Taboo* (London: Routledge, 1992 [1966])

——, *Natural Symbols: Explorations in Cosmology* (London: Routledge, 1996 [1970])

Downing, G., 'Aesthetic Behaviour in the Jewish Scriptures: A Preliminary Sketch', *Journal for the Study of the Old Testament* 28 (2003), 131–47

Droge, A. J. and J. D. Tabor, *A Noble Death: Suicide and Martyrdom Among Christians and Jews in Antiquity* (Harper San Francisco, 1992)

Du Boulay, J., 'Women – Images of their Nature and Destiny in Rural Greece', in J. Dubisch (ed.), *Gender, Power and Rural Greece* (Princeton: Princeton University Press, 1986), 215–33

Dubisch, J., 'Introduction', in J. Dubisch (ed.), *Gender, Power and Rural Greece* (Princeton: Princeton University Press, 1986), 3–41

Duff, P. B., '"I Will Give to Each of You as Your Works Deserve": Witchcraft Accusations and the Fiery-Eyed Son of God in Rev 2.18–23', *New Testament Studies* 43 (1997), 116–33

Dunn, J. D. G., *The Christ and the Spirit* (Edinburgh: T&T Clark, 1998)

Durkheim, E., *Suicide*. English Translation by J. A. Spalding (Toronto, Canada: FreePress/Collier-MacMillan, 1951 [1897])

——, *The Elementary Forms of Religious Life* (London: George Allen & Unwin, 1964 [1912])

Ehrensperger, K., *That We May Be Mutually Encouraged* (New York: T&T Clark International, 2004)

Eilberg-Schwartz, H., *The Savage in Judaism* (Bloomington: Indiana University Press, 1990)

Eliade, M., *Shamanism: Archaic Techniques of Ecstasy* (Penguin Books, 1964)

Elliott, J. H., 'The Fear of the Leer: The Evil Eye from the Bible to Li'l Abner', *Forum* 4 (1988), 42–71

——, 'Paul, Galatians and the Evil Eye', *Currents in Theology and Mission* 17 (1990), 262–73

——, 'Matthew 20:1–15: A Parable of Invidious Comparison and Evil Eye Accusation', *Biblical Theology Bulletin* 22 (1992), 52–65

——, *What is Social-Scientific Criticism?* (Minneapolis: Augsburg Fortress, 1995 [1993])

——, 'The Anthropology of Christian Origins' *Biblical Theology Bulletin* 28 (1998), 120–22

——, 'On Wooing Crocodiles for Fun and Profit: Confessions of An Intact Admirer', in J. J. Pilch (ed.), *Social Scientific Models for Interpreting the Bible* (Leiden: E. J. Brill, 2000), 5–20

Esler, P. F., *The First Christians in their Social Worlds: Social-Scientific Approaches to New Testament Interpretation* (London: Routledge, 1994)

—— (ed.), *Modelling Early Christianity: Social-Scientific Studies of the New Testament in its Context* (London: Routledge, 1995a)

——,'God's Honour and Rome's Triumph: Responses to the Fall of Jerusalem in 70 CE in Three Jewish Apocalypses', in P. Esler (ed.), *Modelling Early Christianity* (London: Routledge 1995b), 239–58

——, 'Models in New Testament Interpretation: A Reply to David Horrell' *Journal for the Study of the New Testament* 78 (2000a), 107–13

——, 'The Mediterranean Context of Early Christianity', in P. F. Esler (ed.), *The Early Christian World, Volume I* (London: Routledge, 2000b), 3–25

——, 'The Context Group Project: An Autobiographical Account', in L. Lawrence and M. Aguilar (eds), *Anthropology and Biblical Studies: Avenues of Approach* (Leiden: Deo, 2004), 46–61

Evans, C. A. and J. A. Sanders, *Luke and Scripture* (Minneapolis: Augsburg Fortress, 1993)

Evans-Pritchard, E. E., *Theories of Primitive Religion* (Oxford: Oxford University Press, 1965)

Exum, C., 'Ten Things Every Feminist Should Know About the Song of Songs', in A. Brenner and C. R. Fontaine (eds), *The Song of Songs: A Feminist Companion to the Bible* (Sheffield: JSOT Press, 2000), 24–35

——, and J. W. H. Bos (eds), *Reasoning with the Foxes. Female Wit in a World of Male Power* (Semeia 42, 1988)

Farberow N. L. (ed.), *Suicide in Different Cultures* (Baltimore: University Park Press, 1975)

Feeley-Harnik, G., *The Lord's Table: The Meaning of Food in Early Judaism and Christianity* (Philadelphia: University of Pennsylvania Press, 1981)

Fiensy, D. A., 'Using the Nuer Culture of Africa in Understanding the Old Testament', *Journal for the Study of the Old Testament* 38 (1987), 73–83

Fischler, S., 'Imperial Cult: Engendering the Cosmos', in L. Foxhall and J. Salmon (eds), *When Men Were Men: Masculinity, Power and Identity in Classical Antiquity* (London: Routledge, 1998), 165–83

Fisher, N., 'Violence, Masculinity and the Law in Classical Athens', in L. Foxhall and J. Salmon (eds), *When Men Were Men: Masculinity, Power and Identity in Classical Antiquity* (London: Routledge, 1998), 68–97

Fitzmyer, J. A., *Luke the Theologian* (London: Geoffrey Chapman, 1989)

Fletcher-Louis, C., *Luke–Acts: Angels, Christology and Soteriology* (Tübingen: Mohr Siebeck, 1997)

Fortna, R., and T. Thatcher (eds), *Jesus in Johannine Tradition* (Louisville: Westminster John Knox, 2001)

Foucault, M., *Discipline and Punish* (New York: Vantage, 1979)

Fox, M. V., *The Song of Songs and Ancient Egyptian Love Poetry* (Madison: University of Wisconsin Press, 1984)

Fox, R. L., *Pagans and Christians* (New York: Alfred A. Knopf, 1987)

Foxhall, L. and J. Salmon (eds), *When Men Were Men: Masculinity, Power and Identity in Classical Antiquity* (London: Routledge, 1998)

Gager, J. A., *Kingdom and Community: The Social World of Early Christianity* (Englewood Cliffs, NJ: Prentice-Hall, 1975)

Garrett, S. R., *The Demise of the Devil* (Minneapolis: Fortress Press, 1989)

Geertz, C., 'Ethos, World-View and the Analysis of Sacred Symbols' *Antioch Review* 17 (1957), 421–37

——, 'Religion as a Cultural System', in M. Banton (ed.), *Anthropological Approaches to the Study of Religion* (London: Tavistock Publications, 1966), 1–46

Gilmore, D., 'Introduction: The Shame of Dishonor', in D. Gilmore (ed.), *Honor and Shame and the Unity of the Mediterranean* (American Anthropological Association 22, 1987), 2–21

——, *Manhood in the Making* (Yale University Press, 1990)

Goodman, N., *Ways of Worldmaking* (Hassocks: Harvester, 1978)

Gottwald, N., *The Tribes of Yahweh: A Sociology of the Religion of Liberated Israel 1250–1050 BC* (Maryknoll: Orbis Books, 1979)

Grayston, K., 'Atonement and Martyrdom', in J. M. G. Barclay and J. P. M. Sweet (eds), *Early Christian Thought in its Jewish Context* (Cambridge: Cambridge University Press, 1996), 250–63

Green, J. B., *The Theology of Luke* (Cambridge: Cambridge University Press, 1995)

Grimes, R., *Deeply Into the Bone: Re-Inventing Rites of Passage* (Berkeley, CA: University of California Press, 2000)

Grunlan, S. A. and M. K. Mayers, *Cultural Anthropology: A Christian Perspective* (Michigan: Zondervan, 1988 [1979])

Guelich, R. A., *Mark 1–8:26 Word Biblical Commentary* (Dallas: Word Books, 1989)

Gundry, R. H., *Mark: A Commentary on His Apology for the Cross* (Grand Rapids, Michigan: Eerdmans, 1993)

Gupta, A. and J. Ferguson, 'Beyond Culture: Space, Identity and the Politics of Difference', *Cultural Anthropology* 7 (1992), 6–23

Gutmann, M. C., 'Trafficking in Men: The Anthropology of Masculinity', *Annual Review of Anthropology* 26 (1997), 385–409

Haas, J., *The Anthropology of War* (Cambridge: Cambridge University Press, 1990)

Hansen, P., *The Trickster and the Paranormal* (Philadelphia: Xlibris Corporation, 2001)

Hanson, K. C., 'Transformed on the Mountain: Ritual Analysis and the Gospel of Matthew', *Semeia* 67 (1994), 147–70

Harlow, M., 'In the Name of the Father: Procreation, Paternity and Patriarchy', in L. Foxhall and J. Salmon (eds), *Thinking Men: Masculinity and Self-Representation in the Classical Tradition* (Routledge: London, 1998), 155–69

Harris, M., 'History and Significance of the Emic/Etic Distinction', *Annual Review of Anthropology* 5 (1976), 329–50

Hartse, C., 'The Emotional Acculturation of Hutterite Defectors', *Journal of Anthropological Research* 50 (1994), 69–85

Hatty, S., *Masculinities, Violence and Culture* (Thousand Oaks, CA: Sage Publications, 2000)

Hearon, H. and A. C. Wire, 'Women's Work in the Realm of God', in M. A. Beavis (ed.), *The Lost Coin: Parables of Women, Work and Wisdom* (Sheffield: Sheffield Academic Press, 2002), 136–57

Hertz, R., *Death and the Right Hand* (trans. R. and C. Needham, New York: Free Press, 1960 [1909])

Herzfeld, M., *The Poetics of Manhood: Contest and Identity in a Cretan Mountain Village* (Princeton: Princeton University Press, 1985)

Hill, M., *The Religious Order: A Study of Virtuoso Religion and its Legitimation in the Nineteenth Century Church of England* (London: Heinemann, 1973)

Holm, N. G. (ed.), *Religious Ecstasy* (Stockholm: Almqvist and Wiksell International, 1982)

Hooker, M. D., *The Gospel According to St Mark* (London: A. & C. Black, 1991)

Horrell, D. G., *The Social Ethos of the Corinthian Correspondence: Interest and Ideology from 1 Corinthians to 1 Clement* (Edinburgh: T&T Clark, 1996)

—— (ed.), *Social-Scientific Approaches to New Testament Interpretation* (Washington, DC: T&T Clark, 1999)

Horrell, D. G., *The Social Ethos of the Corinthian Correspondence: Interest and* 'Models and Methods in Social-Scientific Interpretation: A Response to Philip Esler', *Journal for the Study of the New Testament* 78 (2000), 83–105

Hostetler, J. A., *Hutterite Society* (Baltimore: Johns Hopkins University Press, 1974)

—— and G. E. Huntington, *The Hutterites in North America* (Fort Worth: Harcourt Brace, 1967)

Howard-Brook, W. and A. Gwyther, *Unveiling Empire: Reading Revelation Then and Now* (Maryknoll: Orbis Books, 2001 [1999])

Hurtado, L. W., 'Religious Experience and Religious Innovation in the New Testament' *Journal of Religion* 80 (2000), 183–205

Hutton, R., *Shamans: Siberian Spirituality and the Western Imagination* (London: Hambledon and London, 2001)

Hyde, L., *Trickster Makes This World: Mischief, Myth and Art* (New York: Farrar, Straus and Giroux, 1998)

Jakobsen, M. D., *Shamanism: Traditional and Contemporary Approaches to the Mastery of Spirits and Healing* (New York: Berghahn, 1999)

James, W., *The Ceremonial Animal* (Oxford: Oxford University Press, 2003)

Jasper, D., *Rhetoric, Power and Community* (London: Macmillan Press, 1993)

Jihad Tracy, A., 'Heroes, Lovers and Poet Singers: The Bedouin Ethos in the Music of the Arab Near East' *Journal of American Folklore* 109 (1996), 404–24

Jinbachian, J. M., 'The Genre of Love Poetry in the Song of Songs and the Pre-Islamic Arabian Odes', *The Bible Translator* 48 (1997), 123–37

Johnson, L., *The Gospel of Luke*, Sacra Pagina 3 (Collegeville: Liturgical Press, 1991)

——, *Religious Experience in Earliest Christianity: A Missing Dimension in New Testament Studies* (Minneapolis: Fortress Press, 1998)

Josephus, *The Jewish War*, in *The Works of Josephus*, tr. W. Whiston (Peabody: Hendrickson Publishers, 1999)

Kapferer, B., *A Celebration of Demons: Exorcism and the Aesthetics of Healing in Sri Lanka* (Oxford: Berg Publishers, 1991)

Karp, I. and S. D. Levine, *Exhibiting Cultures: The Poetics and Politics of Museum Display* (Washington Smithsonian Institution, 1991)

Kee, H. C., *Christian Origins in Sociological Perspective* (London: SCM Press, 1980)

Keller, C., 'Mystical Literature', in S. Katz (ed.), *Mysticism and Philosophical Analysis* (London: Sheldon Press, 1978)

Kieffer, R., 'The Implied Reader in John's Gospel', in J. Nissen and S. Pedersen (eds), *New Readings in John* (JSNT Sup Series, Sheffield Academic Press, 1999), 47–65

Kirshenblatt-Gimblett, B., H. Goldberg and S. Heilman, *The Israel Experience* (Jerusalem: Melton, 2002)

Klass, M. and M. K. Weisgrau (eds), *Across the Boundaries of Belief: Contemporary Issues in the Anthropology of Religion* (USA: Westview Press, 1999)

Klassen, W., *Judas: Betrayer or Friend of Jesus?* (London: SCM Press, 1996)

Knauft, B. M., *Genealogies for the Present in Cultural Anthropology* (London: Routledge, 1996)

Korte, A., 'Female Blood Rituals: Cultural-Anthropological Findings and Feminist-Theological Reflections', in K. De Troyer et al. (eds), *Wholly Woman and Holy Blood* (Trinity Press, 2003), 165–88

Kraemer, R., *Her Share of the Blessings: Women's Religions Among Pagans, Jews and Christians in the Graeco-Roman World* (Oxford: Oxford University Press, 1992)

Kraft, C. H., *Christianity in Culture* (New York: Orbis, 1979)

——, *Anthropology for Christian Witness* (Maryknoll: Orbis Books, 1996)

Kugler, R., 'Making All Experience Religious: The Hegemony of Ritual at Qumran' *Journal for the Study of Judaism* 33 (2002), 131–52

LaCocque, A., *Romance She Wrote: A Hermeneutical Essay on Song of Songs* (Harrisburg: Trinity, 1998)

Lambek, M. (ed.), *A Reader in the Anthropology of Religion* (Oxford: Blackwells, 2002)

Landy, F., *Paradoxes of Paradise: Identity and Difference in the Song of Songs* (Sheffield: The Almond Press, 1983)

Lang, B., *Anthropological Approaches to the Old Testament* (Fortress Press, 1985)

Lasine, S., 'Indeterminacy and the Bible: A Review of Literary and Anthropological Theories and their Application to Biblical Texts' *Hebrew Studies* 27 (1986), 48–80

Lawrence, L. J., 'For Truly I Tell You, They Have Received Their Reward (Matt 6:2). Investigating Honour Precedence and Honour Virtue', *Catholic Biblical Quarterly* 64 (2002), 687–702

——, *An Ethnography of the Gospel of Matthew* (Tübingen: Mohr Siebeck, 2003)

——, 'A Taste for the Other: Interpreting Biblical Texts Anthropologically', in L. Lawrence and M. Aguilar (eds), *Anthropology and Biblical Studies: Avenues of Approach* (Leiden: Deo Publishing, 2004), 9–25

——, 'Men of Perfect Holiness (1QS 7. 20) Social-Scientific Thoughts on Group Identity, Asceticism and Ethical Development in the Rule of the Community', in J. Lyons and J. Campbell (eds), *Conference Proceedings on New Exegetical Methods and the Dead Sea Scrolls* (Sheffield: Continuum Press, 2005)

——, and M. I. Aguilar (eds), *Anthropology and Biblical Studies: Avenues of Approach* (Leiden: Deo Publishing, 2004)

Leach, E., 'Anthropological Approaches to the Study of the Bible during the Twentieth Century', in G. M. Tucker and D. A. Knight (eds), *Humanizing America's Iconic Book* (Atlanta: Scholars Press, 1982), 73–94

Lemche, N. O., *Early Israel: Anthropological and Historical Studies on the Israelite Society before the Monarchy* (Leiden: Vetus Testamentum Supplement 37, 1985)

Lévi-Strauss, C., *The Raw and the Cooked: Introduction to the Science of Mythology* (London: Jonathan Cape, 1970)

Levi, P., *The Frontiers of Paradise* (London: Collins 1987)

Lewis, I. M., *Ecstatic Religion: A Study of Shamanism and Spirit Possession* (London: Routledge, 1989)

Liddiard, M., 'Changing Histories: Museums, Sexuality and the Future of the Past' *Museum and Society* 2 (2004), 15–30

Lienhardt, G., *Divinity and Experience: The Religion of the Dinka* (Oxford: Oxford University Press, 1961)

——, 'The Control of Experience Symbolic Action', in M. Lambek (ed.), *A Reader in the Anthropology of Religion* (Oxford: Blackwells, 2002), 330–39

Lindbeck, G., *The Nature of Doctrine: Religion and Theology in a Post-Liberal Age* (Philadelphia: Fortress Press, 1984)

Ling, T., 'Virtuoso Religion and the Judean Social Order', in L. J. Lawrence and M. I. Aguilar (eds), *Anthropology and Biblical Studies: Avenues of Research* (Leiden: Deo Publishing, 2004), 227–58

Loizos, P. and Heady, P. (eds), *Conceiving Persons: Ethnographies of Procreation, Fertility and Growth* London School of Economics Monographs on Social Anthropology, Vol. 68 (London: Athlone, 1999)

Longman, T., *Song of Songs* (Michigan: William Eerdmans Publishing, 2001)

Loubser, B., 'Possession and Sacrifice in the New Testament and African Traditional Religion: The Oral Forms and Conventions Behind Literary Genres', in L. J. Lawrence and M. I. Aguilar (eds), *Anthropology and Biblical Studies: Avenues of Research* (Leiden: Deo Publishing, 2004), 187–207

Loya, A., 'Poetry as Social Document: The Social Position of the Arab Woman as Reflected in the Poetry of Nizar Qabbani', *International Journal of Middle East Studies* 6 (1975), 481–94

Lucien, R., 'Anthropology and Theology: The Emergence of Incarnational Faith According to Mary Douglas', *Eglise et Theologie* 15 (1984), 131–54

Lutz, C., 'Emotion, Thought and Estrangement: Emotion as a Cultural Category', *Cultural Anthropology* 1 (1986), 287–309

——, and G. M. White, 'The Anthropology of Emotions' *Annual Review of Anthropology* 15 (1986), 405–36

MacDonald, M. Y., *The Pauline Churches* (Cambridge: Cambridge University Press, 1988)

MacGregor, N., 'Preface' to J. Mack, *The Museum of the Mind: Art and Memory in World Cultures* (London: The British Museum Press, 2003)

Maclean, J. K. B., 'A Tale of Two Weddings: The Divine Trickster in John', Paper Presented at the Annual Meeting of the Society of Biblical Literature,

Boston 1999. Available online at <URL>http://www2. Roanoke. edu/ religion/Maclean/SBL/DivineTrickster. htm<URL> (accessed 6 June 2004)

Malbon, E. S., *Narrative Space and Mythic Meaning in Mark* (Sheffield: JSOT Press, 1991)

Malina, B. J., 'Conflict in Luke–Acts: Labelling and Deviance Theory', in J. Neyrey (ed.), *The Social World of Luke-Acts* (Hendrickson, 1991), 97–122

——, *The Social World of Jesus and the Gospels* (London: Routledge, 1996)

——, *The New Testament World: Insights from Cultural Anthropology* (Louisville: Westminster John Knox, 2001 [1981])

——, and J. H. Neyrey, *Calling Jesus Names* (Polebridge Press, 1988)

——, and J. H. Neyrey, 'First-Century Personality: Dyadic, Not Individualistic', in J. H. Neyrey (ed.), *The Social World of Luke–Acts* (Hendrickson, 1991), 67–96

——, and J. H. Neyrey, *Portraits of Paul: An Archaeology of Ancient Personality* (Louisville: Westminster John Knox Press, 1996)

——, and J. J. Pilch, *Social-Science Commentary on the Book of Revelation* (Minneapolis: Fortress, 2000)

——, and R. L. Rohrbaugh, *Social-Science Commentary on the Gospel of John* (Minneapolis: Fortress, 1998)

——, and G. Theissen (eds), *The Social Setting of Jesus and the Gospels* (Minneapolis: Fortress, 2002), 135–57

Malinowski, B., *Crime and Custom in Savage Society* (London: Routledge and Kegan Paul, 1926)

Marcus, J., *Mark 1–8, Anchor Bible Commentary* (New York: Doubleday, 2000)

Marcus, M., 'Horsemen are the Fence of the Land: Honor and History Among the Ghiyata of Eastern Morocco', in D. D. Gilmore (ed.), *Honor and Shame and the Unity of the Mediterranean* (Washington: American Anthropological Association 22, 1987), 49–59

Marshall, I. H., *The Gospel of Luke* (Exeter: Paternoster Press, 1978)

Martin, D., *The Corinthian Body* (New Haven, CT: Yale University Press, 1995)

——, 'Social-Scientific Criticism', in S. L. McKenzie and S. R. Haynes (eds), *To Each Its Own Meaning* (Louisville: WJK Press, 1999 [1993]), 125–41

Martyn, J. L., *History and Theology in the Fourth Gospel* (Nashville: Abingdon, 1979)

Matera, F. J., 'The Prologue as the Interpretative Key in Mark's Gospel', in W. R. Telford (ed.), *The Interpretation of Mark* (Edinburgh: T&T Clark, 1995), 289–306

Mauss, M. 'Techniques of the Body' *Economy and Society* 2 (1973), 70–88

McCutcheon, R. T. (ed.), *The Insider/Outsider Problem in the Study of Religion* (London: Cassell, 1999)

McGowan, A., *Ascetic Eucharists: Food and Drink in Early Christian Ritual Meals* (Oxford: Clarendon Press, 1999)

McVann, M., 'Rituals of Status Transformation in Luke–Acts', in J. Neyrey (ed.), *The Social World of Luke–Acts* (Peabody: Hendrickson, 1993), 331–60

Meeks, W., 'The Man from Heaven in Johannine Sectarianism' *Journal of Biblical Literature* 91 (1972), 44–72; Reprinted in J. Ashton, *The Interpretation of John* (Philadephia: Fortress Press, 1986), 141–73

——, *The First Urban Christians: The Social World of the Apostle Paul* (New Haven: Yale University Press, 1983)

Milbank, J., *Theology and Social Theory* (Oxford: Blackwells, 1990)

Montserrat, D., 'Experiencing the Male Body in Roman Egypt', in L. Foxhall and J. Salmon (eds), *When Men Were Men: Masculinity, Power and Identity in Classical Antiquity* (London: Routledge, 1988), 153–64

Moore, S., *God's Gym: Divine Male Bodies of the Bible* (New York: Routledge, 1996)

Moxnes, H., 'Patron–Client Relations and the New Community in Luke–Acts', in J. Neyrey (ed.), *The Social World of Luke–Acts* (Hendrickson, 1991), 241–68

——,' Asceticism and Christian Identity In Antiquity: A Dialogue with Foucault and Paul', *Journal for the Study of the New Testament* 26 (2003), 3–29

Neyrey, J. H., 'The Idea of Purity in Mark's Gospel' *Semeia* 35 (1986a), 91–128

——, 'Witchcraft Accusations in 2 Cor 10–13: Paul in Social-Science Perspective', *Listening* 21 (1986b), 160–70

——, 'Bewitched in Galatia: Paul in Social Science Perspective', *Catholic Biblical Quarterly* 50 (1988), 72–100

——, 'The Footwashing in John 13:6-11: Transformation Ritual or Ceremony?', in L. M. White and O. L. Yarbrough (eds), *The Social World of the First Christians. Essays in Honor of Wayne A. Meeks* (Minneapolis: Fortress, 1995), 198–213. Also available online at <URL>http://www.nd.edu/~jneyrey1/footwash.htm</URL> (accessed 11 Nov 2004)

——, '"Despising the Shame of the Cross" Honor and Shame in the Johannine Passion Narrative', *Semeia* 68 (1996), 113–37

——, *Honor and Shame in the Gospel of Matthew* (Louisville: Westminster John Knox, 1998)

Ng, E. Y. L., *Reconstructing Christian Origins* (Carlisle: Paternoster Press, 2002)

Noth, M., *The History of Israel* (Translated by P. R. Ackroyd 2nd edn. New York: Harper & Row, 1960)

Oakman, D., 'Money in the Moral Universe of the New Testament', in W. Stegemann, B. J. Malina and G. Theissen (eds), *The Social Setting of Jesus and the Gospels* (Minneapolis: Fortress, 2002), 335–48

Olyan, S., *Biblical Mourning: Ritual and Social Dimensions* (Oxford: Oxford University Press, 2004)

Origen, *Origen, Contra Celsum*, ed. and trans. H. Chadwick (Cambridge: Cambridge University Press, 1953)

Ortner, S. B., *High Religion: A Cultural and Political History of Sherpa Buddhism* (Princeton: Princeton University Press, 1989)

Osiek, C. and D. Balch, *Families in the New Testament World: Households and House Churches* (Louisville, Kentucky: Westminster John Knox, 1997)

Ostriker, A., 'A Holy of Holies: The Song of Songs as Countertext', in A. Brenner and C. R. Fontaine (eds), *The Song of Songs: A Feminist Companion to the Bible* (Sheffield: JSOT Press, 2000), 36–54

Overholt, T. W., *Cultural Anthropology and the Old Testament* (Minneapolis: Fortress, 1996)

Overing, J., 'Alterity', in N. Rapport and J. Overing (eds), *Social and Cultural Anthropology* (London: Routledge, 2000), 9–18

Paradellis, T., 'Procreation Metaphors in Rural Greece: Cultivating, Bread-Making and Weaving', in P. Heady and P. Loizos (eds), *Conceiving Persons: Ethnographies of Procreation, Substance and Personhood* (London: Athlone Press, 1999), 201–18

Pardes, I., *Counter Traditions in the Bible: A Feminist Approach* (London: Harvard University Press, 1992)

Pelton, R. D., *The Trickster in West Africa : A Study of Mythic Irony and Sacred Delight* (Berkeley: University of California Press, 1980)

Perkins, L. J., 'Anthropology and the Old Testament', in *Anchor Bible Dictionary* (New York: Doubleday. 1992), 258–62

Peteet, J., 'Male Gender and Rituals of Resistance in the Palestinian "Intifada": A Cultural Politics of Violence', *American Ethnologist* 21 (1994), 31–49

Peter, K. et al., 'The Dynamics of Religious Defection among Hutterites', *Journal for the Scientific Study of Religion* 21:4 (1982), 327–37

Peters, V., *All Things Common: The Hutterian Way of Life* (Minneapolis: University of Minnesota Press, 1965)

Philo, *Hypothetica*, in *Works* Vol. 9, tr. F. H. Colson (Cambridge, MA: Loeb Classical Library, 1941)

Pilch, J. J., 'Healing in Mark: A Social Science Analysis', *Biblical Theology Bulletin* 15 (1985), 142–50

——, 'The Health Care System in Matthew: A Social Science Analysis', *Biblical Theology Bulletin* 16 (1986), 102–6

——, 'Lying and Deceit in the Letters to the Seven Churches: Perspectives from Cultural Anthropology', *Biblical Theology Bulletin* 22 (1992), 126–35

——, 'Visions in Revelation and Alternate Consciousness: A Perspective from Cultural Anthropology', *Listening* 28 (1993), 231–44

——, 'The Transfiguration of Jesus: An Experience of Alternate Reality', in P. Esler (ed.), *Modelling Early Christianity* (London: Routledge, 1995), 47–64

Pilch, J. J., 'Appearances of the Risen Jesus in Cultural Context: Experiences of Alternate Reality', *Biblical Theology Bulletin* 28 (1998), 52–60

——, *The Cultural Dictionary of the Bible* (Collegeville, MN: Liturgical Press, 1999)

——, *Healing in the New Testament: Insights from Medical and Mediterranean Anthropology* (Augsburg Fortress, 2000)

——, 'Altered States of Consciousness in Synoptics', in W. Stegemann, B. J. Malina and G. Theissen (eds), *The Social Setting of Jesus and the Gospels* (Minneapolis: Fortress, 2002), 103–15

Piper, R., 'Satan, Demons and the Absence of Exorcisms in the Fourth Gospel', in D. G. Horrell and C. M. Tuckett (eds), *Christology, Controversy and Community: New Testament Essays in Honour of David Catchpole* (Leiden: E. J. Brill, 2000), 253–78

Pitt Rivers, J., 'Honor', in D. Sillis (ed.), *International Encyclopedia of the Social Sciences, Volume 6* (New York: Free Press, 1968–1979), 503–11

Plato, *Republic*, tr. P. Shorey (Cambridge, MA: Loeb Classical Library, 1935)

Pottier, J., 'Food', in A. Barnard and J. Spencer (eds), *Encyclopedia of Social and Cultural Anthropology* (London: Routledge, 1996), 238–41

Preston, J., 'The Trickster Unmasked: Anthropology and the Imagination', in I. Brady (ed.), *Anthropological Poetics* (Savage: Rowman Littlefield, 1991)

Proffitt, T. D., 'Moses and Anthropology', *Journal of the Evangelical Theological Society* 27 (1984), 19–25

Radcliffe-Brown, A. R., *The Andaman Islanders* (Glencoe: Free Press, 1948 [1922])

——, *African Systems of Kinship and Marriage* (London: Oxford University Press, 1950)

Radin, P., *The Trickster: A Study in American Indian Mythology* (New York: Schocken Books, 1972 [1956])

Raheja, G. and A. Gold, *Listen to the Heron's Words: Reimagining Gender and Kinship in North India* (Berkeley: University of California Press, 1994)

Rappaport, R., *Ritual and Religion in the Making of Humanity* (Cambridge: Cambridge University Press, 1999)

Rapport, N. and J. Overing, *Social and Cultural Anthropology: The Key Concepts* (London and New York: Routledge, 2000)

Rasmussen, K., *The People of the Polar North* (London: Kegan Paul, 1908)

——, *The Netsilik Eskimos: Social Life and Spiritual Culture* (Copenhagen: Gyldenalske Boghandel, Nordisk Forlag, 1931)

Reed-Danahay, D., *Auto/Ethnography: Rewriting the Self and the Social* (Oxford: Berg, 1997)

Reinhartz, A., *The Word in the World* (Atlanta: Society of Biblical Literature, 1992)

Reinhartz, A., 'The Bride in John 3:29: A Feminist Rereading', in M. A. Beavis (ed.), *The Lost Coin: Parables of Women, Work and Wisdom* (Sheffield: Sheffield Academic Press, 2002), 230–41

Rensberger, D., 'The Messiah Who has Come into the World', in R. Fortna and T. Thatcher (eds), *Jesus in Johannine Tradition* (Louisville, Westminster John Knox, 2001), 15–23

Resseguie, J. L., *The Strange Gospel* (Leiden: Brill, 2001)

Retterstol, N., 'Suicide in Cultural History Perspective' (1998). Available online at <URL>http://www. med. uio. no/ipsy/ssff/engelsk/menculture/Retterst013. htm</URL> (accessed 11 June 2003)

Richards, A. I., *Land, Labour and Diet in Northern Rhodesia* (London: Oxford University Press, 1939)

Riches, D., *The Anthropology of Violence* (Oxford: Blackwell, 1986)

Robertson, J., 'Dying to Tell: Sexuality and Suicide in Imperial Japan', *Signs: Journal of Women in Culture and Society* 25 (1999), 1–36

Robertson Smith, W. R., *Lectures on the Religion of the Semites* (New York: KTAV, 1969 [1889])

Rogerson, J., *Anthropology and the Old Testament,* Sheffield: Sheffield Academic Press (1984 [1979])

Rohrbaugh, R. L. (ed.), *The Social Sciences and New Testament Interpretation* (Peabody, MA: Hendrickson, 1996)

——, 'Ethnocentrism and Historical Questions About Jesus', in W. Stegemann, B. J. Malina and G. Theissen (eds), *The Social Setting of Jesus and the Gospels* (Minneapolis: Fortress, 2002), 27–43

——, and B. J. Malina, *Social Science Commentary on the Synoptic Gospels* (Minneapolis: Fortress, 1993)

Rowe, J., 'Response to L. J. Lawrence's "The Joy of Text: Sanctified Subversions in the Song of Songs"' (unpublished paper, 2004)

Rowland, C., *Open Heaven* (Eugene: Wipf and Stock, 2002)

Rozen, R., 'Feminism', in P. S. Boyer (ed.), *The Oxford Companion to United States History* (Oxford: Oxford University Press, 2001) in *Oxford Reference Online* (Oxford University Press). Available online at <URL>http://www.oxfordreference.com/views/ENTRY.html?subview=Main&entry=t119.e0526</URL> (accessed 12 April 2005)

Ruel, M., 'Christians as Believers', in J. David (ed.), *Religious Organization and Religious Experience* (London: Academic Press, 1982), 9–31

——, 'Christians as Believers', in M. Lambek (ed.), *A Reader in the Anthropology of Religion* (Oxford: Blackwells, 2002), 99–113

Rushton, K. P., 'The Woman in Childbirth of John 16:21: A Feminist Reading in (Pro)creative Boundary Crossing', in K. De Troyer et al. (eds), *Wholly Woman, Holy Blood* (London: Trinity Press, 2003), 77–96

Sadgrove, M., 'The Song of Songs as Wisdom Literature' *Studia Biblica* (1978), 245–48

Said, E., *Orientalism* (New York: Vintage, 1979)

Salamone, F. A. and W. R. Adams (eds), *Explorations in Anthropology and Theology* (Lanham: University Press of America, 1997)

——, *Anthropology and Theology: God, Icons and God-Talk* (Lanham: University Press of America, 2000)

Scarry, E., *The Body in Pain: The Making and Unmaking of the World* (Oxford: Oxford University Press, 1985)

Schepher-Hughes, N., 'The Genocidal Continuum: Peace-Time Crimes', in J. Mageo (ed.), *Power and the Self* (Cambridge: Cambridge University Press, 2002), 29–47

——, and M. Lock, 'The Mindful Body: A Prolegomenon to Future Work in Medical Anthropology' *Medical Anthropological Quarterly* 1 (1987), 6–41

Schiavo, L., 'The Temptation of Jesus: The Eschatological Battle and the New Ethic of the First Followers of Jesus in Q', *Journal for the Study of the New Testament* 25 (2002), 141–64

Schüssler Fiorenza, E., *In Memory of Her* (New York: Crossroad, 1983)

——, *But She Said: Feminist Practices of Biblical Interpretation* (Boston: MA Beacon, 1992)

Schweizer, E., *The Good News According to Luke* (London: SPCK, 1984)

Scott, J. C., *Weapons of the Weak: Everyday Forms of Peasant Resistance* (New Haven: Yale University Press, 1985)

——, *Domination and the Arts of Resistance: Hidden Transcripts* (New Haven: Yale University Press, 1990)

Seeley, D., *Noble Death: Graeco-Roman Martyrology and Paul's Concept of Salvation* (Sheffield: JSOT/Sheffield Academic Press, 1990)

Sered, S., *Priestess, Mother, Sacred Sister: Religions Dominated by Women* (New York: Oxford University Press, 1994)

——, *Women as Ritual Experts: The Religious Lives of Elderly Jewish Women in Jerusalem* (Oxford: Oxford University Press, 1996)

——, 'The Domestication of Religion: The Spiritual Guardianship of Elderly Jewish Women', in M. Klass and M. K. Weisgrau (eds), *Across the Boundaries of Belief: Contemporary Issues in the Anthropology of Religion* (USA: Westview Press, 1999), 96–112

Silber, I. F., *Virtuosity, Charisma and the Social Order: A Comparative Sociological Study of Monasticism in Theravada Buddhism and Medieval Catholicism* (Cambridge: Cambridge University Press, 1995)

Sinpoli, C. M., 'The Archaeology of Empires', *Annual Review of Anthropology* 23 (1994), 159–80

Spencer, S., *Mysticism in World Religion* (Middlesex: Penguin, 1963)

Stanton, M. E., 'All Things Common: A Comparison of Israeli, Hutterite and Latter-Day Saint Communalism'. 1992 McKay Lecture. Available online at <URL>http://w3. byuh. edu/academics/ace/Speeches/McKay/M_ Stanton. htm</URL>

Stegemann, W., B. J. Malina and G. Theissen (eds), *The Social Setting of Jesus and the Gospels* (Minneapolis: Fortress, 2002)

Steinberg, N., 'Israelite Tricksters, Their Analogues and Cross-Cultural Study', in C. Exum and J. W. H. Bos (eds), *Reasoning with Foxes: Female Wit in a World of Male Power* (*Semeia* 42, 1988), 1–13

Stipe, C. E., 'Anthropologists Versus Missionaries: The Influence of Pre-suppositions', in M. Klass and M. K. Weisgrau (eds), *Across the Boundaries of Belief: Contemporary Issues in the Anthropology of Religion* (USA: Westview Press, 1999), 7–21

Sutton, D. E., *Remembrance of Repasts: An Anthropology of Food and Memory* (Oxford: Berg, 2001)

Talbert, C., *Reading John: A Literary and Theological Commentary on the Fourth Gospel and Johannine Epistles* (New York: Crossroads 1992)

Tanner, K., *Theories of Culture: A New Agenda for Theology* (Minneapolis: Fortress Press, 1997)

Theissen, G., *The Social Setting of Pauline Christianity* (Fortress Press, 1982)

Tidball, D., *The Social Context of the New Testament* (Carlisle: Paternoster Press, 1983)

Tillich, P., *A Theology of Culture* (New York: Oxford University Press, 1959)

Tonkin, E., *Narrating Our Pasts: The Social Construction of Oral History* (Cambridge: Cambridge University Press, 1992)

Townsend, J., 'Shamanism', in S. Glazier (ed.), *Anthropology of Religion: A Handbook* (Westport: Praeger, 1999), 429–69

Trible, P., 'Love's Lyrics Redeemed', in A. Brenner (ed.), *A Feminist Companion to the Song of Songs* (Sheffield: JSOT Press, 1993), 100–20

Turner, V., *The Ritual Process: Structure and Anti-Structure* (Cornell University Press, 1991 [1969])

Twelftree, G., 'Exorcism in the Fourth Gospel and the Synoptics', in R. T. Fortna and T. Thatcher (eds), *Jesus in Johannine Tradition* (Louisville, Westminster John Knox, 2001), 135–43

Valantasis, R., 'A Theory of the Social Function of Asceticism', in V. L. Wimbush and R. Valantasis (eds), *Asceticism* (Oxford: Oxford University Press, 1995)

Van Aarde, A., 'Jesus as Fatherless Child', in W. Stegemann, B. J. Malina and G. Theissen (eds), *The Social Setting of Jesus and the Gospels* (Minneapolis: Fortress, 2002), 65–84

Van Henten, J. and A. Brenner (eds), *Families and Family Relations* (Leiden: Deo, 2000)

Van Hoof, J. L., *From Autothanasia to Suicide* (London: Routledge, 1990)

Van Rheenen, G., 'A Theology of Culture: Desecularizing Anthropology', *International Journal of Frontier Missions* 14 (1997), 33–38

Van Tilborg, S., 'The Women in John: On Gender and Gender Bending', in A. Brenner and J. W. van Henten (eds), *Families and Family Relations as Represented in Early Judaisms and Early Christianities: Texts and Fictions* (Leiden: Deo, 2000), 192–212

Watts, M. J. 'Space for Everything', *Cultural Anthropology* 7 (1992), 115–129

Weber, M., *The Sociology of Religion* (Boston: Beacon Press, 1963 [1921])

Whelan, C. F., 'Suicide in the Ancient World: A Re-examination of Matthew 27:3–10', *Laval Theologique et Philosophique* 49 (1993), 505–22

Widlock, T., 'Sharing by Default? Outline of an Anthropology of Virtue' *Anthropological Theory* 4 (2004), 53–70

Winkelman M. J., 'Shamans and Other Magico-Religious Healers: A Cross-Cultural Study of their Origins, Nature and Social Transformation', *Ethos* 18 (1990), 308–52

Witherington, B., *Women in the Ministry of Jesus* (Cambridge: Cambridge University Press, 1984)

Wortham, R. A., *Social-Scientific Approaches in Biblical Literature* (Lewiston: E. Mellen, 1999)

PATERNOSTER BIBLICAL MONOGRAPHS

New Covenant, New Community

PETRUS J. GRÄBE

ISBN: 1-84227-248-9

The concept of 'covenant' is a crucial component in understanding God and his actions throughout salvation history. *New Covenant, New Community*, looks at covenant in the Old and New Testaments and the history of Christian interpretation, and makes a substantial contribution to biblical theological studies in this area.

What are the elements of continuity and discontinuity in terms of the covenant concept between the Old and New Testaments? What are the implications of a biblical understanding of covenant for the community of faith – then and now? These are just a few of the many questions Gräbe addresses in this far-reaching, well-researched and highly accessible study.

PATERNOSTER

PATERNOSTER BIBLICAL MONOGRAPHS

Reconstructing Christian Origins?

The Feminist Theology of Elisabeth Schüssler Fiorenza: An Evaluation

ESTHER NG

ISBN: 1-84227-055-9

Elisabeth Schüssler Fiorenza is the most influential feminist New Testament scholar alive. Her work reconstructing the purported egalitarian origins of Christianity has exercised a widespread influence in the academy. Esther Ng's book is the most detailed analysis of Fiorenza's historical reconstruction available. Ng offers a fair-minded but critical analysis of Fiorenza's work, examining her presuppositions and historical methodology, as well as the evidence adduced to support her thesis.

PATERNOSTER

PATERNOSTER BIBLICAL MONOGRAPHS

The Genre, Composition and Hermeneutics of the Epistle of James

LUKE L. CHEUNG

ISBN: 1-84227-062-1

The Genre, Composition and Hermeneutics of the Epistle of James examines the employment of the wisdom genre with a certain compositional structure and the interpretation of the law through Jesus' tradition of the double love command by the author of the Epistle of James to serve his purpose in promoting perfection and warning against doubleness among the eschatologically renewed people of God in the Diaspora.

PATERNOSTER

PATERNOSTER BIBLICAL MONOGRAPHS

Lukan Theology in the Light of the Gospel's Literary Structure

DOUGLAS S. McCOMISKEY

ISBN: 1-84227-148-2

Luke's gospel was purposefully written with theology embedded in its patterned literary structure. A critical analysis of this cyclical structure provides new windows into Luke's interpretation of the individual pericopes comprising the gospel and illuminates several of his theological interests.

PATERNOSTER